MAD MONEY

MAD MONEY

When Markets Outgrow Governments

Susan Strange

Ann Arbor

THE UNIVERSITY OF MICHIGAN PRESS

Published in the United States of America by
The University of Michigan Press

The University of Michigan Press edition published by special arrangement with Manchester University Press, Oxford Road,
Manchester M13 9NR, UK

2001   2000   1999   1998   4   3   2   1

Library of Congress Cataloging-in-Publication Data

Strange, Susan, 1923–
    Mad money : when markets outgrow governments / Susan Strange.
      p.   cm.
    Sequel to Casino capitalism.
    Includes bibliographical references and index.
    ISBN 0-472-09693-1 (hardcover : alk. paper). — ISBN
0-472-06693-5 (pbk. : alk. paper)
      1. International finance.   2. Speculation.   3. International
Monetary Fund.   4. Economic history—1945– I. Title.
HG3881.S773   1998
332—dc21   98-34303
                                                    CIP

Typeset by Ralph Footring, Derby
Printed in Great Britain by Biddles Ltd, Guildford and King's Lynn

Contents

Acknowledgements

Research for this book was supported financially by a grant from the British Economic and Social Research Council.

I have also to thank friends and colleagues for much sage counsel and guidance – notably Carlo Brumath in Monterrey, Mexico, Jerry Cohen in Santa Barbara, California, Lou Pauly in Toronto, Sidney Key, Jane D'Arista and Bob Solomon in Washington, DC, David Lascelles and Marjorie Deane in London, Christian Chavagneux and others in Paris, Giles Merritt in Brussels, Andrew Walter at the London School of Economics, and most of all my colleagues at Warwick, Richard Higgott, Geoffrey Underhill and Tim Sinclair. Any mistakes are my own.

Credit for compiling the extensive bibliography goes to Fridrik Snorrason, who worked evenings and weekends to track down my often cryptic references.

Abbreviations

ATM	automated teller machine
BIS	Bank for International Settlements
CAP	Common Agricultural Policy
CDs	certificates of deposit
CEPII	Centre d'Etudes Prospectives et d'Informations Internationales
CHIPS	Clearing House Interbank Payments System
CIEC	Conference on International Economic Cooperation
EBRD	European Bank for Reconstruction and Development
EC	European Community
ECSC	European Coal and Steel Community
EEC	European Economic Community
EMU	Economic and Monetary Union
ERM	Exchange Rate Mechanism
ERP	European Recovery Program
EU	European Union
FATF	Financial Action Task Force
FBI	Federal Bureau of Investigation
FDIC	Federal Deposit Insurance Corporation
Fed	Federal Reserve Board (United States)
GAB	General Arrangement to Borrow
GATT	General Agreement on Tariffs and Trade
GDP	gross domestic product
GNP	gross national product
HIPC	highly indebted poor country
HKFE	Hong Kong Futures Exchange
ICIC	international credit insurance corporation
IMF	International Monetary Fund
IOSCO	International Organisation of Securities Commissions

KKR	Kohlberg, Kravis and Roberts
LDC	less developed countries
LDP	Liberal Democratic Party (Japan)
LIFFE	London International Financial Futures Exchange
MMDAs	money market deposit accounts
MMMFs	money market mutual funds
MOF	Ministry of Finance (Japan)
NAFTA	North American Free Trade Area
NATO	North Atlantic Treaty Organization
NIC	newly industrialised country
NOW	negotiable order of withdrawal
OECD	Organization for Economic Cooperation and Development
OPEC	Organization of Petroleum-Exporting Countries
OTC	over-the-counter
PRI	Partido Revolucionario Institucional (Institutional Revolutionary Party of Mexico)
S&Ls	saving and loans
SDRs	special drawing rights
SEC	Securities and Exchange Commission
SIB	Securities Investment Board
SILIC	severely indebted low-income country
SIMIC	severely indebted middle-income country
UN	United Nations
UNCTAD	United Nations Conference on Trade and Development
VER	voluntary export restriction
WTO	World Trade Organization

Chapter 1

The casino image gone mad

Why mad? Because to my mind it was, and is, 'wildly foolish' – the dictionary synonym for 'mad' – to let the financial markets run so far ahead, so far beyond the control of state and international authorities. We recognise insanity, or madness in a man or woman, by erratic, unpredictable, irrational behaviour that is potentially damaging to the sufferers themselves or to others. But that is exactly how financial markets have behaved in recent years. They have been erratically manic at one moment, unreasonably depressive at others. The crises that have hit them have been unpredicted and, to most observers, surprising. Their behaviour has very seriously damaged others. Their condition calls urgently for treatment of some kind.

The first step before treatment is diagnosis, assessing the nature and, if possible, the origins of the madness and understanding the stages of its development. That is exactly the purpose of this introductory book. There is a long bibliography at the end for those who want to know more, and to hear different diagnostic opinions. I do not pretend to have the complete answer to what treatment is needed – although I do have a few ideas about where it might start.

The insanity of it all was vividly brought home to me at the end of 1997. The newspapers carried pictures of Wall Street brokers, champagne bottles and glasses in hand, their faces wreathed in crazy grins, celebrating the large end-of-year bonuses they had just been given. Nor were they the only ones in the financial markets being handsomely rewarded: some of the bonuses to investment bankers and fund managers were unimaginably, obscenely large. And meanwhile, in Asia, there was nothing to celebrate. Millions faced job losses and unemployment. Family businesses painstakingly built up over the years were bankrupted. The future looked dark indeed for the once-proud 'tiger economies' of east Asia. It was a coincidence that the book to which this is some sort of sequel, *Casino Capitalism*, had ended with just such a graphic image of the financial operators drinking champagne, while outside the tower-block offices other people were having a hard time of it (Strange 1986). The only difference was that the imaginary picture was set for the millennium in 2000, while the newspaper pictures were three years earlier. The pace of globalisation and of changes in the financial system that lay behind what people thought of as globalisation had got faster.

Globalisation

There are now two serious threats that jeopardise civilisation and the life chances of our children and grandchildren – both 'threats without enemies'. The worst threat – if we take a long-term view of life on this planet – is the environmental one. The depletion of the ozone layer and the build-up of carbon dioxide in the atmosphere, deforestation and the damage to the ecological balance between animals, plants, soil and water have all been studied and understood for the past two decades. The progressively destructive consequences of these processes have been repeatedly debated not only by experts but by governments. But declarations and resolutions have not led on – neither at meetings of the United Nations (UN) in Rio in 1992 nor in Kyoto in 1997 – to serious corrective action – as distinct from vacuous general declarations of intent. There is a small glimmer of hope that, given time, a new and powerful coalition will rise up to challenge the vested interests – the oil companies, the chemical companies, the car manufacturers, the paper and packaging industries and all the others opposed to change. This challenge could come from organised world opinion aided and supported by the self-interest of a few environmental-protection businesses and, probably much more important, by the self-interest of the powerful insurance industry.[1]

But though the ecological threats to humanity are certainly the most serious, they are a comparatively long-term threat. Whereas if confidence in the financial system were to collapse, causing credit to shrink and world economic growth to slow to zero, that is a much more immediate threat. Writing at the end of 1997, it is clear from the public reaction that there is enormous uncertainty even among the experts about how far the contagion that started in Thailand in the summer will spread, and whether the United States and Europe as well as Japan will also suffer. It seems to me that there are more worried people, more public concern this year than last, and certainly more than there was even twelve years ago when *Casino Capitalism* was first published. That concern – which I share – is the reason for returning to the subject of an earlier book.

My concern, now as it was then, is not technical – with the efficiency of the system – but social and political, with the consequences for ordinary people who have never been asked if they wanted to gamble their jobs, their savings, their income in this casino form of capitalism. The fact that some made windfall gains does not assuage the pain and bewilderment of those afflicted with undeserved losses. Today, at the end of the century, the casino nature of the financial system has been widely acknowledged. And what we have today is much more of the same – more volatility, more uncertainty and more anxiety. While many of those engaged in financial markets may regard what is happening as perfectly normal, necessary and therefore acceptable, there are a lot more who think it is all quite crazy. It does not make sense, they think, to gamble in this way with the future of the world market economy. More of the same developments that I described in the 1970s and 1980s have meant worse for those who lost jobs – because it was financially necessary – and for those who lost savings and whose investments failed. Money has indeed gone mad.[2]

That is why there is more need than ever to explore the nature of the problem – its political aspects as well as its technical and functional ones. More need than ever to look for the weak points in the financial system and to ask whether there are possible remedial changes that might be made. And if the prospects for reform, for cooling the casino, for making money sane again are slim, then we should also perhaps look at the alternative scenarios of what could happen to it in the years ahead. Being prepared, even for the worst, is better than being taken totally by surprise. The last chapter, therefore, will briefly review these scenarios.

Meanwhile, the link with the environmental issues is that our chances of acting in time on those are going to be dramatically less if the world economy should fall – as some observers fear it might – into a long-drawn-out depression. For history strongly suggests that at such times governments everywhere tend to focus exclusively on the immediate and the domestic issues. Frustration feeds nationalism and xenophobia at home. Abroad, international collective action is put firmly in second place and little progress is possible. The 1930s are not so long ago that the doldrums of the League of Nations, the impasse in reparations and disarmament talks and the inaction on world economic issues are beyond recall. This is one good reason for not just waiting to see what will happen and hoping for the best. If there is *anything* that can be done, we ought at least to start thinking about how it could be done and by whom. Not having the expert's grasp of the technical details of how financial markets work is no excuse for indifference to the social consequences of casino capitalism.

One thing that has certainly changed since the mid-1980s is the greater awareness of global interdependence. Even as late as 1986, there were still people who thought in terms of the First World and the Third World. The Second World was the Soviet-dominated world of state-planned command economies. Each had different problems. No longer. Now, as 1997 amply showed us, we are all in the same boat. One financial system dominates from Moscow to Manila, from Tokyo to Texas. A large part of the task of this book will be to see how this has come about and what else has changed over the last ten to fifteen years. But first, for some readers, it may be worth recalling the themes of *Casino Capitalism* and the stages by which the relatively stable and predictable world of the 1950s and 1960s had already changed, quite radically, by the 1980s.

Themes of *Casino Capitalism*

The dominant theme of the book to which this is some sort of sequel was – in a word – volatility. That word seemed to sum up how the international monetary and financial system had changed in the twelve years between 1972/3 and 1984/5, when the book was written. The book was not supposed to be a history of that period, but more some reflections on what to make of the history.[3] It seemed to me that, compared with the relatively stable 1960s, the big change had been to far greater instability, and in the pace of change in the basic prices of a world economy: the price of currencies (exchange rates), the price of goods (i.e. inflation), the price of credit (interest rates) and the price of oil as the main traded commodity necessary to industrialised economies. I commented:

> Uncertainty in each has fed the uncertainty and the volatility of the others. And the common factor linking them has been the international financial system. That is the rootstock from whose disorders stem the various problems which afflict the international political economy, just as blight, disease or mildew attack the different branches of a plant. (Strange 1986: 4)

The common problem, therefore, was how to restore – if at all possible – some stability and certainty to the system. The common consequence was to have made involuntary gamblers of us all:

> For the great difference between an ordinary casino which you can go
> into or stay away from, and the global casino of high finance, is that
> in the latter we are all involuntarily engaged in the day's play. A
> currency change can halve the value of a farmer's crop before he
> harvests it, or drive an exporter out of business. A rise in interest rates
> can fatally inflate the costs of holding stocks for the shop-keeper. A
> takeover dictated by financial considerations can rob the factory worker
> of his job. From school-leavers to pensioners, what goes on in the casino
> in the office blocks of the big financial centres is apt to have sudden,
> unpredictable and unavoidable consequences for individual lives. The
> financial casino has everyone playing the game of Snakes and Ladders.
> (Strange 1986: 2)

How had the casino economy come about? That, for a political
economist, was the first question. What were the series of steps, the
decisions and non-decisions, that had led us down this primrose path?
Who had taken those decisions and why? The answers lay in political
as well as economic history, in domestic and in international politics
and markets. Of that there was little doubt, but it was necessary to go
back and list those steps in order to find some satisfactory explanation
for the shift from the relatively stable 1960s to the turbulent, yo-yoing
conditions of the 1970s and early 1980s. Because what has happened
since then goes back to the very same roots, it may be worth sum-
marising what I thought them to have been.

I listed five distant non-decisions, each with far-reaching implications,
drawn from the postwar period up to the end of the 1960s, and then
five political choices taken in the decade 1972–82. Although selection
of 'facts' in history is a notoriously subjective business, as E. H. Carr
(1961) rightly insisted and as the postmodernists have rediscovered for
themselves, I would still stand by the two lists. They can be briefly
summarised.

In the list of distant non-decisions, first came the refusal of Europeans to respond to US pleas for more equitable burden sharing in the
North Atlantic Treaty Organization (NATO), back in the early 1950s.
Opting to be free riders on the security provided by US nuclear weapons
and the tripwires of US ground and air forces, the Europeans – and
Japanese, come to that – gave the United States from that time on the
perfect justification for finding other ways than taxes to have its defence
policies paid for. Thereafter it was no use General Montgomery
complaining that the US got into the Vietnam War without consulting
the European allies, or Jacques Rueff and General de Gaulle complaining
that the US was abusing the exorbitant privileges given it by other
people's use of the dollar as an international currency. European
preference for welfare spending over defence spending shared the blame

with American preferences for spending now and paying later – or never.

The second non-decision was the refusal as early as 1957 to respond to the developing countries' claims for redistributive UN aid. Related to it, third, was the choice of *ad hoc*, case-by-case processes of dealing with international debt.

Also going back to the mid-1950s was the first of many failures to agree strong, comprehensive rules against the use of cheap credit and subsidised export credit insurance to promote competitive exports by the industrialised countries. A recent study by Gunther Walzenbach shows how mutually destructive, politically and economically, has been this ongoing failure (Walzenbach 1998).

Fifth and last, I added the decision by Harold Wilson in the first postwar Labour government in Britain to reopen the City of London as an international financial marketplace. All subsequent history of the management (and mismanagement) of international finance showed the importance to the United States of having London as partner to New York in developing a lively and innovative system for the transnational creation of and trade in credit. In the old sense, it was true even before the Suez debacle that the 'special relationship' of Britain to the United States no longer existed save in the minds of British politicians. But in matters of financial deregulation and re-regulation, the New York–London axis has continued as an indispensable feature of the system (Reinicke 1998; Steil *et al.* 1996).

The five crucial political choices made in the period 1971–85 seemed to me to have been, first, the extreme withdrawal by the United States from any intervention in foreign exchange markets. It was not just that Nixon deliberately abolished the Bretton Woods fixed exchange rate system – though often referred to euphemistically as the 'collapse' of the system, it was actually more like a deliberate act of sabotage. It was the choice in 1972 of total non-intervention with exchange rates – a Treasury decision against the advice of the supposedly independent Federal Reserve chair Burns and the New York Fed's Charlie Coombs (Strange 1986: 38–41).

The second crucial choice was, in effect, to deceive public and professional opinion into believing that international monetary reform was still under serious international discussion. I called this exercise conducted by the Committee of Twenty a 'cynical pantomime', disguising the reality that all rules were erased and the system had reverted to anarchy. I quoted the respected liberal economist John Williamson in support of that judgement (Williamson 1977).

The third crucial choice, again a US decision, was to refuse to negotiate with the oil-producing states and to opt instead for the confrontational strategy of an oil-consumers' coalition armed – that at least was Kissinger's intention – with strategic stockpiles against any repetition of the 1973 oil price rise. At first sight, this might seem to have been a foreign policy decision, having little to do with finance. Yet the close links between oil prices and financial markets, and between both and the indebtedness of the less developed countries (LDCs), form part of the political/economic context of later developments in international finance.

A fourth choice followed from the refusal to deal with the Organization of Petroleum-Exporting Countries (OPEC). It was the stonewalling strategy taken in 1974 against the Conference on International Economic Cooperation (CIEC) – initiated by France on behalf of developing countries hit by higher energy costs. The two decisions together, on top of American tolerant and uncritical support for Israel, help explain why in the Gulf War of 1991 Saddam Hussein could count on so much Arab support against the United States and why Islamic fundamentalism in the Middle East represented a political as well as a religious/ideological protest.

The fifth and final choice was a positive one: to respond to two important bank failures in 1974 – the Franklin National in New York and Bankhaus Herstatt in Germany – by strengthening cooperation between central banks in their dual role as bank regulators and lenders of last resort. Although the system continued to lack a single lender of last resort, the Cooke Committee set up by the Bank for International Settlements (BIS) did at least recognise the problem and the need to be better prepared to meet it (see chapter 9).

Most of these choices were American ones and related to the country's external relations. Equally influential in the long run were US domestic policy decisions relating to banks and financial markets (see chapter 8). Indifference to what US banks did outside the United States went back to the early 1960s. The trend towards deregulation of what they were allowed to do at home started in the mid-1970s with the abolition of fixed commissions for share dealing. In 1980 a further big step was taken in the Depository Institutions Deregulation and Monetary Control Acts (Strange 1986: 47–58). In part this was a response to competition from London, in part ideological. My concluding comment anticipated the bail-outs of the 1990s:

> The end result of 'monetarist' policy may easily turn out to be the exact opposite of its ideological intentions. Instead of freeing the private sector and the market economy from the toils of state intervention, it may actually end – as in Mussolini's Italy – in involving the state more extensively and more permanently in industry and business than it had ever been before. (Strange 1986: 58)

And key decisions of the last decade?

These can be more briefly listed, both because they are fresher in our memories and because the details and the context of them will be found in later chapters of this book. Once again, I could identify just five key decisions, or non-decisions in the case of failures to act when positive action would have been possible.

First, after the October 1987 stock market crisis, there was a tacit decision not to interfere too much. The surprise was the quick recovery both in the stock markets and in the rest of the economy. Hands-off was ideologically welcome and seemed also rationally justified. Carry on, deregulation.

Second, in 1988, governments of the developed economies, Japan included, agreed through the BIS to standardise some of the rules governing the conduct of banks. This was the Basle Accord on capital adequacy in relation to the risks banks ran when they made loans or in other ways issued credit.

Third, after the fall of the Berlin Wall in 1989, there were a bunch of key decisions concerning the former socialist economies. East Germany was to be reunited with West Germany. But the other central European countries would not be similarly reunited with the economy of western Europe. They would have to wait to join the European Community, but in the meantime they – like Russia and the former Soviet Union – would be expected, as proof of their conversion from communism and of good conduct, to open their economies to the world market and to foreign goods and foreign investors. The Second World joined the First – but on unequal terms. (The Third World, meanwhile, by joining the Uruguay Round of negotiations over the General Agreement on Tariffs and Trade (GATT) and later the World Trade Organization (WTO), had also succumbed, for better or worse, to the prevailing ideology of free market economics.) The one world market economy project was complete. What Francis Fukuyama prematurely called 'the end of history' was really the apparent end of intellectual opposition to the dogmas of economic liberalism.

The fourth decision was a reversal. By 1996, the capital–asset ratio as a means of regulating banks according to a common standard as agreed in 1988 was tacitly admitted to be imprecise and therefore unworkable (see chapter 9).

Fifth, in 1997, the response to currency and credit crises in east Asia showed that Mexico, which had had a similar experience two and a half years before, was not the exception that it seemed at the time. The Group of Ten developed countries, by contributing to rescue funds for troubled Asian economies, reiterated more forcefully than ever the conviction that in the modern international financial system, bankruptcy was not an option, at least, not bankruptcy in the sense that a failed business closes down, gets sold off to the best bidder or taken over lock, stock and barrel. The appearance of an immortal, sovereign state was to be preserved – not for its own sake, but for the greater security of the world system.

So what's new? What's dangerous?

I start with five hypotheses about the most important changes that have affected that global financial system – and thus the international political economy – in the past decade or so.

As the next chapter will explain in more detail, a major change since the mid-1980s has been technological – enormous and very fast innovations in the way in which financial markets work, and in which financial traders, brokers and consultants operate.

The other thing that's new is the sheer size of these markets, the volumes traded, the variety of possible deals to be done, the number of new financial centres, the men and women employed directly or indirectly in the business of international finance. There is, in short, more of everything, including the potential victims, the involuntary gamblers in the casino. Their number too has grown.

Third, I would put the 'end of banking' – by which I mean that the bankers no longer occupy the same special, reserved and protected role in the system that they once did. As an erudite and well informed American financial observer, Martin Mayer, has put it, 'Banks as we have known them, from the Medici and the Fuggers to First National This and First National That, have seen their day' (Mayer 1997: 466). Bankers therefore are still with us but they are not what they used to be. Intermediation – taking in deposits and making loans – which was their traditional function is no longer the name of the game. Commercial banks have become investment banks and are increasingly tempted into proprietary trading – that is, betting their own capital in the casino. The trend can be explained by the internationalisation of finance and the consequent break-up of closed shops – the sort of polite cosy cartels, tolerated if not licensed by governments, that were the price of access to the national lender of last resort. Increased competition has brought non-banks, including insurance firms, into the business but has also cut profit margins from regular banking operations.

The fourth big change is the emergence of Asia, and especially of Japan and China, as major components of the system and as

involuntary players in the global casino. There were several references
in the earlier book to the growing involvement of Japanese and
European banks in international financial markets, to their follow-my-
leader behaviour in the kinds of trading they practised, and to US
diplomacy in the late 1970s with Japan as one of the supposed
'locomotive' economies. But these references were dispersed and
unrelated. The 1990s have involved the Pacific Rim to a far greater
extent than the 1980s.

Nor are Asian and other emerging markets the only new players in
the game. We must also note the growing involvement since the mid-
1980s of organised crime in international finance and the importance
of money laundering as one of the many financial services offered by
it. A contributing factor to this change has been the growth of the
transnational trade in illegal drugs, providing a source of wealth to the
mafia far greater than even American prohibition. Organised crime,
too, rose from the ashes of the Cold War. Russians, Chechens and
Georgians have dealt not only in drugs but in arms, illegal immigrants
and even nuclear materials. Liberal economists have tended to take a
curiously neutral view of the mafia as just another kind of business
enterprise – a perspective that obscures the social and political nature
of secret societies and underplays the implications of large-scale money
laundering (Paoli 1997).[4]

Finally, as the brief list of key decisions noted, there has been an
important shift in the basis of coordinated central bank supervision
and control over the markets. Instead of relying on the series of Basle
Concordats thought up and drafted by what started as the Cooke
Committee in the 1970s, the BIS and its member central banks have
shifted to reliance on self-regulation by the banks and non-banks. Why
and how this shift has been made and the implications for the system
is something that must be added to the whole picture (see chapter 9).

Some (conflicting) interpretations

To play fair with the general reader – and incidentally, to show what
a wide variation there is in theories and interpretations of recent
changes and events – there should also be some review of those
conflicting approaches. (If you know this literature already, by all
means skip to the end of the chapter.) In *Casino Capitalism* there was
one long chapter on divergent views of what happened in the interwar
and postwar periods (Strange 1986: ch. 3). Now, the old radical and
marxist voices that were still to be heard then have mostly fallen
strangely silent. Critical comment that is also informed is comparatively

scarce (but all the more welcome – see pp. 13–18). Among observers who broadly accept the system as it is, however, there seems to be more divergence now than there was then between pessimists and optimists. A brief survey of the wide range of opinion will at least signpost the main lines of debate and disagreement.

Within this range, there are plenty of pro-marketeers, those who protest that everything is fine. Markets work well. The more they are left to themselves the better. Globalisation opens up undreamed of opportunities for enterprising people. Nor are these enterprising people, they say, only to be found in the rich countries. Poor developing countries are now part of this great globalised system of international finance and though there are risks the system has also given them new chances for change, new possibilities for escape from poverty, ignorance, disease and early death.

Jeffry Sachs, the Harvard economist and adviser to the Russians on post-socialist transition policies, is one of the best-known champions of the market economy. Capitalist-led development works almost every-where, he argues, and where it does not it is not to blame. Either meddlesome governments have got in the way of globalisation or else the legacies of history and geography impose too heavy a handicap on countries in Latin America or sub-Saharan Africa unable to keep up with the east Asian economic miracles. A 1997 report written by Sachs' Institute for International Development for the Asian Development Bank did qualify the optimism with some cautious predictions concerning the time it would take for the trickle-down benefits of the financial system to reach the poorest. The tropical countries cannot expect to reach even half the gross domestic product (GDP) per head of temperate countries in the foreseeable future – and even that will only be possible if they follow the 'right' economic and demographic policies.[5]

Sachs is not alone in thinking that governments not markets are the problem. David Lascelles, an experienced financial journalist now running the Centre for the Study of Financial Innovation in London, puts it like this:

> The basic causes of instability and speculation in financial markets are irresponsible governments rather than flaky institutions, greedy traders or hectic innovation. Excessive budget deficits, defaults by sovereign borrowers, poor monetary management etc. can be devastating. Admittedly, there has been some improvement in this area since 1986; the US is trying, the Third World is refinanced, and EMU [Economic and Monetary Union] is a sign of a desire at least for better monetary discipline in Europe. But a lot of the markets' behaviour is still driven either by the financing requirements of government borrowers or by the fear of shocks caused by government actions.[6]

A curious convert to what he himself calls a 'market-friendly' approach to financial regulation is a former leader of the French regulation school of left-wing social scientists, Professor Michel Aglietta. He is now director of research at the Centre d'Etudes Prospectives et d'Informations Internationales (CEPII), which is a prestigious French economic think-tank. He describes, apparently with approval, this new approach to prudential policy as based on internal control systems that observe general guidelines for best practice in risk management. Although he notes that value-at-risk systems can break down at times of stress, so that bank supervisors have to be prepared to 'enforce corrective action well before insolvency', he does not comment critically on the chances of them actually doing so (Aglietta 1996, 1997).

Two other experienced and well informed writers, Marjorie Deane and Robin Pringle, concluding their recent study of central banks, conveyed a certain optimism that professional expertise would be able to meet the formidable challenges of financial globalisation: 'Central banks' immediate task in the mid-1990s is to provide price stability – without overdoing it and plunging the world into depression' (Deane and Pringle 1994: 350). They insisted that their study showed that this was not a straightforward task – even assuming central bankers were not frustrated by political interference and were true to the highest principles of public service. But the implicit hope was that the task was not beyond the capabilities of central banks.

Andrew Crockett, long-serving Managing Director of the central bankers' bank, the BIS in Basle, seems to share their defiant optimism. His succinct but comprehensive monograph, *The Theory and Practice of Financial Stability*, ends on an upbeat note. It is worth quoting:

> Recent theoretical work has greatly increased understanding of the forces that cause instability in the financial system. It is no longer necessary to rely on quasi-psychological explanations of why bank runs develop or why financial prices move by more than seems justified by underlying economic fundamentals. This new understanding of the micro-economics of financial-market behavior is an important tool in the policymaker's search for a system that is stable enough to facilitate inter-temporal resource-allocation decisions, yet flexible enough to allow prices and international structures to adapt through time and to provide the proper range of incentives and disincentives for good and bad decisions. (Crockett, 1997: 42)

What of the central bankers themselves? Two of the most eminent and experienced financial diplomats of the last quarter century are Paul Volcker, chair of the board of governors of the US Federal Reserve

System from 1979 to 1987, and Toyoo Gyohten, former vice-president
for international affairs at the Japanese Ministry of Finance. They
wrote a book together based on a joint series of lectures at Princeton
in 1991 (Volcker and Gyohten 1992). Both had suggestions as to how
the management of international finance could be improved and I shall
return to these ideas later. What was interesting in the present context
was that neither was entirely sure what the future held. Volcker
especially ended on a political, not a technical note. American hegemony was not what it was. Yet as the richest and strongest country in
the world, the United States had a responsibility, in its own interest and
that of the system of global finance, to lead others in restoring a sense
of confidence in American strength and stability. Using the word
'restoring' hinted – no more – at some lingering concern whether the
political context in which financial markets operated was robust
enough to meet the challenge.

It goes without saying that the judgements of people like Crockett
and Volcker – even in retirement – must be coloured by their past
experience. Their conclusions, unavoidably, are likely to be moderated
by the wish not to rock the boat, never to provoke needless ner-
vousness in the markets. Operators and unofficial bystanders are
something else. Here, it seems, we find many more than I could find
in the 1980s to voice anxiety and concern for the future. Then, I had
to go looking to long-dead political philosophers of money like Georg
Simmel or Frank Knight to find hints of criticism, or else to extreme
radicals like Ernest Mandel, Samir Amin, Arghiri Emmanuel or
Immanuel Wallerstein, and eccentric economists like the South African
critic of Keynes S. Herbert Frankel, or the late Hyman Minsky, origi-
nator in the 1930s of the Financial Instability Hypothesis, suddenly
rediscovered after the October 1987 stock market fall (Strange 1986:
72–96).

Ten years later, the warning voices come either from the close
observers of the financial scene, or from participants in it – not so
much from the academics. (Like Sachs, liberal economists are
understandably loath to raise doubts about a system based on
liberalisation, deregulation and privatisation.) One of the best-known
such warning voices is that of George Soros, the hedge-fund operator
who became an overnight household name by reportedly making a
billion dollars out of sterling's exit from the Exchange Rate Mechanism
(ERM) in 1993. On several occasions, Soros has given his opinion that
the financial system is inherently unstable and unpredictable, that it
has weaknesses built into it that could cause a major collapse. He
usually adds that while it lasts, he proposes to continue to make
profitable use of his experience and intuitive skills, and to channel

those profits into ameliorating – particularly for universities and students – some of the difficulties of the transition in central Europe and Russia. Soros is not saying collapse will happen, but that it very possibly might. He sustains his opinion with what he calls the reflexive principle, according to which in social science, including economics, what happens (as in markets) is influenced by the spectators and their perceptions of what is happening: 'The participants' thinking is an integral part of the situation they participate in; to treat such a situation as if it were composed exclusively of facts distorts the subject matter' (Soros 1987: 311). This attack on the pretensions of social 'science' together with the account of his hands-on experience in the markets is explained in his best book, *The Alchemy of Finance: reading the mind of the market.* 'We can expect,' he concludes, 'a period of continuing turmoil in financial markets, although the focus of attention may shift from the stock market to the currency market and the bond market and eventually to the market for precious metals.' Arguing that the United States alone has the power to lead but also has the most to gain from a reform of the system, he ends gloomily, 'The alternative is a period similar to the 1930s: financial turmoil, beggar-thy-neighbour policies leading to worldwide depression and perhaps even war' (Soros 1987: 359–60).

Less known than Soros but philosophically quite close to him is the experienced American writer William Grieder. An earlier study of the Federal Reserve System (Grieder 1987) dealt mainly with the financial system of the United States. His more recent book, *One World, Ready or Not: the manic logic of global capitalism* (Grieder 1997), is concerned – as the title suggests – with the global financial system as it affects debtor countries like Mexico, the workers, the Japanese, the environment and the poor. The argument in a nutshell echoes my own in *Casino Capitalism*.

> The steady weakening of government authority alongside its rising debts, suggests an abnormal arrangement that is not sustainable.... Governments ... must now share responsibility with a shrewd private partner who can become quite fickle and overbearing. The result is not the stability and efficiency that market theorists predict. Instead national currencies have become one more commodity in global trade – erratic and undependable, but very profitable for smart traders. (Grieder 1997: 237)

Grieder is, essentially, a global keynesian; the defects of alternating booms and slumps in a capitalist system require political intervention – but this is no longer feasible on a national scale.[7] It has to be done internationally if it is to be effective. The alternative is to go along with the implicit neo-classical liberal economics prescription for stability – through deflation.

> Reforms that simply stabilise the present system by reducing the most visible risks are an insufficient answer to the general economic upheavals and distress. Even if a new currency system worked simply for the interests of finance, it might merely compel governments to adjust their balance sheets by lowering domestic standards of living more swiftly. In that case, if speculators did not blow the system apart, political reactions would. (Grieder 1997: 258)

Two well informed German observers, Hans-Peter Martin and Harald Schumann, are even more pessimistic. Both are editors of *Der Spiegel* and their book, which came out in German in 1996, quickly went into multiple editions and was translated into several languages. In *The Global Trap: globalization and the assault on prosperity and democracy*, they compare the risks of the financial system breaking down to those of nuclear disaster. Quoting Felix Rohatyn's remarks to the same effect, they conclude, 'The probability of a major accident is small but the potential damage it would cause is almost unlimited' (Martin and Schumann 1997: 89). As Europeans, their complaint is not only that the system is dangerous, but that it has already started to undermine the democratic institutions and the welfare provisions for which past generations had fought so hard. 'The superior power of the fund managers allows them to challenge every step forward in social equality that has been achieved in a hundred years of class struggle and political reform' (*ibid.*: 69). The arguments they use for a European counterattack will be discussed later, in chapter 4, but their book reinforces Grieder's point that one of the risks being run is political, not financial. Indeed, its appeal is that it holds out the hope of a backlash by the national and social groups excluded from the benefits but threatened by the risks of financial globalisation.

Historians tend to be more cautious in predicting either disaster or political resistance. If we go back to Kindleberger's classic work, *Manias, Panics and Crashes: a history of financial crises*, for instance, the conclusion from a longer historical perspective was more tentative:

> I do not claim that instability is the rule, only that it has occurred with sufficient frequency in the historical past to keep a good practitioner on the alert for the symptoms. Stability is encountered but so is instability. There is trend and there is, on occasion, financial crisis. (Kindleberger 1990: 248)

Similarly, in 1987 Kindleberger expressed strong doubts about some of the liberal economists' assumptions – that speculation under complete deregulation was stabilising or that short-term capital movements are always helpful in the right direction and amount. The only sane strategy to pursue was a return to fixed exchange rates – one world money – and a more stable system of providing credit to developing countries (Kindleberger 1987: 61–2).

A younger economist who would agree heartily with that neo-keynesian view is Professor John Eatwell, now head of Queen's College Cambridge and formerly professor at the New School for Social Research in New York. In a discussion paper for the UN Development Program, Eatwell has argued forcibly against the deregulation of finance and, specifically, against the lifting of all controls on capital movements. Proof that, as he believes, both have led to poorer economic performance in the real economy may be impossible. Yet he develops a case for thinking that they have increased systemic risks and given a deflationary bias to state policies. As a development economist he cannot agree that it is a good idea to hand over the future of the real economy to liberalised market forces that make systematic policy making impossible (Eatwell 1996).

What about the international political economists – the new hybrid breed who aspire to analyse world economy issues with a synthesis of insights from economics and politics? Influenced by the economists, American political economists have been more optimistic than most European scholars. Ethan Kapstein, for example, wrote a study of international finance in 1992 which concluded that a combination of state regulation and international agreement through the BIS capital adequacy rule would take care of the problem of wild markets and greedy bankers (Kapstein 1993; but see my chapters 8 and 9). By contrast, Geoffrey Underhill, a Canadian ex-patriate political economist in England, says that 'powerful private interests are in a strong position to set the agenda and become the primary beneficiaries of the globalisation process, imposing the substantial costs of risk on others'. He continues:

> This would matter little if it were not for the enormity of the stake for states and their societies at large. The metamorphosis of a series of closed, cartelised, nationally controlled and often segmented financial systems into a transnationally desegmented and marketised space characterised by a high degree of capital volatility and mobility is one of the great and unplanned transformations of the twentieth century. (Underhill 1997: 42)

A long sentence indeed, but in it he summarises the essence of my own views of the international financial scene in the late 1990s. Nor, I believe, would two US ex-patriate academics working in England – Professor Phil Cerny at Leeds and Dr Randall Germain at Sheffield – disagree. Cerny, for example, holds that the global financial economy 'calls the tune for the real economy ... it has developed its own autonomous structural dynamic, a dynamic with regard to which international politics has yet to find a workable consensus on objectives or a feasible method of control' (Cerny 1993: 18).[8]

Like Kindleberger, the political economists would hesitate to predict the consequences. With the historians, they might add that financial crises – even consequential economic depressions – do not necessarily lead to political revolution. But they can do. In the 1930s, many governments were turned out of office; only the most authoritarian European rulers – Stalin, Mussolini, Salazar – survived. And though Roosevelt in 1933 feared social unrest in America, and many young Americans began to look to the Soviet Union as a possible alternative social system, the capitalist system did manage to survive. War, more often than slumps and unemployment, has been the nursery of revolution.

One more observer-participant worth hearing is Paul Erdman, author of a series of financial thrillers all firmly based on the reality of financial markets. In the first of these – written in a Swiss prison while serving sentence for a financial misdemeanour – there were three or four pages of explanation of how foreign exchange markets really work that I have regularly passed to graduate students as far better and clearer than anything written by a professor of economics. His more recent book, *Tug of War: today's global currency crisis*, is short and to the point. His question is whether the 1995 Mexican peso crisis may be the prelude to 'a dollar meltdown that could leave the international currency system in total disarray, resulting in the irreversible decline and fall of the dollar as the world's reserve currency' (Erdman 1996: 6). On balance, his conclusion is that the dollar will survive, that the US economy is fundamentally strong, but that its political leaders in the Congress and the executive show no signs of arresting the expansion of the pool of dollars in foreign hands, increasing with each passing year and rising toward the $2 trillion mark. 'That,' Erdman says, 'would be tantamount to the creation of a "dollar bubble" of unprecedented size which, in turn, could be the precursor of the Currency Crisis of 1997 or 1999' (Erdman 1996: 161). He correctly notes that the Group of Seven, while aware of the dangers, did nothing to rein in the hedge funds that were behind the currency speculation of 1995. Yet markets – and the immense vested interests behind them who want to maintain the status quo – have simply outgrown governments' ability to regulate them. As he says, over the decade 1986–96, bond issues tripled, securities issues have increased more than tenfold and foreign exchange transactions have quadrupled to $1 trillion.

Not everyone involved in this debate would agree with Erdman – or Grieder and Schumann – that the markets have simply 'outgrown' governments. Some would argue that though governments have been left behind, they can always catch up, given the will to do so.[9] This is one of the issues to be gone into in later chapters. For the moment, the point is only that the liveliness of this debate over globalisation in international finance at the very least suggests that it is indeed an issue of some importance. My personal conviction – and my motivation for returning to the themes of *Casino Capitalism* – is that it is *the* prime issue of international politics and economics. Since the end of the Cold War, it has slowly dawned on those engaged in international studies that the prevention of inter-state violence – war – is no longer the top-ranking problematic of the times. Major war between the great powers is still possible but increasingly unlikely (Mueller 1989; Stopford and Strange 1991: ch. 2). Civil war will still produce plenty of violence – but, as in the past, intervention by other states will be the exception rather than the rule because of the basic principles on which international politics and international law have long been founded. Violence we shall still have. Repeats of World War I or II – major wars between rich and strong states – are very unlikely.

Conclusion

The foregoing *tour d'horizon* of contending contributors and observers from different countries, different professions and with different ideological preferences will have shown that, on this subject at least, there is no established conventional wisdom. Each individual can be his/her own pundit. We can proceed now to my particular question. It is this: which of these changes are potential 'threats without enemies'? Where are the truly serious flaws in the system which threaten its stability and even survival? Is it governments that have become weaker or more irresponsible, or markets that have become stronger and more unruly? Some of these flaws, or weaknesses, are technical, some are simply political – but no less important to all involved for that.

The rest of the book, therefore, seeks to look in turn at some of the more obvious of the changes. I start with technology, mainly because I believe it to be important but grossly and erroneously neglected by academics, both economists and political scientists. Neglect by economists explains the next two chapters. They are about politics between governments, what used to be called diplomatic history, an aspect of social relations that has been quite notoriously volatile and unpredictable – think of the Molotov–Ribbentrop pact of 1939, the US–Soviet alliance after 1941, the US reconciliation with China in 1972 – the list of allies who fall out, of enemies who join together, is endless. Today, lacking what US scholars and others would describe loosely as a 'regime', the management of international financial crises will depend – as in the past – on political relationships between states. The two most crucial of such relationships, that between the United States and Japan, and between France and Germany in Europe, occupy chapters 3 and 4. Chapters 6 and 7 look in turn at two major failures of the system – the failure to find a general long-term solution to the problem of transnational indebtedness, and the failure to keep finance honest, free of crime, not only by criminals but by dealers and politicians. Finally in the closing chapters, we get to the heart of the matter. How much financial order is there that we can count on? What rules still hold? Whose authority, if anyone's, still reigns over the markets?

One important note: my purpose is not to predict with certainty that any of these flaws in the financial system will prove fatal, that one or more of its weak links will break, bringing catastrophe upon us. About the only positive thing to be said in favour of the study of international relations as a specialised branch of social science is that it strongly persuades its students of the impossibility of foresight when it comes to the behaviour of states.

My patrons for this book, the Economic and Social Science Research Council of Britain, may not like to be reminded of this but there was a time in the early years of the agency when much money was spent on a project called the Thirty Years Programme. Some time around 1962 or 1963, when I was teaching at University College and my late friend and colleague Geoffrey Goodwin was teaching at the London School of Economics, we were asked by the Social Sciences Research Council – as it was then called – to write a report on the future course of events in international organisation. We should look ahead thirty years, to the mid-1990s. We were honest enough, I am glad to say, to report that we didn't know – and nor did anyone else. Who, we asked, would have dared predict in the mid-1930s what international organisations there would be by the mid-1960s?

For a while in the 1970s, it is true that some American scholars in this subject were misled into forgetting the lessons of past scholarship. Much influenced by behaviouralist thinking – and deeply envious of the popular and official heed (wrongly) paid to economic forecasting – they came to convince themselves that, given enough quantitative data, it would eventually be possible to discover patterns and from them to predict the course of international relations. The result of much painstaking late-night labour by their graduate students was disappointing. Their findings were either banal or inconclusive. For example, much has been made of the finding that democratic states were less apt to go to war with each other than they were with non-democratic states. But the data could not show whether this was because they were democratic – even assuming a definition of the term could be agreed – or whether it was because they were relatively affluent. Fortunately, most younger scholars in international studies today are no longer so sure that more study and better data will bring greater skill or luck in forecasting. For me, at least, a long career as a teacher in international relations and international political economy has only confirmed my scepticism. History, including economic history, is the essential corrective for intellectual hubris. Economists, please note.

None of the above means that scenarios, rather than forecasts, are not worth thinking about. Some consideration of flaws or weak links in the global financial system may serve to alert readers to where the pitfalls may be, so that thought can be given to the appropriate policies and rationales that might help us either to avoid them by anticipation or to climb out of them should we all fall in. The late Robert Triffin used to justify his scathing critiques of the international monetary system in this way: 'My alternatives may not be feasible now,' he would say, 'But perhaps one day, after the necessary catastrophe, they may be rediscovered and made use of'.[10] The same logic was behind the aphorism in international affairs, 'To keep peace, prepare for war'.

Notes

1   Just as insurance firms put their weight behind strict regulation of airports against the danger of fire damage because otherwise they would face ever-larger claims against them, so some are now realising that law suits against some of their most important customers for environmental damage could also be a major problem for the future (Haufler 1997a, b).
2   I am reminded of a tragi-comic story from the German hyperinflation of 1923. My dear friend, the late Willi Guttman, told me about his uncle, a small-time rentier who put his savings into a few Munich apartments. While prices rocketed, rents were fixed. The hyperinflation left him penniless. Only the fact that he was Jewish stopped him joining the one political party – the Nazis – which seemed to understand and sympathise with his anger and frustration. Willi's book of reminiscences of Germany in the hyperinflation was full of similar stories (Guttman and Meehan 1975).
3   A companion volume, *The Political Economy of International Money: in search of a new order*, was edited by Loukas Tsoukalis (Tsoukalis 1985). That book was based on a series of study group meetings at the Royal Institute for

International Affairs in the mid-1970s. As chairman of those meetings, I had had the advantage of listening to a variety of eminent authorities reflecting on the past decade. The project, directed by Professor Tsoukalis, was funded by the British Economic and Social Research Council.

4 The political naïveté, combined with enormous methodological arrogance, of which some economists are capable is well illustrated in a 1995 collection of papers published under the title *The Economics of Organised Crime* (Fiorentini and Peltzman 1995). One considers the comparative efficiency of states and the mafia as 'rival kleptocracies, robbing the people for the benefit of the rulers'; another treats the mafia as models of oligopolistic cartels.

5 *International Herald Tribune*, 14 June 1997.

6 Private communication, 17 April 1997.

7 Some contemporary writers might disagree. Britain's Will Hutton, now editor of *The Observer*, wrote a highly critical book about the shortcomings of Conservative governments in Britain, concluding that keynesian-inspired policies would have been preferable (Hutton 1995). The experience of France under Mitterrand in 1983/4 suggests that, however preferable, such policies might not have been practicable.

8 See chapters 8 and 9. Cerny's edited book has chapters by three Canadians and a Briton, Peter Vipond. Germain's single-authored book is more up to date (Germain 1997).

9 For example, Howard Wachtel (1987) takes this line.

10 One of Triffin's last essays, written when he was over eighty, is available only as a working paper. He called it *IMS – International Monetary System – or Scandal?*. It was published by the European University Institute in Florence in 1992. Triffin, for the benefit of younger readers, first became famous in the 1960s after he wrote *Gold and the Dollar Crisis*, correctly predicting that the gold exchange standard enshrined in the Bretton Woods Agreements was set on an unsustainable path and would not last (Triffin 1961).

Chapter 2

Innovations

Few informed observers would deny that the global financial system in the 1980s and 1990s has been marked by an especially rapid rate of innovation. Change has been constant, fast and contagious as between markets, operators and institutions. The effects on the system have been so extensive that it is not too much to say that the whole story of the decade can be traced to different forms of innovation.

The last chapter briefly reviewed some of the main differences between the system as it is today, in the late 1990s, and the system as it was between 1971 and the mid-1980s. This chapter will list and describe the most important of the innovations which lay behind some of these changes. It will conclude with some comments on the consequences – social and political as well as economic – of recent innovations. First, however, it will help to think more generally about the nature of innovation and the wider implications of different kinds of innovation for the economy and society.

The nature of innovation

People innovate for profit. But profitability is not simply a matter of economics. The opportunity to make a profit out of innovation is given, or withheld, by political authority of one kind or another. Most often, that authority comes from a government. In a state-planned economy like the old Soviet Union, the innovator's profit or reward (if any) comes directly from some agency of the state. In a mixed or market economy, the opportunity to profit from innovation is given by the state more indirectly, by providing guarantees for intellectual property rights and the sanctity of contracts, and by allowing, rather than denying, certain potentially profitable activities. Some examples where political authority has taken different decisions according to time, place and social mores, are over the opportunity to profit from running casinos or brothels, of selling blue movies, alcohol or patent medicines.

In some circumstances, the opportunity can also be given – or denied – by non-state authorities. There have been times when large firms, or trade associations, have opposed and prevented innovations that threatened profits even though they might have benefited consumers. The interest of mafia bosses in money laundering has encouraged them to give new opportunities for profit to compliant banks. Professional associations and labour unions are two sources of non-state regulation that can, and do, make rulings on what innovatory practices are acceptable and what are not. Like governments, both intervene between the innovator and the market.

So much for the necessary and sufficient conditions for the advent of innovations. What about their consequences? Economic historians have been arguing for years about the role of technological innovation in a market economy. The Austrian economist Joseph Schumpeter, in particular, believed that the ups and downs, the booms and slumps of market economies since the early nineteenth century could be correlated with variations in the amount of technological innovation. The building of railroads, the advances in industrial chemistry like the Haber–Bosch process of synthesising ammonia using nitrogen from the air, the discovery of electricity, the internal combustion engine, in his view, all had a galvanising impact on the European economies. They brought in new enterprises and made old ones unprofitable and obsolete (Schumpeter 1961). Periods of expansion on the back of technical progress then alternated with periods of consolidation and slower growth. More recently, economic historians like Chris Freeman in Britain or Nathan Rosenberg in America have elaborated on the importance of technology in relation to economic growth and as a factor explaining the ups and downs in Kondratiev long waves – the fifty-year cycles in wages and prices first noticed by the Soviet economist Kondratiev (Freeman and Soete 1997; Rosenberg 1994).[1]

Most of this work, however, was concerned with technological innovation in manufacturing industry and to some extent with the innovations in transport and communication systems on which industry depended. Comparatively little heed has ever been paid to technical innovations used by the banks and in financial dealing, nor to the technical innovations devised by the banks themselves (and by their competitors) that changed the modes of operation of, and the services provided by, financial markets and institutions, and therefore the distribution of structural power in the political economy. This is the more remarkable in that economic historians have always been well aware of the importance of finance both to trade and to investment, and sociologists have always recognised the changes that money and credit make to social relations.[2]

While a whole chapter could easily be devoted to the technologies used by financial operators and financial markets, for present purposes we can sum them up under three main headings or categories of technology: computers, chips and satellites. Computers – now a major capital investment for any enterprise engaged in finance – have changed the prevailing system of financial settlement out of all recognition. For hundreds of years, current payments and capital transfers were completed in negotiable cash – coins and notes – and in written promises to pay. They were recorded by handwriting in ledgers. Coins and notes gave way progressively to cheques and other promises to pay, such as letters of credit. Since the early 1970s, these too have become obsolete. Computers have made money electronic. This was foreseen by some observers as far back as the 1960s. 'Money had become nothing but guaranteed alphanumeric data recorded in valueless paper and metal. It would eventually become guaranteed data in the form of arranged electrons and photons which would move around the world at the speed of light' (Dee Hock, Chief Executive of Visa, in 1968).[3]

In fact, twenty-five years later, by the mid-1990s, computers had not only transformed the physical form in which money worked as a medium of exchange, they were also in the process of transforming the systems by which payments of money were exchanged and recorded. The United States led with electronic cheque-clearing systems linking banks and their customers. Another electronic system, CHIPS (Clearing House Interbank Payments System), had started with the first use of an early mainframe computer back in the early 1970s. By 1995, what had rapidly grown as a clearing system between US banks had become the largest international clearing system, with 142 domestic and foreign banks using the system to clear roughly 200,000 transactions a day worth in total $1.3 trillion. The new system also allowed any participating bank at any moment of the day to look into its computers and see the state of the accounts of any other CHIPS participating bank, thus giving it the chance to delay or suspend payments to any bank that looked to be headed for trouble. This is only one of the many ways in which computers, communicating with other computers, have made money and banking electronic – and in the process have changed the power relations between the players.

The chips or programmed semiconductors used in computers have also had other technical applications affecting finance. For example, chips have enabled individual consumers to become accustomed to paying in 'plastic' rather than in cash for any but the most trivial amounts (and even those – as with parking meters that accept plastic rather than coins). The credit card has revolutionised shopping in most developed countries and is rapidly spreading to the developing ones. It is already being overtaken by the smart card, which is another piece of plastic, in which a chip records a deposit from a bank account and subtracts from it the value of any purchase or transaction. It is probably still too early to guess the full implications of what has been called 'digital money'. But it is already clear that both the credit card and the smart card have already extended the areas of significant ignorance for monetary authorities, since the amount of outstanding consumer credit on dedicated shop or petrol station cards as well as bank-issued credit cards is a matter of guesswork, although clearly important for the money supply and the velocity of money within a national economy and for its balance of payments with others. Digital money will significantly enlarge these areas of official blindness, according to Professor Kobrin at the Wharton School. Not only will the national money supply become an even more imprecise concept, foreign exchange transactions will be untrackable and untraceable. Innovation in the market will make one more major inroad into the authority of governments (Kobrin 1997).

Thirdly, there are the systems of communication using earth-orbiting satellites. This technology, of course, started in the 1950s with the Soviet Sputnik and was developed by the Americans and Russians for military purposes. By the 1970s and 1980s, the system was being used by private enterprises, especially banks, to link headquarters offices with affiliates and associates throughout the world (Hamelink 1983). While computers could exchange data between themselves, opinions, rumours and advice – more personalised information – still depended on person-to-person communication. Yet by the 1990s, communication by fax and telephones was also becoming obsolete as electronic mail and the Internet became the preferred and habitual systems by which markets, financial and other, were integrated into a single system.

As remarked earlier, very few social scientists have given as much thought as they should either to the technologies of computers, chips and satellites now used in financial business, or to the technology of the financial business itself. This neglect was less important so long as the wealth and economic power were mostly found among the captains of industry – Carnegie, Krupp, Thiessen, Nobel and the like. Now that the great new fortunes are being made in money and banking, and in financial and communication services, it is time to think about the role of technological innovation in finance and on the role of financial innovation in the larger economic system.

But the earlier work is useful because the historians discerned two rather different kinds of innovation. Some innovators introduced new products. Others made money by introducing new processes of production, or new ways of managing or marketing. Sometimes, the two went together – as when Henry Ford revolutionised transport systems by designing a cheap, simplified car, and at the same time devised a new system of assembly-line production breaking down the work so that he could employ armies of relatively cheap, unskilled workers. In finance, a comparable distinction between technological change – as with the use of computers to keep records or make deals – and financial change, as in the introduction of new credit instruments or new market structures, was first made in the 1980s by a Japanese banker, Soichi Enkyo of the Bank of Tokyo. He argued that the financial innovations and the technological ones went together, and that most of both kinds were introduced first in the United States and spread first to London and then to Tokyo (Enkyo 1989). That observation is still true.

Moreover, in finance, there is a further distinction that can be made between innovative products – or services – and innovative processes. We find that some innovations – and highly profitable ones at that – were new financial products or services – like Eurodollar loans in the 1960s or junk bonds in the 1970s. Others were new ways of operating in financial markets, not only by using the technological innovations such as the computers, chips and satellites mentioned above, but also by introducing new players into the game, or by finding new ways of minimising the inherent risks, by diversifying operations or by involving new risk-sharing partners. Sometimes, as in industry, the introduction of a new product coincided with a new way of doing business, so that it becomes difficult to say which brought most benefit to the innovators.

In either case, however, the tacit or explicit permission of one or more political authorities was a necessary condition for the successful introduction of the product, or service, or of the new process or new player in the markets. Usually, permission for the financial innovation, whether tacit or explicit, had to come from government or an agency of government. This is one big difference between innovation in manufacturing and innovation in finance. For the most part, government has not been greatly concerned about what went on in the factory – unless or until it turns out afterwards to affect the health or safety of workers, neighbours or consumers. It has always been much more concerned about who was providing credit, and in what form, on what terms, simply because this affected not just one sector of the economy but all of them, and was also much more open to abuses of partiality or fraud.

It follows that the responsibility for what has been beneficial in recent financial innovations, and for what has put the rest of the economy in dangerous jeopardy, has to be shared between the innovators who thought up the new ideas and the regulators who gave their permission, or failed to impose conditions on the innovators. This is why the distinction made in manufacturing between new products and new processes is still useful. It is so because, in finance, much more than in manufacturing, each might pose different policy issues: regulators might find the product perfectly legitimate and acceptable but might object to the associated process or way of doing business with it, as in insider trading in shares, for instance.

The comparison of innovation in industry with innovation in finance raises another question. It is whether the rate of innovative change is accelerating in the business of finance as it seems to have been accelerating in manufacturing industry and, indeed, in agriculture. In the literature of business management, there is now wide recognition of the fact that technological change in the latter part of the twentieth century has been getting faster and that this has had important implications for corporate strategies and management. Managers are urged by business school professors to make greater efforts to keep up with the accelerating pace of technological change, in order to avoid being overtaken – or indeed, taken over – by their competitors (Dunning 1993; Porter 1990). The argument is directed mostly at manufacturing firms. Here it is pretty evident to all that old technologies, whether relating to the product or the processes of its production and marketing, are becoming obsolete faster than those they replaced, and that current technologies in turn will become more rapidly obsolete than was usual twenty or even ten years ago. It is also pretty evident that, in manufacturing – and indeed in mining and agriculture – the nature of innovatory technology is such that both the products and the processes of their production are becoming more capital intensive and less labour intensive than those they replace.[4] The combination of added costs of investment and diminished time for the realisation of profits from the product or process has effectively pushed firms into seeking larger markets from which to extract the income necessary to amortise the debts incurred for capital investment in time to be ready for the next wave of technological innovation. This, it is now argued, is a more powerful force behind the internationalisation of industrial production than the saving in transaction costs made possible by enlarging the size and scope of the firm (Stopford and

Strange 1991: 77–9). Globalisation and the shift of manufacturing to developing countries is made imperative not just by the availability of cheap labour in these places, but by the prospects of adding new customers and thus additional profits, which will help the firm keep up with the accelerating rate of technological change.

All this has direct relevance to the subject of financial innovation, for it is arguable that the driving forces behind financial innovation are not all that different from those behind industrial innovation. Here, too, accelerating technological change has obliged banks to invest more capital in their business and to seek new markets. They have found it necessary to install expensive computers and equally expensive software in order to manage the business. And the technology of automated teller machines (ATMs) and systems for automatic transfer of money, while it saves labour, is also capital intensive. Nor is it just the mechanical technology that raises the costs of competing. Both banks and their non-bank rivals have to find and pay the people able to provide the new management and consultancy services and products with which to make profits. There are also large costs in setting up the necessary transnational network of offices and partners.

But the appreciation in financial circles of the power of those forces and the analysis of their significance for regulatory policy makers are lagging far behind the management consultants who deal with industrial enterprises. Just as it is not international production that is new, but rather the scale on which it is now practised, so it is not international financial transactions and transnational financial services that are new but rather the scale on which they occur and the rapid pace at which they proliferate.

The blame for this neglect, it must be confessed, lies partly with the business schools, partly with economic theorists and political scientists. The business schools are inclined to concentrate their interest on 'how-to-do-it' questions and therefore to teach their students the technicalities of corporate financing without providing them with any understanding of why and how there have been such very great changes in the range of options open for corporate financing, and in the consequent risks to the system as well as to the individual enterprise. It also lies in part with the economists, so impressed with the seductive logic of the notion of transaction costs that they ignore the dynamism of technology as a decisive factor in a market economy, even when it concerns the production of goods. Instead of the Ricardian concept of land, labour and capital as the three basic factors of production, there are now, in reality, five such factors when technology and energy are added to the list. Moreover, since the pervasive Harvard case study method gives preference to manufacturing business rather than to the production of services, including financial services, the shared myopia has been even more marked. And as for political scientists and other social scientists, their interest in, and understanding of, the niceties of all financial matters is so limited that even when these innovations are seen by financial journalists and practitioners to have fundamental political and social significance, only a few academics have been able to share this important perception.[5]

Derivatives

> Only a decade ago, global derivative markets were small and undeveloped compared with the other international capital markets. Since then, the average annual growth of OTC and exchange-traded derivative markets has been 40 per cent a year. (International Monetary Fund 1996: 25)[6]

If the International Monetary Fund (IMF) judges the growth of trading in derivatives to be the most important innovative change in the international financial system since the mid-1980s, it is by no means alone. The same opinion has been voiced by the Bank for International Settlements (1996: 370–80) and the United Nations Conference on Trade and Development (UNCTAD) in Geneva (Cornford 1995). To explain what derivatives are and how they came to occupy so central a place in the system, a little historical background will be helpful.

Essentially, derivatives are a sophisticated way of managing risk, and have grown to be important as both the risks and the number of potential victims of risk have multiplied. The concept itself is not new. Traders agreed forward contracts for deferred delivery of crops or other goods as far back as the middle ages. Futures contracts – agreements to buy or sell at a future date at an agreed price – were already a developed practice in seventeenth-century Japan, and forward contracts in foreign currencies were available in nineteenth-century Germany. Mostly, however, the trade in futures contracts was predominantly associated until recently with commodity markets, either in crops or in minerals, while special OTC deals in foreign exchange or shares were less common.

Growth came in the 1970s, as the volatility and uncertainty in prices and exchange rates rapidly increased with the inflation associated with the Vietnam War, the Nixon devaluation of the dollar and the consequent 'reform' of the Bretton Woods Agreement on fixed exchange rates.[7] Trading in derivatives allowed banks and transnational enterprises a chance, at relatively low cost, to hedge against losses from changes in exchange rates, in oil or other commodity prices and against unforeseen changes in interest rates.

A good definition of derivatives is that they are 'contracts specifying rights and obligations which are based upon, and thus derive their value from, the performance of some underlying instrument, investment, currency, commodity or service index, right or rate' (Cornford 1995: 347, adapted from a 1993 report by the United States Commodity Futures Trading Commission).

The growth in this kind of financial trading has been truly phenomenal, so that the value of outstanding derivative contracts in twenty-six countries was estimated as amounting to twice the value of world economic output, or some $47.5 trillion in March 1995 (International Monetary Fund 1996: 25). Almost all of the market – all but 2 per cent – was accounted for by contracts in currencies (foreign exchange rates) or interest rates. This survey by central banks revealed that the OTC market was much bigger than previously estimated and was almost twice the size of the exchange-traded derivative market. A bare five years earlier, OTC contracts in total were estimated in total at $3,450 billion, compared with almost $18 trillion in 1995 and $24 trillion in 1996.[8]

What accounted for this explosion of dealing in derivatives? Part of the explanation lies in regulation and the wish of private dealers to get round the regulations. Recall that the growth in Eurodollar trading had been partly motivated by irksome restrictions – like the famous Regulation Q limiting the amount of interest payable on short-term bank loans within the United States. Escaping to London, where the rules did not apply, even to US banks, opened new opportunities for profitable intermediation between depositors with dollars to lend and borrowers in need of dollars. Similarly, governments in the 1960s and 1970s, while they had made their currencies freely convertible for current transactions, had often tried to limit the risks to their balance of payments by putting restrictions on deals that affected the capital account. They continued to restrict their nationals' freedom to borrow in foreign currencies or penalised them for doing so. In response, banks soon devised smart ways of getting round the controls by arranging swaps or back-to-back loans that achieved the same result as lending or borrowing in other currencies. Once this had become common practice, it was a short step to hedging deals between parties with different needs and divergent comparative advantages in lending or borrowing. These swaps could be on interest rates – short or long term – or on spot or forward exchange rates.

The other part of the explanation lies in the coincidence of escalating need and escalating risk. As international trade and international production grew apace, the number of firms which needed to have access to foreign currency, to foreign loans or supplies also grew. But with this increased need went the increased risk that profits could be wiped out by unpredictable changes in exchange rates, interest rates or commodity prices. For example, the profits of a certain successful manufacturer of confectionery were wiped out one year in the 1970s by some unwise dealing in cocoa futures. Derivatives offered the opportunity to hedge such unwise dealing with a contrary bet that prices would not rise but fall.

The third part of the explanation lies – as always – in the opportunity for profit opened up by the innovation. The fact that it was relatively unregulated and untaxed meant that there was plenty of competition, so the cost of hedging, of dealing in derivatives, stayed comparatively low. Effectively, the bet could be made 'on margin', with the dealer in derivatives taking liability only for the difference in exposure between the actual and the traded prices. Thus although the 'notional value' of derivative deals worldwide, as mentioned above, could amount to nearly $50 trillion, the credit exposure of the banks offering derivative deals was only 5 per cent of this sum. True, this was still quite a large exposure, equal in total to three times the aggregate total capital of the seventy-five largest banks. But against the risks entailed, there were also greater opportunities for banks to profit, not only by offering the service of derivative dealing to the clients, but also by dealing for themselves. There was no rule, in short, that said that 'bets' could be placed only on behalf of clients. When markets were moving in one clear direction, whether up or down, a bank or a hedge fund could lay off its liabilities to clients by increasing its converse bets. And it could also, at small cost or risk, take a position on its own account that, if it proved correct, could net large returns. But, of course, if it proved wrong, it could equally result in large losses.

Another striking feature of the derivative business is its dynamism. Innovation in these contracts was never a once-and-for-all kind of change. For example, in May 1997, credit derivatives were one of the most talked about new products in financial markets. These new contracts allowed a bank to sell off to someone else the risk that one of its borrowers might default. First thought up in New York five years before as default swaps or default options, they allowed a bank to pay an investor another kind of insurance premium for taking on the risk and becoming liable to the original lender if the borrower did not pay up – or even if its estimated ability to pay – its credit rating with one of the bond-rating agencies – were to fall. Still small by comparison with the bread-and-butter markets in exchange-traded and OTC derivatives, the credit derivative displays the same essential character of meeting both the customers' needs and the correspondingly great opportunities for profit, and of giving the apparent reassurance that escalating financial risks can be managed. Whether, in truth, the reassurance is real or illusory is a question we shall return to later in chapter 8, in which the adequacy or inadequacy of existing systems of regulation and supervision are examined.

Meanwhile, an important feature of the derivatives business lies in the distinction, reflected in the available statistics, between exchange-traded deals and OTC deals. It is the latter which in recent years have grown fastest. And it is OTC trading which is least transparent, in which the area of significant ignorance of what is really going on is most extensive.[9]

The essential difference is that exchange-traded derivative deals are standard contracts, subject to the rules imposed by the exchange – whether a commodity exchange like the Chicago Commodity Futures Exchange or a financial exchange like the London International Financial Futures Exchange (LIFFE). The exchange itself is a party to every deal, because the contracting parties are usually obliged to operate through a clearing house. These are separate corporate institutions through which all deals must go and be recorded. Their 'shareholders', so to speak, are large financial institutions which provide backing for all the risks in the market. The greater information available to the clearing house means that at the end of each day the amount traded is known and so is the movement of prices for different kinds of deals and the net profit or loss of individual dealers. This is called 'marking to market'. It does not happen in the OTC market, where there is no clearing house and every deal is made in ignorance of other OTC deals. Neither of the parties knows how exposed the other is. Neither of them knows where the market is moving, nor whether any other parties dealing in the market are overexposed to risks of various kinds. Moreover, most national accounting systems do not require firms or banks to reveal their derivatives dealing and whether it adds up to a net asset or liability to the enterprise.

Obviously, the clearing house has to have resources sufficient to meet the obligations of dealers who fail to pay up, for whatever reason. This was evident in the 1980s, when the worldwide stock market collapse in October 1987 hit the newly formed Hong Kong Futures Exchange (HKFE), on which speculative bets on very short-term changes in share prices could be made at low cost. Before Wall Street opened on 19 October, the Hang Seng Index fell 11 per cent. The HKFE was closed, leaving 250,000 deals (equal to one week's normal trading) unsettled. This was too much for the clearing house, the Hong Kong Futures Guarantee Corporation. The government, jointly with the big financial firms, put up an initial HK$2 billion rescue package and, when this was exhausted, a second one. The exchange was saved but an inquiry revealed that the margin requirements on dealers had not always been properly enforced and that the commitment of the members or shareholders in the clearing house was insufficient to meet claims when the going got rough. Almost a third of the brokers belonging to the clearing house went bust. 'This experience,' commented Andrew Cornford, 'illustrates the dangers of shortcomings in legal and institutional frameworks or in supervision for other countries, including developing ones, contemplating the establishment of exchanges for financial futures' (Cornford 1995: 352).[10]

Leveraged buyouts and junk bonds

Two earlier, related innovations that are less important than derivatives but nonetheless interesting for both the factors giving rise to them and the consequences that followed are leveraged buyouts and junk bonds. The potential for profit from both was first discovered in the early 1980s but their heyday – and that of their promoters – was in the latter half of the decade. Junk bonds – more politely referred to as high-yield bonds – were the chosen means of financing leveraged buyouts, mergers and acquisitions in the United States in that period. Like conventional corporate bonds issued by firms wishing to raise long-term finance, the interest was fixed and paid to bondholders twice a year, but the market price could vary. The life of any corporate bond could be as short as three years or as long as twenty years. Where the junk bonds differed was in the yield: instead of the going rate for ordinary corporate bonds at the time of 8–10 per cent, junk bonds paid 11–15 per cent – well above inflation rates of 2 or 3 per cent.

The junk bond story has been told many times as a highly coloured tale of the players who came from nowhere, dazzled the financial scene – and then came to grief (Anders 1992; Burrough and Helyar 1990). But from a systemic angle, it can also be seen as part of a broader political economy story in which the inflation of the 1970s, fuelled by the Vietnam War and the oil price rise, and the cumulative revolution in banking both played a large part. By the revolution in banking, I mean the change that began with the innovation of the Eurodollar in which the old, staid but profitable business of inter-mediating between depositors and borrowers slowly gave way to a new financial services industry in which large profits were made by various means that had nothing to do with traditional intermediation (Mayer 1997: 446). The effect of the inflation of the 1970s had been to change

popular perceptions of banks as safe places to keep personal or
corporate savings. When inflation rates climbed to 6 or more per cent
but the bank was paying 2 or 3 per cent, the depositor was losing
money. His store of value was shrinking. Constrained by old regulations on short-term interest rates, US banks devised new kinds of
bank accounts – like the so-called negotiable order of withdrawal
(NOW) accounts – which got round the regulations and paid money
market rates.

The other effect of the 1970s inflation, especially in the United
States, was to render obsolete the historic valuation of corporate assets
and thus to make firms vulnerable to mergers and takeovers by new
owners who, by revaluing their assets nearer to current market values
and by restructuring the business, could make it more profitable. In
many countries, notably Germany and Japan, there were legal,
institutional and even cultural obstacles to mergers and acquisitions of
one firm by another. Not in the United States. The only problem there
was how to finance the buyout of another company. Enter what Anders
calls the 'merchants of debt', not the inventors but the most successful
promoters of the leveraged buyout (Anders 1992). His account of the
rise and fall of Kohlberg, Kravis and Roberts (KKR) and their
association with Michael Milken and Drexel Burnham Lambert (DBL),
who invented and promoted the junk bonds with which the buyouts
were financed, shows that neither enterprise was either well known or
successful until the mid-1980s. KKR had started in 1976 with just
$120,000 of the partners' capital, but in the course of the 1980s had
managed company takeovers worth nearly $60 billion. Their crowning
achievement, the takeover of RJR Nabisco for a record-breaking price
of $26.4 billion in 1989, also proved their undoing.

If the opportunity for this meteoric success was given partly by the
impact of inflation on banking and on business, it was also given
unwittingly by the government. A tax concession originally designed as
far back as 1909 to facilitate and encourage productive investment in
American industry allowed firms to set payments on debt against the
profits on which they were liable to be taxed. What KKR realised, and
cashed in on – literally – was that this tax concession could help
finance the takeover.

The case of the Houdaille Company, a Florida manufacturer of
machine tools, pumps and car bumpers, and KKR's first big successful
deal, shows how this worked. The KKR partners put up only 0.3 per
cent of the money. They offered to pay $355 million for the buyout –
but – and this was the essential sweetener to the firm's top managers –
to leave the management intact. The rest of the finance was to be
borrowed, a bit from the management, who would put up $25 million

but would then get to own the company, a bit from preferred stock sold to local banks, and the bulk (85 per cent) from new debt – in effect, different kinds of high-yield junk bonds sold on the assurance that the refinanced enterprise would become more profitable and therefore be well able to service and repay the debt. It could do so in part because $22 million or so would no longer have to be paid out to the US government in tax because the debt payments would be set against the firm's operating profits. KKR's profits from the deal came from finding the institutions – banks like the ill-fated Continental Illinois, insurance companies like Prudential and a series of syndicates of lenders keen to profit from the high-yield debt. KKR's success involved all sorts of legal wangles like setting up shell holding companies to give collective consent to the deal. And it could all have fallen apart had the US government, in the shape of the Securities and Exchange Commission (SEC), not agreed to allow the takeover. Its consent was given, subject only to provisions for greater transparency of the new enterprise's accounts.

If the rise of KKR had been meteoric, its fall was even swifter. A combination of causes can be found for it. One, paradoxically in view of the SEC's compliant attitude at the start, was the intervention of a regulator, Robert Clarke. In 1989, he was both the US Comptroller of the Currency and a director of the Federal Deposit Insurance Corporation (FDIC). Clarke persuaded his fellow FDIC directors to award the proposed buyout of a Texas bank not to KKR, which offered the highest price, but to a rival Ohio bank, on the not unreasonable grounds that KKR was, by its past record, likely to break the bank up and sell off the pieces for its own short-term profit. Clarke had come to the conclusion that these sort of deals were not in the long-term interests of US banking.

Another factor was the falling-out between the KKR partners. Kohlberg began suing the two cousins Kravis and Roberts for, in effect, cheating him of his share in deals going back even to the Houdaille case (Anders 1992: 226). But although the cousins played cool, they had bargained without public opinion, both in financial circles and beyond. First *The Economist* and then the *Wall Street Journal* started asking questions. The former wondered whether Kravis had not overdone things; the partners were making annual profits of $100 million each and indulging in much-publicised conspicuous consumption. The latter, very unusually for so conservative a paper, took up arms for the workers. In 1990, it published a long, prize-winning article comparing the fate of sacked workers for the Safeway retail chain – one of KKR's biggest buyout deals – with the profits made by the promoters. It was picking up on testimony by the spokesmen of the

American Federation of Labor–Conference on Industrial Organization
to the Senate Finance Committee blaming leveraged buyouts for the
loss of 90,000 American jobs in a decade.

Coincidentally, two other factors compounded the situation. The
lenders who had bought the junk bonds began to get cold feet. And the
regulators tightened the rules. Clarke's doubts were backed by Alan
Greenspan at the Federal Reserve Board, which decided in February
1989 to require all major banks to make quarterly reports on their
exposure (i.e. holdings) of high-leveraged securities. The final blow
came with the indictment of Mike Milken in February 1989 and a rash
of defaults on junk bonds.

Those defaults also signalled the end of the alliance between KKR
and DBL, which soon after, in February 1990, filed for bankruptcy. It
had been holding $1.5 billion of its own junk bonds. As they lost
market value, it rashly paid the usual lavish bonuses to its top deal
makers. Banks refused to help and the Federal Reserve Board would
not extend emergency loans the way it often had to embattled banks
like Marine Midland or Continental Illinois.

Meanwhile, Mike Milken, who had started it all – and who
eventually went to prison, though not for long – is still recognised as
one of the great financial innovators of the decade: 'One of the great
bankers of the century,' according to Martin Mayer, the respected
American financial analyst and writer, 'The people with whom he
surrounded himself at Drexel Burnham were expert at valuing the
assets that underlay his junk bonds' (Mayer 1997: 466). Their
expertise was a necessary condition for the banking revolution referred
to earlier – that is, to the changeover from banks as a source of credit
in the system to banks as financial management consultants and
facilitators, so that their business overlapped with that of the securities
houses like DBL, Merrill Lynch, Goldman Sachs and others.

Concluding comments

At this point, it becomes clear that the stories of financial innovation
cannot be told simply from the operators' side; their inventiveness and
skills would have brought little profit to them or change to the system
without the connivance – conscious or unconscious – of political
authority. From an historian's point of view, this means that turning
points or benchmarks in the system are as likely to be non-decisions
and failures to act as they are to be active, conscious decisions.

For example, in the above case of the securities houses, the other
necessary condition was a chink in the American regulatory system.

This allowed these securities firms to operate insured non-banks under national or state charters, effectively giving them a licence to operate as sources of credit as if they were banks. The New Deal legislators who had drafted the famous Glass–Steagall Act of 1933 had not foreseen this chink. For the greater stability of the financial system, they had made separate rules for commercial banks and investment banks, while the 1927 McFadden Act had earlier forbidden interstate banking and imposed all sorts of restrictions on what banks could and could not do. But the possibility of competition from those securities houses which promised not to accept demand deposits but to exercise a right to make commercial loans had not occurred to them in the conditions of the early 1930s.

The eventual consequence was that the securities houses slowly crept up on the banks in the business of financial services. Moreover, the borrowers – non-financial businesses in industry and trade – came increasingly to act for themselves, bypassing banks by going straight to the market with their own promises to pay, so that the total amount of bank loans in the US system came to be only marginally larger than the total of commercial paper – that is, securities or promises to pay by governments, local authorities and a great many middle-sized businesses. By the 1990s in the US system, total bank loans amounted in all to $600 billion. Credit in the shape of securitised or commercial paper amounted to $550 billion. This was a truly revolutionary change in the financial system, with consequences that reached beyond far beyond the United States.

An important role in bringing about this change had been played by the earlier innovation of money market mutual funds (MMMFs). These funds had begun back in the 1970s to lend to trading or manufacturing firms at competitive prices. They did so by buying their securitised commercial paper, effectively creating credit, and by packaging the securitised paper in such a way that a diversified bundle spread the risks of loss by any one firm. By 1981, in just one year, the amount invested in MMMFs grew by $100 billion. The investors were happy to earn something nearer a money market rate of interest than they would have been able to get from the banks. The MMMFs were consequently denounced by the banks for 'disintermediation' – that is, taking away the core business of banking (Mayer 1997: 210).

The response from government was the authorisation by the Garn-St Germain Act of Congress in 1982 of money market deposit accounts (MMDAs). By allowing banks to offer MMDAs, the Congress hoped to help them fight back against the MMMFs. To some extent, the licensing of MMDAs worked, but it also encouraged the growth of non-bank banks, which in turn opened new opportunities to the MMMFs (D'Arista 1994: 14, 134).

To cut a long and highly complex story short enough to draw some broad conclusions, the chains of cause and effect again and again lead back to the destabilising effects of the 1970s inflation on established systems of political control over financial operators and their markets – and more particularly on the system of control established in the United States in the 1930s in the aftermath of the 1929 crash and the subsequent tide of bank failures. That system had had two political objectives. One was to rebuild public confidence in banks and savings institutions. This was mostly done by giving more security to the banks' customers by insuring their deposits against loss. This was achieved by setting up the FDIC (see chapter 8). The other objective was to devise ways of protecting the small and weak against the rich and strong, both the small-town banks and their customers, against the big money-centre banks and non-banks of New York, Chicago and the other big cities. Inflation in the 1970s started to undermine this system, starting a move of funds precisely away from the small and weak into the hands of the rich and strong.

For example, one effect of inflation in the 1970s was to raise the costs to small banks of servicing small accounts and small loans, but without any compensating increase in their profits. The result was that enterprising money brokers in the mid-1970s began collecting funds from small banks to lend to the big money-centre banks. Small banks themselves found they could earn a better return by putting larger amounts of their deposits, even overnight, on the interbank market. As D'Arista explains:

> Federal funds and large negotiable CDs [certificates of deposit] paid market rates of interest, and the cost of channelling millions of dollars to a handful of major institutions was much lower than the cost of processing small business loans, car loans, consumer loans etc. to local borrowers. The practice was so widespread in upstate New York that it was referred to by local business people as 'strip-mining' of funds. (D'Arista 1994:136)

Another small innovation in this earlier period was the NOW accounts, offered by US banks to their wealthier clients to help them keep pace with inflation. In 1980, these became more widely available when they were given the same legal protection of deposit insurance enjoyed by ordinary bank accounts. The intention was equitable: to make available to everyone a weapon against inflation hitherto available only to the wealthy. But the result was just further erosion of the 'Chinese walls' by which different kinds of institutions were given privileges while others had constraints put upon them, leading to one more twist in the downward deregulatory spiral.

The New Deal had also aimed to protect small local banks against the competition of larger, stronger money-centre banks, and to channel savings into building houses and into financing small businesses. It was, in short, a politically motivated system to direct private credit for political purposes. It sought deliberately to strike a balance between competitiveness, efficiency and enterprise in the markets on the one hand, and social values of stability and equity as between weak and strong, poor and rich on the other. An important measure of reform was to provide guarantees to depositors that bank failures would not rob them of their savings, as had happened in the early 1930s. The FDIC and the Federal Savings and Loans Insurance Corporation were set up for that purpose, and supplied with funds thought at the time to be more than sufficient to maintain confidence that the guarantees would be honoured. But once inflation took hold, threatening a depreciation of the value of money, cracks appeared in the structure of political control and regulation.

Thus a good many of the innovations of the period 1975 to 1995 were devised by quick-thinking and agile financial entrepreneurs to take profitable advantage of the cracks and chinks in the American regulatory system. But the consequences were not so much due to the innovations as to the failures of the regulators, and of the legislatures that set the rules in the first place, to respond to change with equal agility and quick thinking. This will be clear in chapter 8, when the tragi-comic story of the American savings and loans (S&Ls, or thrifts) is recounted. Mayer (1997: 361) calls it 'the saddest story in the long history of the relationship of American government and American banking'. And it certainly was sad for the US taxpayers who ended up having to find no less than $300 billion to buy out S&Ls. Mayer also observes that the American story was by no means unique. There were strong similarities with the comparable Japanese story of the failed *jusen* or real estate funds in 1996, which may eventually cost the taxpayers even more – perhaps $500 billion. And France, Sweden and Spain had all had the same experience of government in the 1990s overtaken by structural changes in the financial system but feeling obliged to rescue savings banks that had got into trouble. (What was perhaps peculiar to the US story was that the bailout gave an opportunity to financial entrepreneurs aware of the government safety net to buy up bankrupt S&Ls cheaply in the fairly safe expectation of a nice windfall profit.)

As others have noted, the importance of these changes in the American financial system for the rest of the world market economy can hardly be overestimated. The banking revolution started in the United States. But it did not stop there. Some things that the securities houses had done so profitably at home, they soon began to do abroad, first in London, then elsewhere. And some of the things they were not allowed to do at home they were free to do in the City of London and later elsewhere. The role of the City as an easy escape route for profit-hungry US banks under pressure at home of competition among themselves and also from newcomers in the financial services market is a part of the story easily overlooked by writers on financial developments in Britain on one hand and by writers on financial developments in the United States on the other. Where would US banks have gone to expand their international business if London had not offered an open door with 'Welcome' on the mat?

By the mid-1990s the element of contagion in the financial system was much more apparent than it was ten or fifteen years earlier. In the 1980s, the story of financial deregulation seemed to be a national one, mainly concerning changes relating to the American financial laws and institutions, with some belated overspill to Britain with the 'Big Bang' reforms of 1986. By the mid-1990s, and with the advantages of hindsight, it was easier for us to see, first, that the same dilemmas and pressures that were experienced in America would also soon be experienced in some form or other in other countries. Financial innovations did not stop at the water's edge.

The point should be noted by writers in the field of international relations. There has been a growing realisation – obvious to historians but obscured in international relations by obsolete concepts of an 'international society' made up of sovereign states – that the roots and causes of foreign policy decisions often lay in domestic politics.[11] Equally important, but not as yet generally appreciated, is the converse proposition – that the roots of international monetary and financial policy can often be traced to the domestic politics of the United States, especially inasmuch as these relate to banking and finance. Even the S&L story referred to earlier, although it appeared to be an entirely domestic matter for the United States, also had some kind of global contagion effect. If the United States could cheerfully bail out imprudent financial institutions at the taxpayer's expense, why should not others do the same? Certainly, no one outside Japan questioned the wisdom or necessity of the government to make good the banks' losses with the *jusen* in 1995. Nor did anyone stop the authorities in Thailand from stepping in to help those banks which had overinvested and got into subsequent difficulties in 1996. The only difference was that Thailand, unlike the United States or Japan, needed the help of the IMF and had to pay the price by conforming to its demands.[12]

As the story briefly outlined here surely suggests, the banking revolution being experienced worldwide, and the consequently enhanced power of financial markets over the state of the world economy, were, in very large part, 'made in America'. That awareness alone is sufficient reason for students of politics, economics and business – and indeed for politicians and business managers – to pay much closer attention to the significant innovations that were first introduced in the 1970s in the United States but which also cast their shadow forwards, accelerating change in the 1980s and the 1990s, and influencing many of the subsequent developments.

Notes

1 On Kondratiev, see Strange (1986: 62–4) and van Djuin (1983) and Freeman (1983).

2 For a summary of the ideas of Georg Simmel, Walter Bagehot and Frank Knight see Strange (1986: 104–11).

3 Quoted by Mayer (1997: 128). Mayer has two chapters devoted entirely to the technology of the computer age and its impact on banking and finance.

4 This is the connecting theme of Rifkin's *The End of Work*, in which he details how capital has replaced labour in agriculture and mining, in manufacturing and also in service businesses, including financial services (Rifkin 1996).

5 The list, though short, is distinguished and multidisciplinary. Richard Gardner (1956), by training a lawyer, was one of the first. Jerry Cohen (1998) is an economist, now a professor in political science. Another recent writer, Saskia Sassen (1996), is an urban sociologist. Peter Dicken (1992) and Stuart Corbridge (Corbridge *et al.* 1994) are both geographers. Lou Pauly, Phil Cerny, Geoffrey Underhill, Randall Germain and Andrew Walter (see bibliography) are all international political economists.

6 OTC markets stands for markets in over-the-counter, or customised contracts drawn up for particular clients, as opposed to standard contracts traded in commodity, foreign exchange or other markets.

7 For an account of the 'reform' proceedings, see Strange (1986: 41–3), Walter (1991: ch. 6) and Volcker and Gyohten (1992: chs 4, 5, 6).

8 By 1997, while official alarm bells were ringing, it is worth noting that private opinions were possibly somewhat less concerned than they had been a year earlier. The annual *Banana Skins* survey of opinion in the City conducted by the Centre for the Study of Financial Innovation, which had found wide agreement in 1996 that derivatives were the most dangerous of all 'banana skins' for the financial markets, produced a different result in 1997. The consensus this time (and in the wake of the Barings collapse) was that derivatives were less worrying than bad management by the banks – and this consensus was particularly strong among the bankers themselves!

9 The importance of growth in what I called 'areas of significant ignorance' was one of the conclusions made in *Casino Capitalism* (see Strange 1986: 128 ff.).

10 Cornford (1995) also gives detailed accounts of the 1985 default and closure of the London tin market; the strains on the US system in the October 1987 crisis; the Barings collapse in 1995; and the bankruptcies of the Bank of New England and DBL, among other financial firms that dabbled, too riskily, in financial derivatives.

11 See Keohane and Milner (1996); also the influential work of Robert Putnam on two-level games – those played by states in foreign relations and in domestic politics (Putnam 1988).
12 For further discussion on this issue, see chapter 3.

Chapter 3

Political underpinnings:
the US–Japan axis

The political foundations for international financial cooperation are weaker today than they were in the 1970s and 1980s. If we have worries about the stability of the international financial system, it is important to understand in what way these foundations are weaker and how this has come about. For, while the pace of technological innovation in finance (as in manufacturing) has accelerated, and while the size and salience of finance in the world economy have greatly increased, the political capability to adjust to these changes has, if anything, declined. This is an aspect of the problem that economists tend to overlook. They tend to take politics for granted. But, as in sailing in rough weather or riding a nervous horse, when the task becomes more difficult, common sense and experience tell us that there is more, not less, need for a firm pair of hands on the tiller or the reins. The basic problem, however, is that in managing international finance there is not one pair of hands in charge but many – many governments, many international organisations, many national authorities.

For that reason and because, if there is going to be trouble ahead, the political underpinnings of cooperation will be absolutely crucial, this chapter and the next one will attempt a brief analytical survey of those underpinnings and how they have changed for the worse. This is, of course, in contrast to what we are often told by the media. From their reports of those increasingly frequent summit meetings of heads of state, you might assume that everything was under perfect control, that wise heads were being put together and no one need worry. But the fact is – as everyone knows – that summit declarations are one thing, action another. And the reasons for inaction are not technical or economic, but fundamentally political. That is hardly surprising since the same is true for international action on global warming and

43

environmental protection, on the control of nuclear weapons and power plants, on the protection of human rights or the rules for international trade and intellectual property. On all these matters, the international political system, based on an obsolete principle of the sovereignty (i.e. immunity from interference) of territorially defined states, lags pathetically behind a world market economy of great power but little sense of social or moral responsibility.

Why and how the balance of power between market economy and political authority vested in these states has shifted so noticeably in the second half of the twentieth century is another story. The shift often goes under the woolly label of 'globalisation', and is the subject of continuing – and quite fierce – debate, especially among writers on international relations, international business and international political economy (Dunning 1993; Gelber 1997; Hirst and Thompson 1996; Stopford and Strange 1991; Strange 1996). The questions here are more precise and direct. They are: what are the key political relationships that might affect the international financial system for better or worse, have they changed of late, and if so, why and how?

Two such key relationships stand out from the rest. One is that between the United States and Japan. The other is that between France and Germany. In both, the intergovernmental relationships are complicated by changes in domestic politics, so that it is hard to separate the two sides of the coin. Both also spill over on to the decision-making processes of international organisations such as the IMF or the European Union. Let us start with the US–Japan relationship. We shall come to look at the European scene in the next chapter.

A tale of two deficits

Postwar Japanese owe a lot of their prosperity to the Americans. The United States, as the occupying power after the war, was more authoritarian but also more indulgent towards the Japanese than it was towards the Europeans. It imposed agricultural reform and the break-up of the zaibatsu. It not only allowed the Japanese to export freely to the United States while keeping barriers against US exports to Japan – as it had the west Europeans – but it had also allowed – even encouraged – the Japanese to keep foreign firms, including American firms, out of the country. From 1949 on, every US administration was keenly aware that Japan was America's forward base and front line against the Chinese as well as the Russians. Japan had no doubt that it was well protected by the American nuclear umbrella – and therefore had no need to spend its own money on defence and arms.

Around the mid-1960s, US indulgence started to wear thin. The United States was by then aware of a persistent and growing deficit in its balance of payments. Meanwhile, Japan's trade was earning a surplus and it had joined the GATT, the IMF and the Organization for Economic Cooperation and Development (OECD) as a full member. The Americans saw no reason why Japan should not obey the same rules as others, and liberalise controls on capital and allow US firms and goods free entry into the Japanese market. The Japanese were unwilling to do this, and by a combination of procrastination and informal evasion continued to keep their home market more or less to themselves while profiting very substantially from the openness of the US and European economies. The US got some of its own back by engineering the devaluation of the dollar in 1971. This should have cut down its imports from Japan by making them dearer. Yet they continued to grow and Japanese firms continued to out-compete US firms in their home markets for steel, cars, cameras, semiconductors and electronic manufactures. Japanese surpluses – and US deficits – continued to grow. The Japanese government's monetary reserves grew too and were largely invested in US government securities. As the United States in the 1980s raised the ante in its poker game with the Soviet Union, it spent more and more on defence – for which the Japanese paid, in effect, by lending their profits to the United States.

There was thus built up a connection between the two deficits – the fiscal deficit between US savings and taxes and government spending, and the trade deficit between US exports and imports. The US reaction was to put pressure on Japan to redress the trade deficit. A series of bilateral voluntary export restriction (VER) agreements culminated in 1988 with the US Congress passing the Super 301 law threatening to blacklist those countries, including Japan, which it judged to be guilty of unfair trade policies.

A year later, the Berlin Wall came down and the Soviet bloc disintegrated. The Cold War was over. The United States was left as the only superpower. For a while, little changed in US–Japan relations. The implicit bargain – that the United States provided security and Japan paid for it – became more evident in the 1992 Gulf War. In the end, Japan paid some $13 billion of the costs of Desert Storm. Some calculations even suggested that the United States showed a net profit out of the Gulf War (Grunberg 1994). Every year, moreover, Japan was paying almost three-quarters of the non-salary costs of US bases in Japan, most of them in Okinawa, so that it was cheaper for the US Defense Department to keep soldiers in Japan than for them to stay at home. That the Japanese government raised no objection, even when the Okinawans did, could be explained by their continued reliance on the US forces, especially the US Navy, to act as a police force in the Pacific.

Six years after the Cold War ended, there was rising tension between Taiwan and mainland China. In February 1996, the Japanese were understandably reassured by an American show of intermediating force in the shape of the aircraft carrier *Nimitz* steaming through the Taiwan straits. North Korea was another source of insecurity. Would its weak but repressive government, facing a collapsing economy, be tempted to use nuclear weapons against the South? There were also unresolved conflicts between Japan and Russia over the Kurile Islands, and with China over the Spratlys.

There were also other signs that an unravelling of the long-standing implicit bargain was under way, with possible adverse consequences for the global financial system. And those signs lay in the complex economic relations between the two countries.

Quite by coincidence, just as December 1989 marked a turning point in world politics, so did it in the Japanese economy. A downturn in the Tokyo stock market started a series of falls that by the following September had knocked 50 per cent off the value of shares. The bubble economy had burst and the long postwar boom in Japan gave way to a recession that was to last throughout the 1990s.

To understand the interplay of this story with developments in the US economy, we have to go back to 1987 and the stock market collapse that started in London and New York on 'Black Monday', 19 October, and spread to Tokyo (see chapter 5). Had it not been for imposed circuit breakers suspending dealing in shares that fell in one day by more than 15 per cent, the panic in Tokyo would have been unstoppable. That just gave time for the Ministry of Finance (MOF) in Tokyo to mount a concerted buying campaign by the big four securities firms – Nomura, Daiwa, Yamaichi and Nikko. It did so as much in self-defence as out of concern for the stability of global stock markets. By 1987, Japan's current account surplus was rising to $96 billion – three times what it had been in 1983. The surpluses were mostly invested by Japanese banks on behalf of successful exporters in dollar assets – shares, bonds and government securities. It was not in their interest, nor in the national interest, to let these assets become worthless.

What to do to stop such losses, however, was no easy question. Between 1985 and 1988 the top five Japanese insurance firms had lost more than $25 billion on their US investments (Murphy 1996: 178). While the Plaza Accord of January 1986 between the G5 finance ministers had apparently been effective in checking the dollar's appreciation, their next agreement, reached at the Louvre in February 1987, had completely failed to stabilise exchange rates despite the collective declaration that the rates were 'consistent with economic fundamentals'. Markets were quick to see the signs of divergent aims and interests among the ministers and acted accordingly. As Funabashi observed afterwards, 'To be durable and effective, the positive effects that may accrue from an ad hoc process of coordination must be accumulated and transformed into a permanent structure' – or else they would not convince the markets (Funabashi 1988: 226).[1]

After the Black Monday crisis, the Japanese MOF was still concerned lest private divestment of dollar assets by Japanese investors brought the dollar still lower and the yen stronger – thus hurting export industries. Faith in official policy coordination had gone. Popular criticism in America of 'unfair' Japanese competition mounted in 1988, threatening yet more US protectionism. The MOF decided, acting through the central bank, on a deliberate lowering of interest rates in Japan. This made keeping profits at home so unprofitable that it effectively pushed them abroad. Two things resulted. Cheap money at home fuelled inflation, accelerated the rise of asset prices and helped set off the bubble economy that finally burst in 1989/90. Secondly, Japanese firms and investors went in for a buying spree in America that landed many of them with overpriced, almost unsaleable or unprofitable real assets – like the Rockefeller Center in New York or Columbia Pictures (Murphy 1996). According to Paul Erdman, between 1985 and 1991, Japanese firms invested about $77 billion in US property; he instances, among others, Mitsubishi Bank's $94 million loan for a shopping centre, finally sold for $6 million when the developer defaulted (Erdman 1996: 126). They got little thanks and no apologies from the Americans. Instead, many Americans were encouraged by extreme nationalists to believe the Japanese had concocted some evil plot to buy up and control the American economy.[2]

Many Japanese, meanwhile, were persuaded that the Americans were behind an equally evil plot to handicap their banks in competition with the Americans and Europeans. In July 1988, led by the United States and backed by the British, the Bank of Japan was persuaded to go along with the Basle Accord – so-called because it was done through the BIS in Basle – on tighter rules on the capital adequacy of banks in relation to their assets (loans). It was certainly true that western banks felt the low interest rates the Japanese had to pay on deposits gave them an unfair competitive advantage in pricing loans. But Paul Volcker's initiative – as head of the Fed – for such an international agreement on capital adequacy standards had first been made in 1984, and followed the near-disastrous failure of Continental Illinois. The same year, the Bank of England had similarly felt obliged to bail out the Johnson Matthey banking group. Both central banks understandably felt it was time, for the sake of the global financial system, to raise the standards of capital adequacy in all the major economies. At that point, however, the Accord still left rather vague what exactly should be counted as 'core capital' and what as 'supplementary' capital, or how broadly or narrowly to define the 'international banks' to whom the rules applied (Deane and Pringle 1994: 163–5). In Japan, the 1–8 capital assets ratio, however interpreted, still meant that banks had to sell some of their hidden assets and at the same time to issue more shares to raise capital to back their loan portfolios. (Their shares already accounted for a quarter of the Tokyo stock market.) This 'double whammy' was an important trigger for the fall in Tokyo share prices that started late in 1989 and thus for the bursting of the bubble economy (Murphy 1996: 190–2).[3] Not surprising that some Japanese thought the *gaijin* (foreigners) were to blame.

But not them alone. The easy money that blew hot air into the bubble fuelled a real estate boom as well as a stock market boom. Like the real estate investment trusts (REITs) that nearly brought some US banks to grief in America in the 1970s, Japanese banks forgot that real estate property prices could fall even faster than they rose. Another unrecognised weakness in the system, peculiar to Japan, came from the large and popular market in equity warrant bonds. These were a kind of option to buy shares at a predetermined 'exercise price' and to hold the option for as much as five or seven years. On a rising stock market, paying 1 or 2 per cent above the current share price looked like a good deal, especially as the bonds offered bonuses if they were held to maturity. When the bubble burst, however, the overhang of equity warrant bonds and the need to unload losses on US real estate investments both dried up the demand from Japanese investors for long-term US government bonds. In short, the stock market collapse in the early 1990s brought dollars hurrying back to Japan to keep banks and firms solvent and in business (Murphy 1996: 214).

This part of the story relates directly to the two US deficits, the trade deficit and the fiscal deficit. The fiscal deficit had been financed in the 1980s by private Japanese investors buying US government securities – in effect lending the US government the money to pay its bills. The deficit on trade had similarly been balanced by a reverse flow of (mostly private sector) capital from Japan to the United States. This equalising flow kept the dollar–yen exchange rate more or less stable but only so long as both governments wanted to keep it that way, as in the Plaza and Louvre Accords. This changed with the 1992 US presidential elections. Bill Clinton was elected on a mandate to cut taxes, bring in a costly health-care system *and* cut the mounting budget deficit. Either raising taxes or spending more government money was going to wreck the already overloaded market for US bonds. The answer seemed to lie in attacking the trade deficit by making the yen more expensive in terms of dollars. This was what Nixon had managed in 1971 by the negotiated revaluation of the Smithsonian Agreement. This would make Japanese exports to the United States more expensive and US exports to Japan cheaper – or at least so economic logic promised. When Clinton took over the White House in January 1993, the yen stood at 125 to the dollar. By March/April 1995, it had gone to 79 or 80. But the US trade deficit persisted, although by the mid-1990s it was no longer exclusively with Japan, but with China, South Korea and other Asian tigers. Japanese firms were borrowing dollars to expand production inside US trade barriers – like the North American Free Trade Area (NAFTA) – and in lower-cost locations on the Asian mainland. So the capital flow was actually going into Japan, not out of it. And only about half the US payments deficit was with Japan, although Japanese firms in Asia probably accounted for another 25 per cent.

By the end of 1995, the US economy had finally climbed out of recession, while the Japanese economy had not. The politically significant change was that financing the US fiscal deficit now depended not on private capital inflows from Japan but on official ones. To keep the yen from appreciating too fast, the Bank of Japan had bought massive amounts of dollars and had invested them in US government securities – $100 billion in 1995 alone. It became the largest single lender to the US government, to the tune of over $200 billion (Erdman 1996: 127). By 1997, Prime Minister Hashimoto had only to hint at the possibility of selling its US government bonds for the market to shiver. There are good reasons of self-interest why the Japanese government would hesitate to use such a dangerous deterrent. But just having it does change the politics of the US–Japan relationship.

And meanwhile the US strategy of talking down the dollar had unintentionally done the Japanese bureaucracy a good turn. As Taggart Murphy explains, 'Thanks to American whining, Japan's bureaucrats escaped the political heat for a soaring yen which was almost entirely their responsibility' (Murphy 1996: 226). What he means is that the MOF strongly opposed tax cuts or any effective keynesian stimulation of the post-bubble economy and shunned the reforms in land tenure or restrictive business practices that might have revived economic growth. MOF bureaucrats did, however, want to put a floor under the Tokyo stock market, and in doing so encouraged foreign portfolio investment which, as capital flowed in, pushed the exchange rate higher. Once again, it was easier for the Japanese press and public to blame the *gaijin* for low growth, rising unemployment and failing businesses than to blame the bureaucrats.

Domestic politics on both sides played an important part here. The bubble economy had – as in all inflationary periods – opened tempting opportunities for fraudulent businessmen and corrupt politicians. In summer 1989, there was the Recruit scandal in which a successful entrepreneur tried to stave off a law that would have put him out of business by bribing politicians. He had no lack of takers; for politicians, the bubble was also pushing up the costs of getting re-elected and the rising stock market provided the financial means. Exposure brought down the government and brought politicians into disrepute. In 1991, the story came out of how securities companies were compensating their biggest clients for losses on the stock market, while small investors got nothing when their shares were worth half what they had paid for them. In resigning to show his contrition, the president of Nomura Securities remarked in passing that MOF had known all along about this kind of fat-cat insider trading. It was these insiders who habitually financed the ruling Liberal Democratic Party (LDP). The revelations of a cosy – not to say scandalous – understanding between politicians, bureaucrats and financial leaders surely contributed to the movement for political reform which began to gather support, even from within the LDP, by the mid-1990s. The further association of all three with leaders of organised crime, which came to light in the course of 1991 and afterwards, tarnished some of the big names in Japanese finance – the Industrial Bank of Japan, Sumitomo, Fuji Bank (Murphy 1996: 198–202; see also chapter 7).

It also started a move by disgusted small depositors away from the banks to the already large Japanese postal savings system. By 1996, this already held more in deposits (equivalent to some $1,750 billion) than all of Japan's commercial banks combined. But of course, the larger its role, the greater the leverage of any Japanese government over the flows resulting from the country's comparatively high savings rate. At the time of writing, the leverage had not been used. But it remained a latent political factor in the crucial US–Japan relationship. And meanwhile the change in the nature of Japanese institutions' preferences for short-term US Treasury bills instead of long-term securities makes the US balance of payments on capital account highly vulnerable to change in market conditions, relative interest rates and exchange rate expectations. As Taggart Murphy observed, 'While Japanese institutions go on financing a lot of American national debt, they are no longer willing or able to bear the currency and interest rate risks of American profligacy' (Murphy 1996: 244–5).

That is a big and significant change in the US–Japan relationship, as big in its way as the end of the Cold War. How it will affect the international financial system will depend, in part, on the outcome of an ongoing debate within Japan on the subject of political and economic reform. Roughly speaking, the economic debate is between those who think reform is both desirable and cannot be avoided, given the competitive nature of the world market economy, and those who think Japan and other Asian tigers have done pretty well by developing their own model of capitalism, in which the state necessarily plays a far larger part than it does in the United States, and should not be in too much of a hurry to change. By 1998, the turmoil in Asian markets and in Japan had strengthened the pro-western view and downgraded the 'Asian values' school. The US economy, moreover, was doing well, the dollar was strong and the fiscal deficit was set to decline.

Both reformers and conservatives in Japan include some strange bedfellows. The political reformers want to curb the power of the elitist bureaucracies and to break the hold of the LDP on Japanese politics.[4] The economic reformers are more keen on breaking restrictive business practices and introducing more competition for the benefit of consumers and small business. But they do not necessarily want slavishly to copy the American model, which seems to go against Asian values and notions of social responsibility. Sometimes political liberalism and economic liberalism can pull in different directions.

Comparable tensions exist among those opposing reform. Some are simply old-fashioned nationalists, resentful of American bullying and hypocrisy. Others are fearful of the risks involved in abolishing the old structures of bureaucratic guidance and control before thoroughgoing electoral reforms and the development of a properly functioning judiciary system, able to deal openly and expeditiously with conflicts of economic interest, can be put in place.

As Funabashi perceptively argued back in 1987, clipping the wings of the bureaucracy without strengthening the power of the Prime Minister would be a recipe for anarchy rather than reform. 'Bureaucratic intransigence,' he wrote, 'and the lack of strong initiatives from political circles will leave to market forces the task of rectifying imbalances and will therefore constitute a destabilising force in international economic peacekeeping' (Funabashi 1988: 247).

And while political change is painfully slow – as in Italy – economic changes are already weakening the guiding influence of Japanese bureaucracies over industry and finance. The surge in the value of the yen in 1995/6 accelerated the move of many Japanese companies' manufacturing capacity offshore to China, Malaysia, Thailand and South Korea. As the British and Americans had found out long before, and as French and German governments were finding out at about the same time, a company with offshore operations is much less dependent on its home government and soon acquires a spirit of independence in corporate decision making that makes it readier than ever before to put corporate survival first and the national interest second.

Comparable confusion, meanwhile, reigns in the United States. There is continuing deep disagreement among academics and politicians on how best to deal with Japan. To oversimplify once more, the debate is between the so-called 'revisionists' and the modernisation school, which sees Japan as an eager pupil and follower of the United States, successfully managing a transition first from a feudal to an industrial economy and, second, a transition from an hierarchic and obedient society to an open, democratic one. President Kennedy's ambassador to Japan, former professor Edwin Reichsauer, was the father of this school and had done much to increase American cultural and intellectual influence over Japan, and in so doing to reduce Soviet influence and the appeal of marxist ideology to Japanese intellectuals. From this perspective, while differences between American and Japanese forms of capitalism remained, they were diminishing and American patience would, it seemed, be rewarded by gradual conformity to the American model.

The revisionist school is so called because, around the late 1980s, its adherents questioned the assumptions of the modernisation school and demanded US policy be revised accordingly. The basic assumption challenged by them was that Japan was just another capitalist political economy with some minor differences from the American model. On the contrary, they argued, Japan was much more of an outlier than France or Germany. Chalmers Johnson (1982) had argued that Japan's economic success owed much to the guidance and direction of the Ministry of International Trade and Industry. But it was only in the late 1980s, when Japanese success in gaining market shares at American expense seemed unstoppable, that the revisionist analysis caught public attention. Clyde Prestowitz (1988), Karel van Wolferen (1989) and a respected senior Japan specialist, James Fallows (1994), all wrote books and articles that emphasised the importance of Japanese institutions and, in particular, its authoritarian bureaucracies, in helping Japanese firms to out-compete their American counterparts. By the time Clinton was elected, political support had grown in America for 'strategic trade policy'. This was really a euphemism for a more protectionist attitude towards Japanese imports into the US market and for a more aggressive, coercive attitude towards the barriers keeping US firms and US goods out of the Japanese market. It found expression in Clinton's appointment of Laura Tyson, a former colleague of Chalmers Johnson at UC Berkeley, to the Council of Economic Advisers, and in subsequent reports to the Congress from the Office of Technology Assessment.[5]

These people were called Japan-bashers by the modernisation school – and (in private) by many Japanese. Inevitably, it provoked a backlash in Japan. For the first time ever, a US–Japan trade negotiation, in February 1994, ended without agreement. Agreement was reached in September 1994, but it was a vacuous document and made no mention, for once, of cars or car parts, nor of the discriminatory procurement practices of Nippon Telephone and Telegraph (NTT). Quite apart from growing American concern – largely political because of looming Congressional elections – over the exchange rate and interest rates, the fact was that Washington, too, like Tokyo, was divided over the best strategy. Clinton's Secretary of Labour, Robert Reich, had argued cogently, and publicly, that an industrial policy that tried to protect US firms against foreign competition was misdirected. Competition policy, rather, should look with favour on foreign firms that came to the United States and gave jobs to unemployed American workers (Reich 1990). Reich, however, was something of an odd-man-out in the Clinton Administration and left office after the 1996 elections.

The divergence of perceptions in the United States regarding Japan was still not resolved at the time of writing. Until some kind of consensus emerges, American ambivalence towards Japan will remain, as will Japanese ambivalence towards the United States. The balance between conflict and cooperation, therefore, is likely to continue to shift, first one way and then another. The determining factors are both economic and political, both domestic and international. As American economic growth swelled tax revenues in 1997, the shadow of the fiscal deficit was somewhat lifted. Yet every US government is still vulnerable to an exodus of Japanese money. Since the turbulence in Asian markets in 1997, the sense of shared vulnerability to the markets has been strong enough to get agreement on the bailout not just for Thailand and Indonesia but also on the much larger IMF rescue for South Korea. Some divergence obviously remains between Japanese and American views of what steps are needed in both Korea and Japan to restore confidence in their respective banking systems. But on the whole fear of the fragility of the markets in both New York and Tokyo has moderated mutual recrimination by the politicians.

One important and unpredictable variable is the future direction of Chinese policy towards Taiwan and other neighbouring states. The more threatening China seems to Tokyo, the less anxious the Japanese will be to offend the Americans.

Meanwhile, as the political–economic seesaw in US–Japan relations persists, we can expect some spill-over to the work of international organisations and meetings. Unresolved debates in Washington and in Tokyo will be reflected in reluctance, especially by the United States, to take any decisive action on outstanding conflicts. There are proposals, official and unofficial, coming from Japan – to call these 'demands' would be too strong – for a larger voice in international organisations like the UN Security Council or the IMF Executive Board. In both, the US has the controlling power either to resist or to promote change. So far it has resisted, or at least failed to respond – at the UN, for example, blaming the British and French for refusing to give up their national right of veto as permanent members. At the IMF, new demands are being made on the organisation – to manage a massive new rescue fund, the New Arrangements to Borrow, replacing the 1962 General Arrangement to Borrow – and to monitor and supervise banking regulation in emerging markets. Both require positive cooperation from Japan. Whether that cooperation will be forthcoming – and quickly enough to cope with a crisis of any kind – is far from certain.[6]

The point was made in chapter 2 that financial innovation and the integration of financial markets worldwide speed up the onset of financial crises. Governments now need to be able and prepared to react much more quickly and decisively than they did in the 1960s or 1970s. And yet two of the key governments whose economies are most deeply involved in the international financial system are not more but less able to do so now than they were in the past. Both are beset by domestic problems to which they cannot find quick solutions. Japan especially has promised a 'Big Bang' reform programme for its banks and financial markets, but faces enormous difficulties in substituting a new system of regulation for the old monolithic MOF (see chapter 8). Both are more interested and engaged in their respective regional relations, Japan in east Asia, the United States in NAFTA, than they are in 'global governance'. As in Europe, that is partly because, when the problems of restructuring the world economy prove too intractable, it is natural for politicians to look instead to what might be done by neighbours and for neighbours. In finance, though, regional solutions are no substitute for collective action on a global scale (see chapter 4). And such collective action is possible only on the basis of strong, well established mutual trust. The story of US–Japan relations, and especially since 1990, however, is one of growing mutual mistrust and misperception.

Remember the 1930s: politics mattered then too

It would be well if everyone concerned, in markets, government or the media, took the time and trouble to reread the history of the 1930s, especially the period after the Wall Street crash and up to the failure of the World Economic Conference of 1933. They would surely be struck by many points of similarity – both political and financial – between those times and our own.

As everyone knows, the American 'bubble economy' of the late 1920s burst in spectacular fashion with the fall of share prices on Wall Street in October 1929. But the record is clear that during the next year, especially in the first half, the fall in the stock market levelled off, employment and production picked up and international lending resumed – the second-quarter total actually more or less matching the same quarter of 1928. On 1 May, President Hoover said he was confident the country was over the worst (Kindleberger 1973: 128). Why was he so wrong? And why, more particularly, did the failure of a bank in a small central European country (see below) set off a new slide into depression and deflation from which it took the world economy years – and a world war – to recover fully?

Economists, predictably, have given a variety of answers. Friedman blamed the Federal Reserve System for failing to increase the money supply to raise prices and encourage confidence in growth (Friedman and Schwarz 1963). Arthur Lewis blamed the continued decline in commodity prices (Lewis 1949). Schumpeter, propounding theories of business cycles, fell back on the psychology of panic (Schumpeter 1939). Kindleberger developed a concept of hegemonic stability which required the system to be managed by a leader who was lender of last resort and who would keep the market open to distress goods. His conclusion therefore was that the old hegemon, Britain, was financially so weak that it could no longer fill the role, while the United States was able but unwilling to do so (Kindleberger 1973: 303–6).

For us in the 1990s, it seems to many experts that Kindleberger was right: the system does need management or 'governance' when things start to go wrong. Yet these days, no single hegemonic leader is strong enough or rich enough to fill the role unaided. Instead, we may have to pin our hopes to the chances of a collective leadership as a substitute for the national hegemon. Also, there are two parts to the problem of hegemonic stability. One is how to prevent a global economic depression starting in the first place. The other is how to escape from it once it has happened. And the first ought to be easier than the second, just as it is easier to avoid a traffic accident by prudent driving than to repair the damage after the crash. And this is where the similarities between our own times and the story of 1930–1 become striking, and where perhaps lessons may be learned concerning preventive action.

The story began with the failure of one bank in a small indebted country – Austria's Kreditanstalt. The inherent dangers to the system had, however, been foreseen and some precautionary steps had been taken. Kreditanstalt failed in mid-May 1931. But before then, central bankers had already consulted each other at the very beginning of 1931 after some French banks had failed. They had come up with various proposals for a safety net in case it happened again. The Germans proposed official funding of their short-term debt, the French of their sterling holdings. The Bank of England proposed a collective fund managed by the BIS and financed by private loans to assist 'those borrowers whose relief and rehabilitation are an agreed object of policy'. This was not unlike the General Arrangement to Borrow of 1962 – essentially an agreement in advance to provide the liquidity necessary to restore financial confidence. But the French and the Americans both mistrusted the British, suspecting that this was an elaborate scheme to refinance Britain's major export markets, and gave it no support. Thus, when Kreditanstalt failed and the Austrian government was unable to underwrite the bank's foreign debts, Austria appealed for help to the League of Nations Financial Committee. Austria had already been helped by a League loan in the 1920s and to turn to it again was natural enough. But the Financial Committee referred Austria to the BIS. Over the next two or three weeks, a pitifully small loan from eleven central banks was put together. Historians disagree as to whether the reason for this delay was political – that the French wanted Austria in return to renounce its proposed customs union with Germany – or simply the lack of any sense of urgency. Either way, Kindleberger observed, 'The niggardliness of the sum and the delay together proved disastrous' (Kindleberger 1973: 151).

Part of the reason for a failure to understand the size of the problem may have been that, a few years before, Kreditanstalt had taken over another bank, which later turned out to have debts almost twice as large as its capital. This is the sort of problem that could easily recur in Japan or some other Asian markets, where one of the anticipated effects of financial deregulation is a spate of bank mergers and takeovers. Since Japanese banks are notorious for their skill in disguising bad debts and 'non-performing' loans that will never be repaid, such nasty surprises could easily happen. Another familiar feature of the story was the contagiousness of financial failure. Even before Kreditanstalt fell, trouble had spread through most of central Europe and to Germany. There, major banks like Dresdner and Deutschebank suffered heavy withdrawals and the Reichsbank steadily lost gold from its reserves. This meant that the prospect of reparations ever being paid to France – and therefore of France paying its war debts to the United States – disappeared over the horizon. President Hoover came up with a proposal for a temporary moratorium on all intergovernmental debts. But this overlooked the political scene in

France and the changing scene in Germany. While the politicians argued, new loans to Germany through the BIS melted away and when France eventually agreed early in July 1931 to Hoover's moratorium, it was too late to stop the crisis spreading to Britain. Britain was particularly vulnerable because other Europeans – the Swiss and the Dutch, for instance – had invested their monetary reserves in sterling, which until 1931 was convertible into gold but paid interest while gold did not. These sterling balances, however, could be withdrawn and some were. The market became nervous and, to calm it, the Bank of England raised loans from the US Federal Reserve and the Bank of France and French commercial banks. Once again, the loans were too small; losses from the reserves in late July were twice the size of the loans. Moreover, the loans were never actually used, because drawing on the private sector lenders would have alerted the markets to the trouble (Kindleberger 1973: 159). While the Bank of England tried to straighten out the terms of the loan, the pressure on sterling continued. Politics also came into it, because of disagreements between the Labour government and the deflationist Bank of England. Foreign bankers agreed with the Bank of England and insisted on correction of the fiscal deficit as the price of a further loan. Their insistence made the government propose a cut in the dole to the unemployed, whereupon the trade unions withdrew their support and the government fell. Ramsay Macdonald and Philip Snowden stayed on as Prime Minister and Finance Minister in a National government, but their proposed budget cuts failed to restore confidence. More funds were taken out of sterling and finally, in September 1931, Britain 'came off gold' – that is, pound notes could no longer be exchanged for gold.

To sum up the lessons of the story, many of which have a contemporary ring:

- Trouble can easily start in a small country.
- It is almost always foreshadowed when foreign funds shift from long-term assets into more liquid, shorter-term ones.
- International support in the shape of new loans must be swift, large and ready to use, not just for show.
- Such support must come first from governments; commercial banks may themselves be vulnerable and can therefore be risk averse when it comes to backing other countries or other banks. Their help may be needed, but it may not be forthcoming unless national governments use their power to coerce them.
- Governments must appear absolutely united and wholly determined. This is more difficult where there is a division of responsibility between the governing party and the central bank.

When it comes to acting swiftly and decisively against the markets, therefore, an independent central bank may not be the best instrument for effective policy.

•   Central banks also have an innate tendency to prefer deflation to inflation, and to judge monetary stability more important than keeping people in jobs and troubled businesses from closing down.

In 1931, the deflationists were wrong. Bringing down a government that depended on the support of organised labour was not in any one's long-term interest. Towards the end of his life, the British economist Lionel Robbins admitted in his autobiography that, like Montagu Norman and the majority of his profession at the time, he had been wrong (Robbins 1971). And Maynard Keynes was almost alone in a Chatham House study group that met in 1932 in being far more concerned with the real economy than with the question of sterling's link to gold, a topic on which the others were almost neurotically obsessed.

Above all, the source of all subsequent troubles in the world economy was financial, not commercial. Prices were low because demand was low or non-existent. Demand was low because too many people had too little money to spend, and those who did have it preferred neither to spend it nor to invest it for fear of losing it. Higher tariffs and quota restrictions were symptoms of this situation, not a cause. They were a response to political pressure on governments to do something. But the net effect on the volume or direction of trade flows was negligible. Trade blocs, such as they were, were also a response to economic pain, not a cause of it. Yet to this day, more research and writing have been devoted to international trade than to international finance, and there has been more passionate advocacy of trade liberalisation than of preventive financial arrangements (Strange 1986).

Notes

1   An observation shared by some financial analysts in Europe and the United States. M. Brender, for instance, has consistently argued that central banks are still able to control financial markets even though their resources may be dwarfed by the vastly greater turnover in the markets. But only, he adds, when they are visibly and convincingly agreed on what they want, or do not want, to happen. If they are not, the markets will be quick to test their resolve (interview, Paris, May 1977).

2   As suggested, for example, in the popular and successful novel (and film) *The Rising Sun* by Michael Crichton (1993).

3   This author, a former investment banker in Tokyo, also argues that, ironically and by a quirk of regulatory rules, some of the money that could have gone

     to recapitalise Japanese banks was lent by non-banks in Japan to non-Japanese banks in New York, London, Sydney and Europe, which were also under pressure to comply with the new rules (Murphy 1996: 190, footnote).

4   The elections in 1993 resulted in a humiliating fall in support for the LDP. But in 1996, it returned to power when Ryutaro Hashimoto formed a government which benefited from deep and continuing divisions between the Democratic Party and Mr Ozawa's breakaway New Frontier Party.

5   Tyson's *Who's Bashing Whom? Trade conflict in high-technology industries* came out in 1992. It followed *Politics and Productivity: the real story of how Japan works* (jointly authored with John Zysman, 1988). She was a colleague of John Zysman and his Berkeley Roundtable on the International Economy. Zysman, with Stephen Cohen, had written *Manufacturing Matters* (1987), arguing that the United States could not afford in its own long-term national interest to allow its manufacturing enterprises to be wiped out by Japanese competition. The Office of Technology Assessment was an agency uniquely responsible to the Congress, not the Executive. It was closed as a result of budget cuts in 1996.

6   *IMF Survey*, supplement, September 1997.

Chapter 4

Political underpinnings: disunited Europe

At least until 2003 – and possibly thereafter – the euro is likely to cause trouble in the currency markets. Even if it starts on time and despite the fudging of the conditions laid down in the Maastricht Treaty, it is going to be an ongoing source of uncertainty. And uncertainty, as we all know, is meat and drink to the markets. How much trouble the markets will cause and how governments will respond are the big unanswered questions.

The second point is that the uncertainty is political in nature. At the end of the day, it is about the domestic politics of France and Germany and the impact of both on relations between them. It has little or nothing to do with the technicalities of the arrangements for setting up a common European currency, or with the economic indicators set out in the Maastricht Treaty and in subsequent agreements at ministerial level. In short, Franco-German relations are the second important political underpinning for the stability of the international financial system to which observers must pay attention. The other, as argued in the previous chapter, is US–Japanese relations.

Once again, the best way to appreciate this is to recall the historical background to the issues at stake for the European Union in the closing years of the twentieth century. Many readers will already be familiar with the story so that they can easily pass on to the next chapter. Even for others who are less familiar with it, a detailed narrative is not necessary here. It will be enough to pick out the politically significant highlights and to draw some conclusions from them. For the details of the various attempts at monetary integration in Europe, there is a large and well researched literature to which readers can refer.[1]

In my estimation, the origins of the story lie in that small fought-over corner of western Europe known as the Saarland. Since the earliest days of a united Germany in the 1870s, it had been a football between the French and the Germans – the more so since its coalfields were seen by both as an important resource, adding to the economic power of a modern industrial state, for which energy was the essential input for most manufacturing enterprises. Taken by Germany from France in the 1870s, it was reclaimed by France again after Germany's defeat in 1918. Only President Wilson, with his faith in the principle of self-determination rather than territorial annexation as the basis for future peace in Europe, stood in France's way. Disagreement over the Saar in 1919 almost led Wilson to wash his hands of the entire Paris peace conference and go home in disgust. The result – predictably since France still hoped for an American guarantee of European security – was a compromise. This put the Saar in France but under temporary trusteeship governed by a League of Nations commissioner for fifteen years, after which its people could choose by popular referendum which state to join. Thus Wilson's principle was not overturned and France got the use of the coalfields to make good the energy deficit left by the wartime devastation of the coalfields of northern France.

The Saar question resurfaced again after the World War II. Since the referendum in 1935 had gone for Germany, France was once again keen to reclaim what French politicians regarded as theirs. Another referendum in 1946 gave the hungry Saarlanders the chance to opt for skimpy German rations or more ample French ones. Sensibly choosing France, they still had the option five years later to change their minds. By then, the French hoped that their efforts to knit the province permanently into the French administration and educational system would succeed in persuading people to stay with them. German political parties thought and hoped language and culture would bring the Saar into the Federal Republic. The impending row put in serious jeopardy all the heartfelt efforts on both sides to ensure that France and Germany never again came close to war. Federalists and function-alists alike saw the Saar question as a land mine in the path of European peace and integration.

That, in brief, was the background to the Schuman Plan of 1951 for a European Coal and Steel Community (ECSC), a body with supranational powers over both industries, which would take the place of both French and German administrations where coal and steel were concerned (Diebold 1959; Milward 1984; Strange 1951). While both governments lost control over the Saar, both also won. By indefinitely subordinating German basic industries to a European authority, France won. By making France subject to the same authority, Germany regained equal status, even though still under military occupation by US, British and French armed forces. The scheme therefore had the support of both governments. They also agreed on the appointment of federalist Jean Monnet as the ECSC's first chief. A Franco-German compromise had laid an early foundation for what was to become the European Union.

Better known and documented was the Franco-German bargaining that was the basis for the Rome Treaty of 1957, which set up the European Economic Community (EEC) and anticipated the creation of a common market that transcended political frontiers among the founding Six – France, Germany, Italy, Belgium, the Netherlands and Luxembourg. Behind all the European rhetoric was an exchange of concessions – by the French to the Germans, and by the Germans to the French. France agreed progressively to open its market to German manufactures, Germany progressively to allow French farm products to compete in the German market, while both agreed to develop a Common Agricultural Policy (CAP) to protect the EEC from US imports, especially of cheap cereals. Furthermore, the Germans agreed to take a share in supporting what was left of French Africa in return for equal access to these ex-colonial but still dependent markets.

When deals like this and the Schuman Plan could be made, which reconciled differing French and German national interests, the European project prospered and progressed. But when a workable compromise that satisfied both sides could not be found, it faltered and stood still. For example, in 1954 there was a proposal for a European defence community, a sort of first step to a federal army. This would have been a stronger foundation for a federal state than the free trade area that was the essence of the EEC. But while the Germans – and the French government – were in favour, it was rejected by the French National Assembly. The idea was anathema both to communist deputies and, for different reasons, to the Gaullists. Their combined votes were enough to defeat the proposal. Indeed, in the 1960s, General de Gaulle actually took France out of NATO, professing a *tout azimuths* defence strategy that proclaimed France's determination to distance the country from the United States and leave its leaders free to negotiate direct with the Soviet Union.

The next political clash between French and Germans came in the mid-1960s, over the future development of the EEC. The early years since the Rome Treaty (1957) had seen progress towards a lowering of intra-EEC trade barriers and the building of common institutions – the Council of Ministers, the European Parliament and Court of Justice, and the European Commission. By the mid-1960s, with the US-inspired trade negotiations that became known as the Kennedy Round, and the return of Charles de Gaulle to power in France, the Six had reached a kind of watershed. De Gaulle thought European federalism was a foolish dream. The Europe he wanted was a '*Europe des Patries*', a strong alliance of national governments. He distrusted the European Commission – which he called 'this embryonic technocracy, for the most part foreign'. The European federalists, by contrast, believed the time had come to move from what John Pinder later called 'negative integration' – taking down intra-European barriers – to 'positive integration' – the formulation of common policies towards the outside world and common rules on everything from taxation to company law.

In 1965, with the support of the Bonn government and of officials in the European Commission in Brussels, the federalists wanted to move towards majority voting in the Council of Ministers and the delegation of trade diplomacy in the Kennedy Round to a single European negotiator. They were frustrated by General de Gaulle. In July 1965, France actually withdrew from all EEC discussions. For six difficult months, they stayed away from Brussels and official meetings there. Then finally, in January 1966, a bargain that came to be known as the Luxembourg Compromise was struck.

What had happened over the intervening six months was that the French began to realise that the longer they stayed away from Brussels, the more likely it was that the Five would start to make their own decisions, leaving France out of it. The Five, meanwhile, began to realise that the EEC without France was unworkable. The French knew this. For, as the late Miriam Camps explained:

> Even after it became clear that the French government was determined to build up the crisis rather than to overcome it, the Five and the Commission were at pains to keep open the lines of approach to the French, to avoid anything that could be interpreted as provocation or ganging up and to make it as easy as possible for the French to return to the negotiating table. (Camps 1967: 73–4).[2]

Actually, the sticking points over which France and the Five were at loggerheads were really rather trivial compared with the larger project of European integration. They concerned the date at which the Six would move towards a customs union for manufactures and a common policy for agriculture. How to fund the latter, since existing funds were running low and national subsidies would have to be replaced by standard European ones out of a single fund, was a related question (Camps 1967: 42). The most important issue arose out of some ambiguities in the Treaty of Rome's provisions for majority voting.

While all decisions to extend the scope of the EEC to new fields, beyond those listed in the Treaty, required unanimity in the Council of Ministers, proposals coming from the Commission could be voted down by a majority. The only provision safeguarding the interests of the smaller member states was that when the big three were not agreed among themselves, the majority had to include at least one of the small ones – Belgium, the Netherlands or Luxembourg (Camps 1967: 120). Because the Commission's interest was naturally in expanding its own role in policy making, and governments did not like to vote against each other on what seemed relatively minor matters, a tendency to *engrenage* had developed.[3] De Gaulle thought this dangerous, if only because it tended to increase the power of the Commission at the expense of national governments.

The compromise eventually struck in Luxembourg acknowledged that this might not be the last time opinions differed within the EEC. But it dealt with the majority voting question by assuring France that when issues very important to one or more member countries were at stake, the others would try, within a reasonable time, to reach a unanimous decision. The French agreed, in effect, not to walk out again in a huff, but to carry on talking until unanimity was reached – a promise that led on other occasions to the EEC habit of 'stopping the clock'. In the long run, it also set precedents for fudging difficult questions and for allowing rhetoric about European union to substitute for hard decisions.

Indeed, about that time, in the mid-1960s, there were two other important issues on which French and German inclinations and perceived interests were at odds with one another. One was over NATO and European defence arrangements – in effect, divergence over their respective relations with the United States. De Gaulle began by announcing that he would visit Moscow and that France would ease up – against American guidelines – on trade with the Soviet Union. As mentioned earlier, he ended up a few weeks later by withdrawing from NATO decision making and declaring the independence from it of a French nuclear *force de frappe*, thus distancing France not only from Britain but also from Germany for whom the US nuclear tripwire against a Soviet attack was generally thought a vital national interest.

The split over defence was mirrored by a split over money. In February 1965 de Gaulle attacked the 'extraordinary privileges' of the dollar in the international gold exchange standard, set up under the Bretton Woods Agreement back in the 1940s.[4] He compared this system unfavourably with one traditionally based on gold. But his fond dream of a united European front against the United States and the almighty dollar soon faded away when the Germans failed to stand by the French in the debates on international monetary reform. Germany owed its security from the Red Army to the US nuclear umbrella; the price, as the United States repeatedly made clear, of the implicit bargain was German membership and support for NATO and compliance with US interests in the management of money and finance. German leaders all understood this, so that, later, before Nixon unilaterally devalued the dollar in 1971, Germany was the first western ally after Canada to agree not to embarrass Washington by asking for gold in return for the dollars it held in its growing monetary reserves (Calleo 1982; Solomon 1977; Strange 1976).

The split indeed was deep rooted in geography and history. France lay to the west of Germany and could therefore better afford to be a partial free rider on American Cold War strategies of containment towards the Soviet Union. Its relations with the United States, going back as far as 1919 and the Paris peace conference, had been persistently antagonistic. This showed up, again and again, in the two basic issue areas of security and finance. The old days of Lafayette and Ben Franklin and the coincident opposition of France and the newly independent United States to Britain were long gone. America had taken the place of Britain as the hegemonic world power inimical to French culture, traditions and perceived interests. For west Germans, the US Army standing in the path of the Red Army in 1945 had saved them from Russian occupation and the depredations that had gone with it to the east. They could not help but recognise that, having escaped one totalitarian regime, it was the Americans who had saved them from falling into the hands of another. And it was US protection and postwar economic aid that had been a necessary condition for the 'economic miracle' of German recovery in the 1950s and 1960s.

That said, one important lesson from the Luxembourg Compromise was that while differences of perceptions, opinions and interests existed, both French and Germans were acutely conscious that they also shared perceptions, opinions and interests. Two European wars in a generation made them agree that it should never happen again; that a market economy was not incompatible with state intervention; and that Europeans should hang on to their free democratic institutions. As with human relations within families, within a business or between firms, there was always both conflict and cooperation in their relationship. And as with these, the necessity of cooperation was likely to be greater when a common danger threatened and when both parties experienced uncomfortable turbulence coming from outside.

That was precisely what generated the first moves by governments towards closer European monetary integration. By 1966, about five years of mainly US–European discussions about reform of the international monetary system had got nowhere. The US deficit on the balance of payments had continued to grow, financed by other countries' holdings of dollar IOUs. These trends confirmed Robert Triffin's prediction that the dollar–gold exchange system was unsustainable in the long run because the markets would eventually recognise that US gold reserves were insufficient to sustain faith in the mounting pile of dollar claims in foreign hands (Triffin 1961). The Americans did finally give in on the creation of special drawing rights (SDRs) on the IMF but only because they realised that SDRs would help take the heat off the dollar. By 1969, the Bretton Woods system was creaking but no one knew how long it would last or when and how it would crack up (Calleo and Strange 1984; Strange 1976).

It was this uncertainty in the wider international monetary system that pushed European Community (EC) governments toward the Werner Plan of 1970. The Plan emerged from an *ad hoc* committee set up the year before. It proposed a three-stage progress towards fixed exchange rates in a monetary union within ten years, accompanied by free movement within the EC of goods, people and capital. (It was significant that an earlier proposal along similar lines coming from the Commission in 1962 had been ignored by governments.) The Werner Committee could agree on the final objective – but not on how to get there. The 'monetarists', led by France, insisted that the first step was to commit member countries to fixed exchange rates. The rest would follow. The 'economists', led by Germany, insisted that this was unrealistic. Economic convergence based on anti-inflationary monetary policies – like Germany's – had to come first. Once again, the issue was fudged. And not for the last time, it was outside events and forces that doomed the Werner Plan.

President Nixon in August 1971 came to believe that a dollar devaluation adroitly managed might solve the Triffin dilemma and to realise that it could be done unilaterally, without consulting its allies but with the help of nervous foreign exchange markets. The Europeans were thrown into disarray. When, in December 1971, Nixon agreed with Pompidou the Smithsonian Agreement, setting new exchange rates based on market valuations between, especially, the yen and the dollar and the mark and the dollar, the fixed rates proposed by Werner had been blown away. A European attempt in 1972 (often called the 'Snake in the Tunnel') to set them up again by keeping to narrower margins of fluctuation than the 4.5 per cent margins agreed in the Smithsonian Agreement was equally vain. Britain and Ireland had to leave early, in 1972, soon followed by Denmark. By 1974, the French franc could no longer keep within the 'Snake' and for the next four years, the EC was split, monetarily, between what was recognised as a

Deutschmark zone and the weaker floating currencies (Tsoukalis 1991: 164).

The reason for this split has never been very well understood in Europe.[5] The explanation lay with the power of financial markets over national governments. The latter were not really prepared either to resolve their differences nor to commit themselves to treating national reserves as common property, to be used collectively to defend weak currencies against attack in the markets. This was true in the 1970s. And it was still true in the 1980s and 1990s when, after a relatively easy birth and infancy, the ERM finally started to come apart. Although the ERM agreement – like the Werner Plan – had contemplated a final stage in which reserves were pooled, this had never been reached. The markets could see this as a sign of weakness – and acted on the knowledge.

To cut the story short, the French and Germans agreed at Copenhagen in 1978 to try again. One partial explanation lay in domestic politics. Volatile exchange rates played hell with the agreed intervention prices in the CAP. Managing the CAP took up much time and most of the EC budget, but it had important constituencies in both countries. Exchange rate stability was thus indirectly necessary to maintain political support for the CAP and indirectly the EC. More important than this internal reason was the vulnerability of European exchange rates to US policy – and especially to American indifference – what Americans liked to call 'benign neglect'. For five years up to 1978, the Germans had suffered from an unstable dollar–Deutschmark exchange rate, sudden surges of capital flows in and out of marks, and from large and unpredictable shifts in US intervention strategies. As Hans Feddersen commented in his historical study of US–German monetary relations after 1973:

> Preoccupied with domestic economic objectives US policy makers were inclined to disregard depreciations and appreciations of the dollar for long periods. Only when an extremely weak or an extremely strong dollar threatened some important policy objectives, Washington's attitude shifted from indifference to concern. (Feddersen 1986)

Dr Otmar Emminger, then head of the Bundesbank, concluded from the experience of those years that earlier German assumptions that by good management the country could enjoy low and stable inflation rates, stable exchange rates *and* low interest rates were no longer to be relied on. Under pressure from the markets, one of the three might have to be sacrificed. A similar point was made later by the Italian economist and central banker Tommaso Padoa-Schioppa. After the

1990 agreement to abolish capital controls within the EC, he warned against the 'incompatible quartet' of policies – full capital mobility, free trade, fixed exchange rates and national monetary autonomy. Introduce the first, he said, and the markets may speculate that you cannot at the same time maintain the fixed exchange rate. He turned out to be right, but not all would agree that the *only* alternative then was to move on to full monetary union (Padoa-Schioppa 1994).

On top of what, in Bonn and Frankfurt, looked like frivolous and irresponsible American behaviour on monetary matters, the United States also seemed in Europe to be more and more inclined to act unilaterally in defence and foreign policy, without bothering to consult the Europeans. An example was the US Defense Department's proposal, revealed in 1977, to develop a neutron bomb – a weapon which might deter the Russians but at the possible cost of German lives. In that sense, there was a paradox about the ERM. The Americans unwittingly pushed the Europeans to try again, but by sheer coincidence helped them to make a go of it – at least for a time. The coincidence was that in the United States, the generals and politicians decided they could no longer tolerate policies that led to high inflation and a weakening dollar. Volcker was appointed to lead the Federal Reserve Board and advocated a radical shift in monetary policy, effectively restricting credit, shrinking the money supply and causing interest rates to rise sharply. The resulting strong dollar made it possible to launch the ERM without threat from the markets. Moreover, Volcker's deflationist strategy to bring down American inflation had repercussions beyond the United States. It became easier for Europeans to follow suit and keep a lid on inflation, thus removing one of the causes of exchange rate volatility.

In short, the ERM was lucky to last as long as it did. It was also fortunate in being able to add Spain (1989), Britain (1990) and Portugal (1992) to the original eight (Germany, France, Belgium, the Netherlands, Luxembourg, Denmark, Ireland and, with wider bands, Italy). It did not altogether prevent devaluations – most notably France in 1983 – and the weighted basket-of-currencies unit named the ECU played a lesser role than intended. By the mid-1980s, the ERM came to look more and more like a Deutschmark zone, extending beyond the EC to Austria and Switzerland, and led, unchallenged, by the Bundesbank.[6]

The story of how it finally collapsed with the British and Italian devaluations forced on it by the markets in 1993 is well known and much written about.[7] Most of those stories were written by economists and some of them tended to leave out the political and institutional factors that played an important part, both in the collapse of ERM and in the subsequent resolve in the Maastricht Treaty (1991) to try again, and harder, to move to EMU.

It will be enough therefore if I briefly mention four of these non-economic, non-technical factors. I do so in order to show why so little attention was given in Brussels, Paris and Bonn in the mid-1990s to the uncertainties that surrounded EMU and the dangers that lay in its path. For the lesson that perceptions count in politics, whether national or international, is one of the fundamental axioms learned by every student of international relations (Jervis 1976). It is apt to be over-looked by economists, although, as noted earlier, it is central to Soros' concept of the reflexive principle in social science (see chapter 1). Having established that within the European Union (EU) such perceptions may have been skewed by a combination of non-economic factors, we can then move on to the important question of whether these dangers also threatened the larger global financial system.

The first factor was the mood of optimism, even of euphoria, that followed the launching of the single European market initiative in 1986. Until then the mood in Brussels had been one of euro-pessimism. The high hopes of the 1960s had faded. Functionalists as well as federalists saw progress on European integration as painfully slow, the problems of working out a common industrial policy, energy policy, transport policy, fishing policy – let alone foreign or defence policies – seemed insoluble. The CAP was running into difficulties. Only on steel and some trade issues did the member states unite. Big business in Europe was muttering gloomily that their chances of survival as European-based firms competing successfully with the Americans or the Japanese were slim so long as European governments were so sluggish in their pursuit of a true common market. In 1995, for example, the European Commission found 258 cases of national restrictions on the free movement of goods to which all member governments had agreed; 54 were by Germany, 48 by France, 32 by Italy and comparatively few, only 10, by the much-maligned British.

The mood of gloom lifted when a British Commissioner, Lord Cockcroft, with backing from the European Round Table of Indust-rialists, proposed a big new push to sweep away the hundreds of impediments to trade still adding to costs for all kinds of European industries and businesses and handicapping them with obsolete form filling and other kinds of administrative hassle. Knowing that big business was behind the single European market initiative then put new determination to move forward into government delegates and bureaucrats alike.

The second factor was institutional. By the mid-1980s, relations between Paris and Brussels were the reverse of what they had been in de Gaulle's time. Jacques Delors was President of the Commission, and Emile Noel, former *chef de cabinet* to Guy Mollet in the 1950s and a senior French official, was head of the EC secretariat. There was every chance therefore of success for a French strategy of guiding the EC in such a way that French national interests were safeguarded. Instead of the enemy that de Gaulle had perceived, the Commission was a potential tool through which France could control Germany, in what the French considered the general European interest. The French finance minister, Edouard Balladur, consequently wrote to his counterparts in 1988 arguing for 'the rapid pursuit of the monetary construction of Europe' and, indeed, that eventual monetary union was desirable. The result was that Delors was asked to chair a committee to report on the proposal by June 1989. When it did, it advocated liberalisation of capital controls, fiscal harmonisation and the delegation of monetary policy making by national governments to 'a federal form, in what might be called a European System of Central Banks'.[8]

A third factor was geopolitical. By late 1989, the Soviet bloc in eastern Europe was crumbling. The Berlin Wall came down and effectively the Cold War was over. The Red Army was ready to go home and east Germany could be reunited with the west. The security structure which had put Germans in the front line and made them so much more susceptible than the French to pressures from Washington, not only on matters of defence but also over monetary matters, had fundamentally changed. Though it took time for both the French and Germans to adjust to the new situation, in the long run it looked as though the chances of collaboration had greatly improved.

One final source of optimism for the EMU project was the paradoxical argument that the ERM had been unlucky in having to carry a number of 'passengers'. It was their weakness that had alerted market dealers to the possibility of making nice profits out of taking one-way bets that they could not hold their exchange rates. Britain and Italy were the biggest of these suspect passengers in the ERM boat. But there were others and the trouble began long before the fatal days of September 1993, when both were forced to devalue. In January, the Irish were forced to devalue their punt by 20 per cent. In February, the Danish krone was under such pressure that the price of holding krone overnight was raised to 100 per cent. In May, despite intervention by other central banks, the Spanish and Portuguese both had to devalue. By July, there was more market pressure, not only on the smaller and weaker currencies but even on the franc. At the end of the month, in order to make the speculators more careful, it was agreed to widen the permitted bands from 2.25 per cent to 15 per cent. When the serious trouble started in September, Britain and Italy had to come out of the system and only some very determined intervention saved France from the same fate.

Afterwards, the plausible explanation was given that Britain had unwisely gone into the ERM at an unsustainably high exchange rate; and that the political turmoil in Italy made it hard to believe that the country's finances could be brought under control or inflation arrested. What a reformed system had to have, therefore, were strict conditions of entry that kept out the potentially vulnerable currencies and arrangements that assured the markets that monetary authorities not only would but could intervene to maintain the fixed rates.

But while it was legitimate to blame both the British and the Italians, that was not the whole story. Some of the pressure on the weak currencies originated in Germany as a result of reuniting the former East Germany (DDR) with the Federal Republic. For what were clearly political reasons and against the strong advice of the Bundesbank, Chancellor Kohl had insisted that Ostmarks could be exchanged for Deutschmarks on a one-for-one basis. This gave East Germans much more spending money than if the rate had been fixed more realistically. They were also promised heavy government funding for their dilapidated infrastructure. This was going to mean larger budget deficits for the federal government and renewed inflationary pressures. One option would have been to raise taxes – but this was considered politically unpalatable in the west. The other was to raise interest rates to finance the deficit – and this, in the aftermath of unification, it did. The unintended effect was inevitably to strengthen the mark.

The German government could then have chosen to force a re-valuation of the mark against the franc. If the French objected and refused to cooperate, the Germans could have made it clear to them that the Bundesbank would not intervene in the markets to support the franc at the old rate.[9] Whether they liked it or not, the French would have had to give in. But to have chosen that option, though logical, would have completely destroyed faith in Maastricht and the common currency. Whatever the Bundesbank may have thought, Chancellor Kohl was emotionally and politically committed to pursuing the dream of EMU. No wonder he chose to shut his eyes to the contradiction pointed out in Emminger's essay and in a later letter (see note 9).

At the time of writing, it is still unclear whether that contradiction still holds good for the common currency agreed on at Maastricht and planned for in subsequent years. Opinions differ, with the Commission in Brussels, the majority of politicians in the member states – the British Conservative Euro-sceptics excepted – and a good many economists convinced that it will disappear once euros – the common currency – are in circulation. Others remain doubtful. Peter Kenen, for instance, draws parallels with the Bretton Woods system of fixed exchange rates. His comments are worth quoting:

> In both cases, the country at the center of the system suffered a large political shock, underestimated the fiscal implications, and declined to pay the political price of correcting its mistake.... Unable to arrange an orderly exchange rate realignment (both) resorted instead to methods that undermined the system. Their tactics were different but the outcomes were quite similar. In 1971, Richard Nixon and John Connally acted provocatively in shutting the gold window and imposing an import tax. In 1992, Helmut Schlesinger and other Bundesbank officials expressed their doubt about certain EMS currencies, mobilising market forces to put pressure on them. (Kenen 1995: 160–1)

That view was supported by a survey of foreign exchange traders' interpretations of the collapse of 1993. Some 68 per cent blamed the crisis mainly on high German interest rates, and almost the same percentage thought political reasons had caused central banks to stop defending their currencies.[10]

The EMU plan

The chances for and against the success of Europe's common currency are a subject of deep disagreement, and not only in Britain. Much hinges on the details of the arrangements made for effecting the transition, first from national currencies linked by fixed but flexible exchange rates to national currencies locked into each other and freely convertible into a common currency, and then the further transition, as agreed at Maastricht, to a single common currency replacing the national ones. The sceptics' case largely rests on the argument that the Maastricht agreement provided for the introduction of the euro as a parallel currency in January 1999, but that the replacement of the national currencies by the euro would not happen until January 2002. The sceptics thought this was too long a transition period, given the known political disagreements over the management of the common currency and the economic divergence between the member states. It was asking for trouble in the markets.

To explain how and why this caused many observers in the late 1990s to believe that EMU would start on time – but that it would not long survive – I cannot do better than to quote briefly from a 'fairy story' written early in 1997 by David Lascelles. Lascelles is a former editorial writer for the *Financial Times* and is now co-director of the

London Centre for the Study of Financial Innovation. His fairy story took the form of a fictitious report written in 2003 for the British government in the wake of the euro's collapse earlier that year. The report recounted the whole history of EMU from the beginning, in Maastricht; nine bullet points led up to the conclusion. This was:

> Our final conclusion is that EMU was a well-intentioned but premature stratagem. It aimed to raise European union to new levels. But it was driven by political imperatives which ignored the full practical implications, and in the end, those imperatives were not sufficiently powerful to see it through economic problems that were evident from the outset.

The nine bullet points put the argument in a nutshell. Paraphrased, they were:

- EMU participants were insufficiently unified politically for the task they set themselves;
- because political leaders wanted EMU to happen they overlooked many practical difficulties, such as the difficulty of maintaining common policies against inflation;
- financial markets were perplexed and already putting out conflicting signals on EMU prospects before it started;
- participating governments fudged the agreed convergence criteria and were not strict enough in enforcing them;
- instead of creating jobs, as its advocates had promised, EMU brought more unemployment both before and after it started;
- the costs borne by banks and taxpayers therefore greatly exceeded the promised benefits;
- at first, the euro was rated strong in the financial markets – stronger than expected or was desirable;[11]
- the 'stability pact' agreed at the Dublin and Amsterdam summits in 1996/7 added to austerity measures in the EMU economies, lowering growth instead of raising it;
- as the consequent political pressures mounted, EMU states began to put national priorities above those of monetary union.

Thus the fairy story ended with the French government's doomed attempt to escape the straitjacket of the stability pact by issuing French government debt denominated in US dollars. The markets reacted by devaluing French government debt as compared with German. The situation could have been saved only by a wide open commitment by the German government to underwrite French national debt. In the summer of 2002, Lascelles imagined, with great political realism, the Bundestag refused to do this, so that the markets – as Kenen and others had always insisted – began to place more and more one-way bets on the collapse of EMU.

Now though it may not happen quite like this, and the collapse could come sooner, or later, both the logic of political economy and the historical experience of fixed-rate regimes between autonomous national governments point in the same direction.

Euros, dollars and yen

And even if they did not, the important question for the rest of the world was how the euro would affect the relative market prices of euros, dollars and yen. This was something given little serious thought in Europe and on which American opinions were divided. The Europeans have always had a tendency to overlook the global context and consequences of what they do inside the EU, whether on trade or monetary or other matters. European official and much conventional opinion therefore has always tended to exaggerate the euro's chances of rivalling the dollar. They chose to ignore the fact that they had no control over the market's relative valuation of euros, dollars and yen. If EMU did not start on time, or if political trouble were to start to build up between Paris and Berlin, the reaction of the markets could be as sudden and as extreme as they were in east Asia in the summer of 1997. Even assuming that EMU, like the ERM, has an easy birth and infancy, and encounters no market turmoil in the dangerous transition period to 2003, it could very well be that German monetary hegemony in the EU will doom European economies to prolonged slow growth, high unemployment and low competitiveness. The question to consider, therefore, is whether a weak euro would set off further turbulence in global markets.

In such a scenario, holders of assets denominated in euros would seek a safe haven, presumably in the US dollar. They were hardly likely after 1997 to change into Japanese yen, and US interest rates were unlikely to fall so substantially that the dollar would weaken. A weak euro, therefore, would tend to generate an inflow of funds into America and to raise the exchange rate of the dollar. In theory, this would impose a burden on US export industries. But in the late 1990s, when the dollar strengthened against the yen, we have seen that this does not apparently greatly worry them, as American exports of grain, cotton, and other primary products are priced in dollars anyway. And in manufacturing, most of the big firms able to export are already established overseas in Europe and Asia and thus benefit from lower production costs compared with their local competitors. European and Asian firms with subsidiaries in the United States would find their costs increased. But equally their sales, in terms of their home currency, would be more valuable.

The alternative scenario is a strong euro. This is more dangerous for the currency markets – and would consequently offer more opportunities for hedge fund managers and others to profit from speculative dealing. A strong euro implies a weaker dollar. The relevant experience here would be from the 1970s, when inflation took hold in the United States. The result then was to polarise the strong and weak European currencies, since dollars fled into Deutschmarks but not into francs or lire. Until the end of the transition period, therefore, when national currencies would still circulate alongside euros, and perceptions persist – as they probably would – that there might be a qualitative difference in the value of, say, German and Italian government bonds or shares, a weak dollar can pose dangers to EMU.

Since British entry remains subject to a referendum and is therefore problematic, EMU also poses problems for sterling. Sterling has tended to shadow the dollar in relation to third currencies, so a weak dollar would mean a weak pound. Other things being equal, this would be good for British export industries and British farmers. But in the long term, a strong euro might give Europeans the political muscle they hope for – always provided their perceived interests in making use of this muscle can coincide – whether in reforming the IMF, assisting Russia and central Europe or dealing with the Middle East oil producers.

Some would also see pointers to the consequences of a strong euro in the dollar–yen exchange rates of the 1990s. Until 1997, when the yen had fallen to 130 to the dollar – and some forecasters thought it could fall further, to 150 – the exchange rate had yo-yoed up and down, first falling then rising briefly to around 85 to the dollar then falling once more. Governments come under pressure from interests adversely affected and tend to take it out on other governments. It is always easier to blame foreigners for domestic pain. International economic relations sour in consequence. As argued in *Casino Capitalism* and more recently by Paul Erdman and others, such volatility is apt to produce friction over trade, over competition between firms – Kodak and Fuji, Boeing and Airbus – and over the running of international organisations and the management of international crises. Nor does it help towards the solution of other problems in the world economy. We come to a consideration of some of these issues in subsequent chapters.

Notes

1   Of the many books and articles that have been written on the subject, I would
    highly recommend Loukas Tsoukalis' *The New European Economy* (1997).
    Written by an economist, it is unusually accessible to non-economists, being
    based on his courses for graduate students at the College of Europe in Bruges.
    Second, I would recommend Peter Kenen's *Economic and Monetary Union in
    Europe* (Kenen 1995). It too is balanced and non-technical.

2   Camps' book was a masterly exposition of a complex situation in which
    divisions of opinion and conflicts of interest within the member countries
    complicated negotiations on multiple issues. A former rising star in the State
    Department who married a Cambridge (England) professor and worked at
    Chatham House and the Council on Foreign Relations in New York, she had
    access to good sources. Her interpretations, based on a combination of
    documentary evidence and personal interviews, have not, so far as I am
    aware, been confounded by subsequent research. There are some recent
    theorists on European integration who would do well to reread, if they have
    not already done so, Camps' study.

3   *Engrenage*: the process of setting something going, of getting gears to mesh
    with each other as national governments were starting to mesh with the
    Brussels bureaucracy.

4   Even then, the French had put forward their own gold-based alternative to the
    plan worked out between Keynes and White. Jacques Rueff, as de Gaulle's
    financial adviser in the 1960s, was only harking back to an old argument
    (Rueff 1971). It was one with which quite a few other Europeans sympathised.
    They included some of the leading economists at the BIS and – ironically – the
    former head of the Bundesbank, Hjalmar Schacht (Schacht 1950).

5   A notable exception was the *Le Monde* columnist Paul Fabra. He consistently
    argued that the rational market reaction to a weak dollar in the mid-1970s
    was to move funds out of dollars into Deutschmarks – but not into francs or
    Italian lire. No wonder, he said, the snake got pulled apart. Few listened to
    him then, probably because European politicians and most of the media liked
    to think that European governments were in charge of their own destinies and
    could not be pushed off course by US policies or by the markets.

6   The consequent commitment in the Basle–Nyborg Agreement of 1987 to tie
    their interest rates to those of the Bundesbank by agreeing to use these to
    maintain the ERM grid made German leadership explicit.

7   Notably, Gros and Thygesen (1988), Kenen (1995) and Tsoukalis (1997).

8   Quoted in Kenen (1995), where the details of the report are fully set out.

9   Peter Kenen raises this possibility, drawing attention to the German refusal to
    support the Belgian franc in 1981 when the Belgian government resisted a
    devaluation, and to a letter from Otmar Emminger as head of the Bundesbank
    in which he had pointed out that there was a contradiction between the
    constitutional obligation of the Buba to maintain monetary stability and its
    obligations under the old ERM to intervene on behalf of its fellow member
    states. Emminger wrote that if the need to choose ever arose, he assumed the
    German government would either release the Buba from its obligations under
    the ERM or negotiate a correction of the vulnerable fixed exchange rates. The
    politicians had never acknowledged Emminger's logic.

10 As reported by Eichengreen and Wyplosz (1993) and quoted by Kenen (1995).
    They also suggested the Bundesbank had threatened to limit its intervention,

adding to market suspicions that they were unsustainable. For a short example of the arguments between sceptics and believers, see Sam Brittan's column in the *Financial Times*, 12 September 1997, and the reply by Richard Portes some days later.

11 This prophetic point was predicated on an imagined Wall Street crash in 2000 (Lascelles 1997: 16). Reality anticipated the prophecy with the crash of 1997, brought on by the unexpected trouble in Asian emerging markets that summer – a salutary reminder of the dangers of economic forecasting, even by the well informed.

Chapter 5

Wall Street and other casinos

History and the media between them have spread the idea far and wide that Wall Street – or perhaps stock exchanges generally – are the weakest point in the international financial system. If there is going to be trouble in the world market economy, that is where it will start.

Whether this is a correct reading of history and the right conclusion to draw from more recent developments is the question that will be examined in this chapter. What is abundantly clear is that opinions on this question vary widely. At one extreme, there are Jeremiahs who argue that what goes up must come down – and that when it does, the crash will herald deep recession in the world economy. At the other, there are Pollyannas who argue with equal conviction that history need not repeat itself and that the underlying strengths of the world market economy today are proof against the ups and downs of stock markets. Since the experts themselves are deeply divided in their views, there is no right or wrong interpretation. Readers will have to make their own judgement, based on the strengths and weaknesses of the conflicting arguments and on the available evidence.

The case for optimism

This rests heavily on the experience of October 1987. For a week or so, the worldwide collapse of share prices seemed to be a rerun of October 1929. By the end of the year, it looked in retrospect like nothing more than a 'healthy correction' of inflated prices, a kind of therapeutic bloodletting. Firms whose shares had rocketed over the summer found themselves back where they had started six months before – neither worse nor better off. Within three months, stock exchanges in London and New York were enjoying the beginning of a sustained recovery.

Yet the experience had been scary enough at the time. The worst of the fall – 23 per cent of total share values in a day – happened on Black Monday, 19 October. The rush to sell might have started in London the Friday before, but a freak hurricane over the south of England, felling trees and blocking railways and roads, had kept commuting traders at home, all the more eager to unload their clients' stocks the following Monday. Then, the rush to sell started in Tokyo, spread from there to London and hit Wall Street as soon as the market opened. In two hours, the Dow index fell by 200 points. At the SEC, there was talk of closing it, even temporarily, to stop the panic. Fears of being caught with unsold loss-making shares followed. The rush to sell reverberated round the world. Tokyo fell by 13 per cent. Hong Kong was closed. Traders could not keep up with the rush of orders to sell, sell, sell.

Why then did the stock market fall in 1987 not herald a general loss of confidence in the economy, as it had, apparently, in 1929? Today's optimists find a number of reasons. One is that the authorities in the United States acted promptly and effectively to stop the panic in the markets. Their intervention to provide liquidity to banks and market traders was predicated on a belief in the so-called 'wealth effect' of a fall in the value of shares. Some time before the crash, economists at the Federal Reserve had calculated that for every dollar decline in the market value of their wealth, American consumers would cut their current spending by 4 to 5 cents and this would be enough, they believed, to trigger a recession. A vicious spiral of declining orders from retailers to manufacturers, and from manufacturers to their suppliers, would set in, bringing unemployment, lower wages and a credit squeeze. Not everyone shared this belief in the wealth effect. There is still disagreement on whether it was really necessary to inject so much liquidity into the financial system. Because of the omnipresent counterfactual problem – what would have happened otherwise? – no one can be sure for certain. Some say that by 'getting behind the curve', that is, by reinforcing a trend that was already there, the Federal Reserve Board laid up trouble for the future. Others – including Alan Greenspan, who ultimately was responsible for the decision – argued that, in a crisis, financial authorities could not dare take the greater, more immediate risk of doing nothing – just in case the wealth effect did not work.

What the Fed did therefore was to interrupt their earlier strategy of gradually increasing US interest rates. In the weeks before Black Monday, they had raised the Fed funds rate from 6.5 per cent to 7.25

per cent. The injections of liquidity after the crash – supplemented by possibly coordinated action by corporations intervening to buy back their own shares – brought the rate down again by 0.5 per cent, to 6.75. In January 1988, it was lowered again to 6.5 per cent. In short, the wealth effect presumed by economic research had not materialised. Private savings did indeed increase as consumers prudently paid off some of their credit card debt. But to compensate for slacker demand in the home market, US exports did well; for whatever reason, they doubled the growth rate of previous years. Economic growth in the US economy in 1988 came back to 3 per cent of gross national product (GNP). The following year, 1989, the Fed once again feared inflation more than recession, so that it reversed its easier policy and put rates back up again.

The conclusion could be drawn from this experience that in a financial crisis in the stock exchanges, fear of 'meltdown' and a total collapse of confidence in the credit system overcomes the fear of inflation. This leads central banks to use their credit-creating powers to protect the private institutions put in jeopardy by the volatility of the markets. It would seem to be a generalisation borne out by the reaction of Japanese authorities to the bursting of the bubble economy in 1989/ 90. Rather than let the banks suffer the consequences of imprudent investments in the real estate boom of the 1980s, the central bank and the MOF preferred to impose on the public sector – ultimately the taxpayers – the major cost of paying off the *jusen,* and meanwhile to allow the banks to conceal many of their bad and non-performing loans, storing up trouble for the future (see chapter 3). In Thailand, and in South Korea too, governments have preferred rescue operations, bailouts and nationalisation (as of the troubled Kia car firm) to letting the market deal out punishment in its own way.

Marxists would say that this only proves their case that governments are the tools of finance capitalists. But the truth is surely a bit more complex: there is a sort of symbiosis that works both ways between business and the state. In a market-based economy, neither can exist without the other. Each has to compromise its preferences with those of the other as the price of its own survival. But it seems that fear works more powerfully on government than on business and that only governments – or intergovernmental institutions like the IMF – can create the liquidity required to prevent financial panic. Traders and firms operating in the market cannot act collectively and therefore still look for a lender of last resort to come to their rescue. The result is that, in the end, it is society that pays the price for the rescue.

Besides the quick recovery of the American and world economy after Black Monday, the other argument on the side of optimism has been that of geography. What happened in Asia in 1997, it was argued, could be explained by local factors peculiar to the economies of the newly industrialised countries (NICs). Each case was slightly different, yet all had in common an overvalued currency, recent and over-hasty liberalisation of controls over capital and investment, a consequent inflow of 'hot money' from abroad from investors in search of quick and easy profits and a banking system inadequately monitored and controlled.

Asian currencies were overvalued, especially in relation to trading partners in Europe and Japan. This was because they were tied – closely for Thailand or Hong Kong, loosely for Indonesia – to the US dollar. Yet between 1995 and 1997, the dollar had appreciated by 50 per cent against the yen. The Deutschmark had also lost 20 per cent of its dollar value, the franc 23 per cent, according to calculations by Professor Jeffry Sachs in a Brookings study (Sachs 1996). The figures were based on the divergence between local consumer prices and the prices prevailing in, for example, Thailand's trading partners. This overvaluation tended to bring foreign funds into Thai banks or the stock exchange, and into construction and real estate rather than manufacturing or agriculture, on which exports depended. The result was a stock market and property boom – or as a former prime minister put it afterwards, 'a soap bubble based on greed, speculation, con-sumption, buy-now-pay-later and plastic cards'.[1] As with Mexico, much of the speculation was financed by borrowing cheaply in US dollars – which proved far from cheap when the local currency crashed in the late summer of 1997. In retrospect, the over-hasty liberalisation of financial flows allowed too many foreign funds to come in faster than the government or the banking system could handle. Not only were the banks inadequately monitored or regulated, but they were often closely linked with corrupt politicians who looked to them to supply the funds necessary for their re-election. Coalition governments were too weak and too fragile to reform the political system or to impose discipline on the banks. As in Mexico, Thai banks and enterprises had borrowed cheaply in dollars to finance short-term speculation in the local currency (see chapter 6).

In Indonesia, the rupiah was less closely tied to the US dollar, having been allowed to fluctuate within a 12 per cent band. Yet beyond that limit, the central bank stood committed to intervening in support of the currency. The result was still that speculators could be sure it would not get stronger than the dollar and might possibly get weaker, even beyond the band. They therefore – as with other fixed exchange rates in the past – could take a one-way bet from which they could not lose and might, with luck, gain quite substantially. Derivative markets gave the opportunity to do so, in effect, on margin, at minimal immediate cost. Add to that the many fundamental weaknesses in Indonesian politics and economics, not least the nepotism and corruption on which the Suharto regime depended.

In Malaysia, the real economy was highly rated by development economists as one of the success stories of south-east Asia (Stopford and Strange 1991). The country had avoided overexposure to foreign creditors. It had welcomed the entry of foreign firms, especially the Japanese, and had consequently benefited from the pressures on costs at home that drove them to transfer manufacturing offshore. Their confidence was strongly reinforced by the long-standing Malaysian policy of putting no impediments in the way of firms who might decide to repatriate their profits to their home base.[2] Why then was Malaysia not secure against the contagion of failing confidence in its currency? Prime Minister Mahathir's explanation pointed the finger at foreign speculators, notably George Soros – just as Harold Wilson in the 1960s had accused the 'gnomes of Zurich' for speculative attacks on sterling. Both chose blindly to overlook the role of local financial interests, which are often the first to abandon ship, so to speak, and to ignore the factors that raised doubts in the market about the sustainability of the country's exchange rate. For one thing, Malaysia's strong export record was under threat from new Asian competitors – especially China, where labour costs in electronics and consumer electrical products like air conditioners were much lower than in Malaysia. For another, Mahathir had announced some grandiose plans to build an Asian Silicon Valley, launch a transcontinental railway to link the Indian Ocean with China, and generate electric power on a grand scale. All this would involve foreign capital. Could Malaysian exports meet the bill or would the country have to take on expensive and risky foreign debt?

A similar story of early optimism followed by sudden doubts in the markets can be told of the Philippines. Early in 1997, financial commentators on emerging markets were inclined to point to the Philippines as the next 'miracle economy'. Japanese investment there had boomed; wages were low but the population was relatively educated and skilled; although government was notoriously corrupt and democracy pretty much of a sham, US connections at the sub-state level were still strong and there was easier access to the North American market.

The optimists naturally argued, first, that these Asian economies were fundamentally strong and were capable – given appropriate reforms – of quickly resuming their economic growth and restoring the confidence of foreign investors. They recalled that over the preceding quarter of a century, east Asian economies had grown more than twice as fast as the rest of the world economy. Poverty rates had dropped. An affluent middle class sustained a savings rate equal to more than a third of GDP and six times the inflow of foreign investment. The stock exchange and currency crisis was primarily due therefore to weak regulation of the banks and financial markets. The sudden inflow of short-term foreign funds had allowed the banks to make too many risky loans. When these were dollar-denominated and the exchange rates with the dollar could not be held, these local banks were in trouble. Closer monitoring and stricter regulation were all that was needed for the Asian miracle to resume its upward path.

Secondly, the optimists argued that these Asian problems had no relevance – or very little – to what happens in the rich industrialised countries, especially the United States. Wall Street is so big a market, sustained by so strong a national economy, that falling share prices in Bangkok or Manila – even in Hong Kong – have little impact on the big global stock markets. It used to be said that when the United States catches a cold, Britain (or Europe, or Japan) gets pneumonia. Now the reverse argument was used: when east Asia gets pneumonia, Wall Street gets a sniffle. Tough luck for the Chinese and other Asian investors – but they only reap the punishment for their own follies – financial and political.

That particular source of optimism took a bad knock in late October 1997 – but, as in 1987, the fact that, after a nail-biting few days, Wall Street bounced back rather strongly restored the optimists' faith in the resilience of the global system. Recall that the turbulence in Thailand, Malaysia, Indonesia and the Philippines spread to Hong Kong, bringing share prices on the Hang Seng Index sharply down and putting the Hong Kong dollar under pressure in the foreign exchange markets. It was true that the property market in Hong Kong – as in Bangkok – was grossly inflated, throwing doubt on the authorities' promises to build new public housing. But the currency was much stronger than the other Asian currencies. It was run by a currency board which required the local money supply to be 100 per cent backed by US dollars and which commanded very large reserves of foreign exchange – some $80 billion – with which to intervene against speculation in the market. However, there were political reasons for doubting whether, over the longer term, this would suffice to save the exchange rate established back in 1993. Before the British hand-over to the People's Republic in July 1997, Beijing had promised that its own reserves, totalling a massive $180 billion, were available to support the Hong Kong dollar. But in October/November 1997, that categorical assurance was not repeated. Some said it still held. Others were not so sure. The ambiguity aroused some suspicions that some factions on the mainland – in Shanghai, for instance – might think it would be in the longer-term interests of the government to let Hong Kong spend its reserves in a futile defence of the exchange rate, thus depriving the territory of a major economic source of political independence from Beijing.

However that may be, the turbulence in the markets spread to London and Wall Street, affecting not only the shares of firms deeply involved in Asia, but the entire share market. Another Black Monday ensued. In terms of points on the Dow, there was the biggest ever fall in share prices. Under new rules introduced after 1987, the market suspended trading in the early afternoon and again half an hour before the scheduled close. In response, share prices fell another 11 per cent in Hong Kong, over 7 per cent in Singapore and 10 per cent in Australia. Share prices also fell in Europe and in Russia.

The next day, Tuesday, 28 October 1997, Wall Street rallied and was followed by London. What turned it round, it seemed, was the re-entry of big firms like IBM, which started to buy back their own shares. This was probably more important to traders than the reassuring noises from President Clinton and Treasury Secretary Rubin. The optimists reaffirmed their faith in the underlying strength of the US economy, the low inflation, relatively low unemployment (compared with Europe), technological leadership in a number of key sectors and a generally buoyant mood among consumers. At least for the time being, the optimists were reassured.

The case for pessimism

Today's pessimists would not agree. They follow a long tradition, reaching far back into the ancient world. Recall Pharaoh's prophetic dream about the fat cattle and the lean cattle, the full ears of corn and the withered ones (Genesis, chapter 41). It inspired Joseph to advise Pharaoh that seven fat years in Egypt would be followed by seven lean ones, and a grievous famine would eat up the land. The wise ruler therefore would anticipate the lean years and hard times to come by stockpiling grain in order to moderate the sort of scarcity prices that could be politically destabilising.

Ever since, there have been pessimists who have argued that good times do not last for ever; prudence in business and in government counsels preparation for the hard times to come. Such ideas are seldom welcome. However much supporting evidence they may find in economic history, they are hardly consistent with the ideologies of left or right, with either the critics of the prevailing system of political economy or with its equally dogmatic defendants, for whom markets always know best and government interference is always counter-productive.

The marxist dogma, taking the extreme of pessimistic views, insisted on the inherent tendency in a capitalist political economy for the rate of profit to fall, and therefore for the ultimate and inevitable decline and collapse of the whole system. Kondratiev's historical research into wages and prices in the nineteenth century had led him to detect (without seeking to explain) a fifty-year cycle during which upswings followed downswings in wages and prices. The implication of such findings was that capitalism had its ups as well as its downs. There were fat years even for wage slaves as well as lean ones. Stalin found such a notion pure heresy. It was not what Marx and Lenin had taught and what justified the dictatorship of the proletariat as represented by the hierarchy of the Party. He therefore condemned poor Kondratiev to the gulags and an unmarked grave. In the West, however, Kondratiev's research seemed to support Joseph Schumpeter's argument that economic growth tended to accelerate in response to technological advances that introduced new products or new production processes. Although the concept of the long wave appealed to many economists, those who made a study of the evidence tended to conclude that the long wave was not the only factor affecting economic performance in a capitalist system (van Duijn 1983: 143).[3] Wars, for instance, or demographic changes or the state of financial markets also mattered. Yet van Duijn also thought that the integrative forces of globalisation probably meant that more and more countries would feel the effects of long-wave cycles. The only problem – but a major one for our purposes – was that the fifty-year pattern was neither regular nor precise. There was therefore no way of foretelling when the upswing would give way to a downward movement. Too many other factors entered into it, including even human psychology.

Today's pessimists have other, less intuitive, grounds for believing that there are fatal flaws in the present financial system that put in jeopardy the prosperity of the world market economy. Chief among these, in my opinion, is the argument that stock market crashes can – but may not – be the triggers setting off a long economic slump. This belief is very much based on the interwar experience. The crash of October 1929 did not immediately lead to the slump of the 1930s. That required certain other coincidental circumstances. Since recent years have witnessed two rather large stock market falls, one in 1987 and the other in 1997, from which each time the world economy recovered rather quickly, it is important to determine what these other circumstances might be.

Easier said than done. Once again, the experts disagree. According to their political predilections and/or their previous experience and area of specialised knowledge, economists have tended to pick on one or two specific reasons why, despite the rather strong recovery in the stock market in 1930 and 1931, world trade and investment slumped, developing countries were unable to pay their foreign debts and in-dustrialised ones unable to cure the mass unemployment that marked the entire decade of the 1930s. Once again, wary and intelligent readers have to make up their own minds between the conflicting explanatory theories.

Outside the United States, many will already be aware that the conventional wisdom parroted in innumerable American texts on international political economy is by no means unchallenged. Drawing heavily on the economic literature of monetarist and liberal free-trade doctrine, this conventional wisdom put the weight of blame for the world depression, first, on monetary policy as the cause of the boom and slump on Wall Street, and secondly on the protectionist Smoot-Hawley Tariff Act of 1930. The first account rested heavily on the magisterial work of Milton Friedman and Anna Schwarz in their *Monetary History of the United States, 1867–1960* (1963).[4] According to this account, the Fed's decision to raise US interest rates in 1928 had contributed to the gadarene rush of foreign money into Wall Street in the months before the crash. Then, after the crash, and certainly in the winter of 1930–1, it should have undertaken massive open-market operations in order to enlarge the money supply of the United States. But it did not. The origin of the slump lay in US policy rather than in Europe, in the commodity markets or the structure of the international financial system. This very US-based interpretation is contested by Kindleberger, among others. He argues that the money supply alone was an insufficient factor; credit conditions both in the United States and internationally were inimical to recovery (Kindleberger 1973: 136–7).[5]

Liberal conventional wisdom – heavily endorsed by Secretary of State Cordell Hull in the 1940s – put heavy blame for the length and depth of the slump on protectionism – by the United States in 1930 and also by Britain and its Commonwealth partners in the Ottawa Agreements of 1932. This was the main line of argument by the Australian economist Hans Arndt in his *Economic Lessons of the 1930s* (1944). It was certainly true that protectionism in many forms – tariffs, quotas, exchange controls and exclusionary trading deals like the Sperrmark scheme of Nazi Germany for the poor indebted countries of central and eastern European – did indeed proliferate in the 1930s. But as I have argued elsewhere, the evidence is not conclusive that this was the *cause* of economic stagnation and unemployment. Rather, the record suggests that everywhere protectionism was a political response to electoral discontent, a symptom of economic pain, not a cause of it (Strange 1986: 61–2).[6] By the late 1930s, even liberal economic historians found little evidence that any of these higher tariffs had had much effect either on the volume or on the direction of trade flows.

Next to protectionism, later conventional wisdom often put competitive devaluations as another form of beggar-thy-neighbour policies that had frustrated recovery in the 1930s. For this, too, there is little firm historical evidence. The devaluation of sterling in 1931 or, later, of the franc or the lira in the 1930s was not engineered by governments. Indeed, the British Labour Chancellor of the Exchequer, Philip Snowden, is alleged to have observed rather plaintively afterwards: 'Nobody told us we could do that!'[7] Rather – as with European and later Asian devaluations in the 1990s – they were forced on governments by the decision of foreign exchange dealers in the market.

If neither protectionism nor competitive devaluation, then what were the reasons for the long miseries of the 1930s? Both Friedman and, paradoxically, Galbraith concentrated on factors within the United States – but not the same factors. Where Friedman and Schwartz blamed inappropriate monetary management by the Fed, Galbraith pointed to other failings in the system. Some of these – financial dishonesty, for example – may be relevant to our own days. Galbraith recalled the stories of three financial figures – Albert Wiggin of the Chase Bank, Charles Mitchell of National City Bank and, worst of all, Richard Whitney, president-elect of the New York stock exchange in 1932, whose arraignment by District Attorney Thomas Dewey on a charge of grand larceny did not take place until 1938. The laxity of financial morals and regulations was recognised early on in the New Deal by such reforms as the Securities Act of 1933 and the Securities Exchange Act of 1934 (Galbraith 1955: 166–85).

Another factor Galbraith identified – also relevant in the 1990s – is the distribution of income in the whole economy. In 1929, the richest 5 per cent of Americans were receiving a third of personal incomes, much more of it in unearned income than in the 1940s. Another factor was the prevailing corporate strategy of cutting back on investment in order to maintain dividends and thus the valuation of shares on the stock exchange. A third was the structure of US banking, which in the 1920s was not too different from that of some Asian countries in the 1990s. There were too many small, independent and vulnerable banks. When one found itself illiquid thanks to imprudent or speculative investments, it not only provoked a panic flight by unfortunate customers, but it also started a domino effect on other small banks. Between 1930 and 1933, almost 9,000 US banks went bust, over 4,000 in 1933 alone. For many communities, this meant not only that many depositors' savings were wiped out, but that a local source of credit was closed.

It is also worth recalling, as Galbraith did, that in the 1930s fear of inflation prevailed over fear of deflation for far too long after the crash, and that even Roosevelt campaigned in 1932 with a firm pledge to cut government spending and balance the federal budget.

True as it was that the depression originated in America, the interpretations offered by Galbraith and by Friedman tended to concentrate exclusively on systemic and policy weaknesses in the United States as the reason for its long duration. Other economic historians took a wider, more global view. As noted in chapter 3, Charles Kindleberger came out with an explanation that later became known as the Hegemonic Stability Theory. Briefly, this was that a world economy characterised by substantial flows of traded goods and capital between national economies needed one country to act as hegemon. The hegemon had to be able and willing to provide an open market for distress goods (i.e. goods that could not find an unprotected market elsewhere); to maintain a steady outward flow of capital to generate growth in poorer countries; and – most important in times of crisis – to act as lender of last resort to a fragile or fearful banking system. He argued that in the crucial years 1930–3, Britain, which had acted as global hegemon for most of the pre-1914 century, was no longer able to do so, while the United States, which was capable of so acting, was unwilling to do so (Kindleberger 1973: ch. 14). His was not the only world-system explanation. The West Indian economist Sir Arthur Lewis, writing in the late 1940s, pointed to the weakness of commodity prices – wheat, sugar, cotton, coffee, tobacco – in the late 1920s and especially from 1927 on (Lewis 1949: 302). The US economist Walt Rostow, writing in the 1970s, also believed that declining incomes for primary producers everywhere – the south-east of Europe and the south-west of the United States as well as South America and Australia – had predisposed the system to depression in the 1930s as it had in earlier times (Rostow 1978).

Where this argument links with Kindleberger's explanation is that the primary producing countries were also the very ones worst hit by the dearth of credit after 1930, especially of credit provided by London and New York. Australia, Argentina and others were in the same plight as the Third World debtors of the 1980s. Even though capital markets recovered somewhat in 1930, the recovery was short lived. After 1932, neither short- nor long-term capital was to be had at any price.

Just to complete the survey of conflicting opinions, I might mention those who insisted on underlying demographic factors as fundamental weaknesses revealed by the shock of the stock market crash. One was an American, Alvin Hansen, who saw the levelling-off of US population numbers as a check on the demand side. It was true, of course, that from 1924 the United States had introduced immigration quotas, making a mockery of the message inscribed on the Statue of Liberty 'Bring me your tired, your poor, / Your huddled masses yearning to breathe free'. Coming on top of the closing of the frontier to the west, this may indeed have played a part, just as, conversely, the influx of Germans from the east after 1945 may have given an important boost to the Erhard 'miracle' in the West German economy in the 1950s. A more Atlantic theory was put forward by the Welsh economist Brinley Thomas, who correlated emigration from Britain (then including Ireland) in the nineteenth century with upturns in capital flows westwards, which in turn sustained construction booms in America (Thomas 1954).

The only trouble with such theories, of course, is that demographic change tends to be slow and to persist over long periods. It can coincide with good times as well as bad. It is never the *only* factor in the political economy. Indeed, Galbraith, in summing up his account of the crash, observed, 'Far more important than the rate of interest and the supply of credit is *the mood*' (Galbraith 1955: 187, my italics). Economic factors alone cannot explain why in the space of two years the optimism of the speculative boom turned to the pessimism of the depression. Some later, rather sophisticated econometric research actually concluded that most of the fall in spending in 1929–31 was due to non-monetary factors; monetary conditions explained only about a quarter of the fall.[8] What no econometric study can do, of course, is to measure and explain why there should have been such a change in popular mood.

At the time of writing, most independent financial commentators are self-consciously ambiguous. They are unsure whether to come down on the side of optimism – in Hoover's memorable phrase, 'Prosperity is just around the corner' – or on the side of pessimism – the turmoil in Asian markets and the slide in London and Wall Street are over, but only for the moment; expect further slides in the months to come. In the concluding section of this chapter, therefore, it may help to suggest the main points of similarity and of difference between the international financial and economic system in the 1990s as compared with the

1930s. Are we better placed, or worse, to prevent another stock market collapse turning the general mood from optimism to despair?

What has changed?

The most significant difference, in my opinion, is that in the 1930s there was little understanding of what ought to be done; in the 1990s, there is – or should be – more understanding, but no more willingness and less capability to do it. Let me explain.

Keynes' great work, *The General Theory of Employment, Interest, and Money* (Keynes 1936), had explained how and why a market economy could fall into deep economic depression. (Already in the 1920s, he had analysed the failings of capitalism from a social and political point of view (Keynes 1926) – it was not capitalism so much as the capitalists, and more particularly the financial markets, that were to blame.) The final chapter of *The General Theory* put it succinctly. 'The outstanding faults of the economic society in which we live,' he wrote, 'are its failure to provide full employment and its arbitrary and inequitable distribution of income and wealth.' Public policy, therefore, had to be directed to 'increasing and supplementing the propensity to invest' whenever the 'animal spirits' of the investing classes deserted them. 'The central controls necessary to ensure full employment will, of course, involve a large extension of the functions of government.'[9] Merely lowering the price of credit by cutting interest rates was not enough; the state had to step in, alone or in collaboration with private interests.

Now, although *The General Theory* did not appear until the very trough of the slump, so that keynesian-type policies were either too timid, as in the US New Deal, or were eventually undertaken, as in France, Germany and Britain, for quite other reasons – to prepare for World War II – the understanding of what to do was widespread in America and Europe only by the end of the decade. The most dramatic demonstration of their effectiveness, indeed, was in the United States after Pearl Harbor. In the space of a year, most of the United States' 13 million unemployed were back at work. Government credit for defence production was readily available. Some industries, even, were effectively nationalised. The 'arsenal of democracy' showed what could be done given the spur of war.[10]

The next demonstration of keynesian logic – again taken more for reasons of state security than concern for employment and income equality – was in postwar Europe, in the European Recovery Program. Instead of the postwar slump feared and predicted by left-wing keynesians like Henry Wallace, the injection of $20 billion of US credit into flagging economies in western Europe restored the confidence of governments, people and business not only in Europe but also in the United States.[11]

When I said there was little understanding of keynesian logic in the 1930s, I should have added that in the 1930s and in the 1940s there were, however, the necessary and sufficient conditions for governments to apply that logic *within national economies*. This is worth noting because those conditions are no longer there. One was the low level of capital mobility. Not only were few bonds or shares for foreign borrowers issued in London or New York, in many countries exchange controls cut the national economy off from the rest of the world. Keynes himself recognised the importance of this relative financial insulation as necessary to effective national economic management. It allowed a government to fix interest rates, to expand or contract the money supply as it thought fit and to use fiscal measures to redistribute spending power to stimulate demand.[12] In wartime, all these controls acquired even greater force and legitimacy. And for over a decade after the war, until about 1960 and the development of Euro-currency markets, conditions existed that allowed countries to practise keynesian demand management. French indicative planning, as described by Shonfield in *Modern Capitalism*, was a prime example (Shonfield 1965).

By the mid-1980s, the old insulating fences around most national economies were gone. Even France had discovered that government borrowing to finance counter-cyclical pump-priming measures carried too high a price. Foreign exchange markets attacked the exchange rate and Mitterrand was obliged in 1983/4 to give up his keynesian strategy. As economists – and central bankers like Otmar Emminger – came to recognise, in the new open financial system, states could not control both the rate of inflation *and* the exchange rate *and* the national rate of economic growth. One of the three had to be left to the markets.

The logic of the *General Theory* still held. But henceforth if counter-cyclical intervention were to be effective, it would have to be global and collective, not national. In the 1980s, however, there was little support in the rich countries – and especially the United States – for a demand-creating redistribution of income to developing countries as demanded by the G77 developing countries and the Brandt Commission. American opinion was that they expected too much, should do more to help themselves – and anyway no payoffs for US foreign policy could be expected.

But by 1990 a golden opportunity appeared as the Berlin Wall came down and the Soviet empire collapsed. For a speedy and successful transition from a centrally planned to a mixed economy, some sort of Marshall Plan for central and eastern Europe was needed. Such a proposal was strongly urged by the veteran Dutch economist Max Kohnstam and by many European economists familiar with the situation in central Europe.[13] But it was not to be. Germany was totally absorbed by the problems of German unification. The United States, when finally it agreed to set up a European Bank for Reconstruction and Development (EBRD), dogmatically insisted that 60 per cent of its loans should go to private borrowers, even though the obvious crying need – as in western Europe in 1948 – was to improve and modernise the infrastructure of transport, communications and power generation. Secondly, the United States also failed to privilege discriminatory trading between the former Council for Mutual Economic Assistance (CMEA) states over trading with the more affluent and competitive west (see also chapter 6).

The result of that missed keynesian opportunity was that central Europe and the former Soviet Union have been slow to make the transition to an effective market system. Their demand for imports has been constrained by their limited access to foreign exchange and by the leakage of profits abroad or into hoarded dollar notes. They did not turn out to be the engines of growth for the world economy in the 1990s that they might have been.

For the world economy, therefore, a great deal more would depend on what happened in the one strong area of growth, east Asia. How quickly or slowly were those economies going to recover from the currency and stock market crisis of October 1997? Were the political conditions, national and international, good enough to restore investor confidence in their economies? Had the 1997 crises revealed underlying weaknesses in the world economy which would make it hard, as in the early 1930s, to stop a stock market crisis turning into a long economic depression? Could further stock market falls, as before, change the general mood from optimism to pessimism and despair?

Each of these crucial questions deserves examination, if only because the circumstances of the 1990s are very different from those of the 1930s, so that although interwar and postwar history is a useful, it may not be a sufficient, guide to the present.

The first question concerns the role of the IMF and the uses that will be made of the rescue packages put together for, in particular, Thailand and Indonesia. For Thailand, the first and largest rescuers were its Asian neighbours. The IMF contribution to the $17.2 billion package was less than a quarter of the total. Yet because non-intervention in domestic affairs was a cardinal principle of cooperation within the Association of South-East Asian Nations, the neighbours were unlikely to put much serious pressure on the government in Bangkok. This at least was the view in the US Treasury. It was therefore going to be up to the IMF to ensure that the aid was not wasted. That was even more the case in Indonesia, where the IMF put up twice as much and together with the World Bank and the Asian Development Bank made sure that the bulk of the rescue – $18 billion out of a total of $23 billion – came not from the neighbours but from multilateral organisations. Not only the IMF officials but also the US government had decided that conditions had to be attached to the rescue (see chapter 6). The question was, first, were they the right conditions; and second, could they be made to stick?

The IMF's prevailing philosophy, developed over many years, was monetarist rather than keynesian, anti-inflationary, opposed to fiscal deficits, state ownership and welfare subsidies. It did not always go down well among Asians, since it smacked too much of American ideas and western colonialist attitudes. More important, the kind of regulatory reforms of banking practice that the IMF was asking for in Thailand could be administered only by a strong and determined national administration. As in many African countries, even when they signed up for the IMF's structural adjustment loans, national bureaucracies were simply too weak, too corrupt and ineffectual to carry out their promises. This was the danger in Thailand. In the long history of foreign lending, creditors had constantly tried to make the money conditional. Only very rarely had the debtors met their conditions.[14]

An exception had been the US Marshall Plan. But the circumstances then had also been exceptional. Congress had granted the money only out of fear of Soviet expansion westwards. The recipients depended on the Americans not only for the hard currency but also for their defence by NATO forces – mostly American. On top of this, the US administration imposed on the receiving countries the responsibility for agreeing among themselves their individual shares, month by month. Unless they agreed, they got no more dollars. And control over national policy was bilaterally enforced through special US missions inside each country. These 'negotiated' with each government how the counterpart funds set aside to match the dollars were to be used. The IMF missions have no such powers.

The second crucial question concerning the likelihood of a stock market collapse being the harbinger of worldwide recession was about the sort of underlying weaknesses that the historians of the 1930s had found to explain the slump after 1931. Then, one such weakness had been the weak commodity prices. In those days, world trade was mostly trade in primary products. Today, cars and car parts and electric consumer goods occupy the same dominant place. Already in 1997, there were signs of falling prices in wheat and other commodities, and of gross overproduction of cars. Investment in new plant was often based on rosy estimates of growing demand in east Asia, including China. And even then, industry experts were predicting that the market would not be able to support all the big established car firms; some would have to merge or close.

Another underlying weakness might be demographic – the so-called greying of populations in Japan, America and Europe. These ageing men and women were adding their savings to pension funds, which fed the pool of footloose and volatile capital that had flooded into Thailand before flooding out again. But those savings were not spent, so it was possible that estimates of demand and of economic growth would turn out to be overoptimistic.

The last crucial question concerned the stock exchanges themselves. Even after the autumn of 1997, were shares still seriously overvalued? Does a roller-coaster ride to the bottom lie ahead, in which each dive is preceded by a slight but deceptive upturn? Some financial analysts think so and find justification for their view in certain indicators. One is the relation of present share prices to the long-term secular trend. By late 1997, even after the shake-out in late October, share prices in the London market were 45–50 per cent above this trend. When in the past they have dropped back or below the long-term trend, it has been either because of some political conflict, as when in 1987 the Americans and Germans disagreed about interest rates; or else, as in the mid-1970s, because of a major shock like the quadrupling of oil prices.

Another indicator, some say, is the *p–e* or price–earnings ratio. This measures the gap between a firm's share price and the dividends paid on them. By the late 1990s, this was certainly unusually high. But this could have been in response to Wall Street, where US tax law penalised earnings from dividends so that shareholders looked rather for capital gains, which were not taxed. Yet another possible indicator is the ratio of a firm's assets, as reflected in its balance sheet, to the market price of its shares. In 1997, most share prices had shot ahead of 'book values'. But again this could be explained by long-term changes in production, from manufacturing to services, from heavy industry with high fixed capital costs to light and high-tech business in which the assets are in skill, human capital and information, and are therefore hard to measure.

Or, more broadly, the key may lie in the simple old relation between demand and supply. Most analysts agree that recent years have been marked by 'financial glut' – a superfluity of credit. For this, many of the financial innovations described in chapter 2 are largely responsible. Credit in many forms has been created. Its creators have reaped big profits and the profits in turn have fuelled the rise in share prices. While the supply of tradable credit instruments has increased, so has the demand for them. And demand has been further increased by the opportunity to buy on margin through the derivatives markets.

Perhaps the most worrying thing is the uncertainty of the experts. Many more of them than even a few years ago are heard raising doubts about both the prospects for shares and the likely responses of people in the real economy. To quote one such comment, 'A downturn thus cannot be far away. Whether it turns into a serious bear market depends on whether the real economy remains robust in the face of precipitous falls in the markets'.[15] Which is rather like saying that if it doesn't rain, it will stay fine!

Notes

1 Quoted in the *Sunday Times*, 10 August 1997.
2 On this see Stopford and Strange (1991) and on the repatriation of profits policy also see Strange (1971), where it is explained that this was part of a political–economic deal with Britain by which Britain provided military back-up to Malaysia against civil disorder and local interstate conflicts, as with Indonesia.
3 For a comprehensive review of the long wave concept, see Freeman (1983).
4 Of which chapter 7 was later published separately as *The Great Contraction* by Princeton University Press in 1966.
5 See also the work of Peter Temin, an economic historian, *Did Monetary Forces Cause the Great Depression?* (Temin 1976).
6 An argument I made in the Adam Weiler Lecture at the University of Sussex, 1992. Note though that the evidence on quantitative trade restrictions – quotas – is more ambiguous. To check imports, nineteen European countries and nine others used them in the 1930s, often in conjunction with exchange controls.
7 The remark has also been attributed to Beatrice and/or Sidney Webb (Lord Passfield).
8 The researchers were R. Gordon and J. Wilcox. Their results were published in Brunner (1981) and mentioned by Kenwood and Longheed (1983). For a cool but comprehensive survey of the literature, their chapter 15 is hard to beat.
9 For some brief but insightful commentaries on Keynes' thought, see Skidelsky (1977).
10 The story is well told by Vatter (1985).
11 This has been contested by the revisionist historian Alan Milward on the grounds that, in 1947, European economies were recovering well and therefore had no need of the Marshall Plan (Milward 1984). True, but he forgets – or chooses not to recall – that their reserves by then were all but exhausted, and without American help they would have been unable to pay for the food, raw materials and capital goods so vital for reconstruction.

12 This was explicit in a letter from Keynes to Roy Harrod in 1942 (see Bernstein 1987: 219).
13 Kohnstam had been a colleague of Monnet, an early member of the European Commission and the first president of the European University Institute in Florence.
14 Some obvious examples are the US British loan of 1945, the Soviet loans to China in the 1950s and, further back, the French loans to Tsarist Russia or the Ottoman empire, or British loans to Portugal under the monarchy (Feis 1954).
15 John Plender, *Financial Times*, 20 July 1997.

Chapter 6

The debtors

The debtors and how best to deal with them is surely one of the continuing but unresolved issues for the international financial system. The present chapter will argue that the evolution of that system has changed the nature of the debt problem, but that neither governments nor markets are any nearer a final solution to the question of how to manage transnational debt than they were in the 1980s. Indeed, the evidence suggests that they may be even further away from a sustainable solution. If so, this is a conclusion that throws serious doubt on many optimistic incremental assumptions about the progressive improvement of 'global governance' through the increased role of international organisations – assumptions often cherished by some academics – and (of course) in bureaucratic circles.

By transnational debt, I do not mean only the financial credits extended by governments to other governments. They are but a small part of the story. The term covers all the forms of debt across state frontiers: all the liabilities incurred, and claims established, between institutions or individuals under one political jurisdiction, and institutions or individuals under another political jurisdiction. It would thus include assets claimed by foreign shareholders in enterprises in another country, interbank loans across frontiers, bonds issued to non-nationals both by governments and other institutions and firms, as well as credits or guarantees extended by states or multilateral organisations like the IMF or World Bank or the regional development banks in Asia, the western hemisphere or Africa.

The purpose of the present study, I would remind the reader, is not to give a comprehensive survey of all the recent developments in the international financial system. That would be a vast undertaking. Even to survey all the developments in the treatment of transnational debt would be a massive task. Rather, my aim is the more limited purpose of analysing – and if possible explaining – how the system has changed in recent years, and with what consequences for social classes, for creditors and debtors and for institutions, including firms as well as national governments. The main purpose is neither descriptive nor prescriptive, but analytical and interpretative. It can be boiled down to finding the answers to three rather straightforward questions.

The first, obviously, is what has changed since the 1980s, and what is the same – and why. The next is who, in the 1990s, has been involved in transnational lending and borrowing – which players, new and old, political and financial, have to be taken into account when it comes either to state or intergovernmental policy making or for that matter corporate strategy. The third question is whether transnational debt is in any sense a threat or potential danger to the international financial system. It certainly was believed to be so in the early 1980s. By the late 1990s, it is not so clear whether and when it is, or is not, threatening the financial foundations of the world market economy.

One basic point in political economy has to be remembered. The phenomenon of borrowing – getting money today in exchange for money tomorrow – is economic. But how such transactions are managed is political. To political economists, it is clear that how national societies manage debt within the borders of state authority differs fundamentally from how the collectivity of national governments manage transnational debts. Within national market economies, it became clear even in the nineteenth century that the national economic interest was not well served by a legal system that relied on deterrence, by punishing debtors when they failed to meet their obligations to creditors. Prison was no solution. Some other arrangements had to be evolved: either ways had to be found to rehabilitate the indebted enterprise or individual, usually by agreement with the creditors to accept only part repayment; or else ways had to be devised that would allow others to take control in exchange for assuming the debtor's liabilities in whole or in part. Either arrangement had to have the legitimacy of an enforceable legal contract. Bankruptcy, therefore, whether temporary or permanent, could be imposed on debtors (and their creditors) only with the authority of the state.

That is much more difficult when the debt is transnational, involving two or more state authorities and legal systems (see chapter 9). It has been particularly difficult when one of the parties to the borrowing was itself a supposedly sovereign state. The international political system had developed no general rules for the treatment of bankrupt states. Such states there had been, in the nineteenth century as in the twentieth century (Feis 1964). Each had been dealt with in an *ad hoc* manner. In rare cases, like Egypt in the 1880s, or Central American banana republics in the early 1900s, creditor states intervened and acted as receivers, temporarily taking over the country's financial management from the indebted government. A kind of delegated collective form of receivership was developed in an *ad hoc* way in the 1920s for the administration of countries getting loans from the League of Nations – although in fact the funds were subscribed by the British and French. More commonly, creditors' governments either ignored their nationals' losses as bad luck, or practised the exclusionary strategy of simply closing off their credit systems to the government and nationals of the defaulting state. This was the western response to the Soviet Union's renunciation of Tsarist foreign debts in the 1920s.

The preference for uncertainty and *ad hoc* solutions goes back a long way. It was Lord Palmerston in 1848 who first devised the smart policy of leaving open and undecided whether in any particular case of bad transnational debt the British government would or would not intervene, possibly with naval force, to recover unsettled claims by British investors. This uncertainty addressed the problem of moral hazard at both ends. It discouraged rash investors – usually bondholders at the time – from thinking that their government would always be ready with military or naval force to come to their aid. At the same time, it left the debtors in some doubt as to whether their country might suffer the humiliation and disruption of military intervention if they failed to honour their foreign debts.

Pragmatically, creditor governments since 1945 have followed the same strategy of leaving undecided what punitive measures would or would not be applied against foreign defaulters on transnational obligations.[1] They have not, until recently, contemplated developing a systematic, legal process for the treatment and possible rehabilitation of bankrupts. Only in a partial fashion, as we shall see, have they come close to doing so by the device of negotiating Multi-Year Rescheduling Agreements (MYRAs) with LDC governments and by offering Structural Adjustment Loans (SALs) as the way out for indebted governments. Both are negotiated in a more or less *ad hoc* fashion. This is as close as the creditor governments have dared come to the sort of collective colonialism feared and predicted by Kautsky in his famous disagreement with Lenin in 1915. Where Lenin predicted the inevitable clash of national capitalist–imperialist states, Kautsky argued that their common interest in maintaining a stable but open world economic order would lead the imperialist powers to collective intervention in what were then, still, colonies. On the whole, Lenin has been proved wrong, and Kautsky – and the late Ernest Mandel – right.[2]

Compared with the treatment of transnational debt in the 1980s and before, the treatment in the 1990s has not substantially changed. It has not changed because the logic of the international political system of states does not easily permit international agreement on the terms and conditions of a legally enforceable system of bankruptcy. So, while some – mainly Asian – countries have escaped the debt trap, the problem of how to deal with debtors – and especially poor African countries and former Soviet states and allies – remains and, in a long-term perspective, it is rather worse than it was a decade earlier. Such a conclusion would go far to explain the paradox of official support for an enhanced role for the IMF and the World Bank. The IMF in particular lost its chief *raison d'être* when the United States decided in the 1970s to abandon the fixed exchange rate regime it was set up to oversee and enforce. Finding an alternative role in the surveillance of developing countries brought it by stages into partnership with the World Bank, whose image in Latin America and Africa was somewhat more benign. Then, in the 1990s, when the technological and financial innovations described in chapter 2 allowed the integration of new financial centres in Asia and other emerging markets into the financial system, the problem arose of how these were to be supervised and regulated. Hence, perhaps, the popularity in official government and central bank circles of bringing the IMF into the picture (see chapter 9).

So if this is new, what is still much the same? In *Casino Capitalism* I observed,

> The sorry state of the financial system is undoubtedly aggravating the difficulties in the path of economic development for poor countries, while conversely the difficulties of the deeply indebted developing countries, so long as they persist, will aggravate the instability of the banking system. (Strange 1986: 181)

This judgement is still valid, even though some of the poor developing countries since the mid-1980s have managed despite the financial system – or even with help from it – to achieve very rapid economic growth, and even though not all the sources of instability in the banking system can be laid at the door of indebted LDCs. In short, there is still a complex interaction between the system by means of which credit is created and allocated and the prospects and opportunities open to countries seeking greater wealth and economic development. But there are important respects in which this complex interaction has changed, producing new winners and new losers.

The Mexican story

As it happens, there was one country, Mexico, which experienced two acute crises arising from its foreign debts, one in 1982 and the other in 1994/5. By comparing the two, we can observe both some similarities in the two incidents and some important differences. From this empirical experience, we should be able to draw at least some wider conclusions about what was the same and what was different as between the 1980s and the 1990s. Fortunately, there is a large and exhaustive literature, in English and Spanish, on both crises, so that the salient points can be picked out without going into too much tedious detail.[3]

Responsibility for bringing about the 1982 peso crisis must be shared between creditors and debtors. Foreign banks lent unwisely and too much in Mexico, and the leaders of the Mexican ruling party, the Partido Revolucionario Institucional (PRI; Institutional Revolutionary Party), allowed a fatal flight of capital out of the country which eventually made it impossible for the government to service – let alone repay – its foreign debts. For years, the PRI as a party and its successive leaders had profited from a bizarre constitution which gave each President a once-in-a-lifetime opportunity to amass a personal fortune by means of fraud, patronage and protection. Presidents could only ever serve one six-year term and, in earlier times, the fortunes they made were mostly invested in land, property or businesses *within* Mexico. Political power was used regressively to redistribute wealth within the country, but the balance of payments and the value of the currency were not affected.

But by the 1970s and 1980s, the financial innovations and the integration of financial markets almost invited Mexican Presidents to stash their loot where it was safer from successive peso devaluations. President Portillo (1976–82) and his friends and relations led a fatal flight of capital out of Mexico, mostly to the United States and into real estate and financial assets. Foreign exchange to service the debt was borrowed at shorter and shorter term. The probability of eventual default was obvious – but ignored until it was too late.

The second Mexican debt crisis, in 1994/5, did not involve foreign banks as creditors. They had learnt a lesson the hard way since the rescue operation mounted by President Reagan in 1983 used the threat of total loss eventually to coerce the major creditor banks – US and foreign – into contributing to an emergency rescue package. They were later pressured into accepting a Brady Plan deal, launched in 1989 and first negotiated with Mexico. This succeeded where the earlier Baker Plan, launched in 1985, had failed. It effectively persuaded the banks to cut their losses, by writing off about a third of the interest they would have been paid (Bowe and Dean 1997: 13). In return they acquired Brady bonds backed by the US government, the World Bank and the IMF – each contributing $12 billion – and the Japan Export–Import Bank, which added another $10 billion. Over the next seven years, twenty-six countries signed up for Brady deals. On balance, the banks had been helped out with public money. This had triggered a recovery in the value of secondary-market debt, making the banks substantially better off than they were at the start in 1989.

One long-term result was that the international financial institutions – the World Bank and the IMF – averted *de facto* default by lending out, year after year, more than they were owed (Bowe and Dean 1997: 53). Another was that the banks belatedly recognised that past performance by debtor countries was not necessarily a safe or reliable guide to present and future performance. Once bitten, they were twice shy of risking their own money on LDC loans. But the alternative strategy, of acting as a conduit for OPM (other people's money), could be profitable as well as less risky. The Mexican experience also gave a fillip to political risk analysis, a new service industry born out of the political upsets (as in Iran) and expropriations of the 1970s, which now found new clients in investing circles.

In the second peso crisis, as in the first, responsibility was not all on one side. Mistakes were made by both the Mexican debtors and the foreign creditors. The PRI and its leaders, first Salinas and then Zedillo, were certainly responsible for clinging too long and too hard to an unrealistic exchange rate which grossly overvalued the peso; and then for adding to the danger by issuing *tesobonos* – Mexican government securities denominated in US dollars. Before the collapse in December 1994, it had issued no less than $30 billion *tesobonos*. These constituted about a half of the whole foreign debt, of $60 billion (Aglietta 1996: 13). As Martin Mayer commented, 'When Mexico blew again in late 1994, it was almost a non-event to the banks which had suffered so in 1982. They had brokered customers' money into Mexican securities at the customers' own risks, but had made few direct new loans to Mexican borrowers' (Mayer 1997: 446).

If the banks had learnt the hard way to be cautious, why were other creditors quite so ready to invest in Mexican securities? Like the banks before them, these new investors were led to do so by the prospect of profit. There was a divergence between the interest rates to be earned in the United States and those to be earned in Mexico. Thus, it was possible in 1994 to borrow money in New York at 5 or 6 per cent, and invest it in Mexico at 12 to 14 per cent. This game is called arbitrage. In a sense, it is not new. Even in the nineteenth century, there were opportunities to borrow money at home, in London for example, and invest it more profitably abroad – but at a higher level of risk. What was new was the ease with which large funds could be employed in this way and the rapidity with which they could be moved.

And Mexico was not the only country to experience this shift, although it did get more than its share. In the 1990s, the managers of British and American insurance and pension funds led a wave of portfolio investment into the emerging markets of Asia and Latin America, especially to Mexico, Brazil and Argentina. Between 1990 and 1993, Mexico received $91 billion, which was one-fifth of all net capital inflows to developing countries. Two-thirds of this was portfolio investment and most of that was invested in the Mexican stock market, setting off a boom in share prices. The market rose 436 per cent in dollar terms in that three-year period (D'Arista 1994: 16).

But it was not only Mexicans who were blowing hot air into this dangerous bubble. As William Grieder has commented, politicians, the media and market dealers outside Mexico played a large part in encouraging the false optimism that allowed the issue of the *tesobonos* (Grieder 1997: 259). President Clinton especially had a political axe to grind in promoting popular belief in the myth of a newly modernised Mexico as partner to the United States and Canada in NAFTA. In his election campaign in 1992 he had ridiculed the objections of Ross Perot and others to the NAFTA strategy, discounting the risks not only to Mexico but also to the United States. Politically, NAFTA and the enlarged market it represented gave Americans a new and more powerful weapon when it came to bargaining over trade terms with both the Japanese and the Europeans.

Grieder also pointed out that a more proximate factor behind the bursting of the bubble in December 1994 could be found in the monetary policies of the US Federal Reserve. As the US economy started to grow again, the Federal Reserve Board, fearing inflation, began to raise interest rates. The spread between returns in the United States and Mexico would have narrowed, but to keep the flow going and to sustain confidence in the peso Mexico raised its own interest rates and began to spend its monetary reserves to boost demand for pesos. The alternative strategy of putting some controls on capital inflows and outflows was suggested to President Zedillo but rejected (Grieder 1997: 263). Grieder suggests this was for ideological reasons although, given the size of the foreign debt, there were also practical difficulties.[4] Mexican reserves started to run out rather fast even before the 1994 elections; the Chiapas revolt and the assassination of presidential candidate Luis Colosio shook confidence. The unravelling, when it came, was much faster than in 1982. There were just three

days between 19 December 1994 when Zedillo lowered the guaranteed
dollar rate for *tesobonos* and 22 December when he gave up
supporting the exchange rate and let the currency fall. The country
faced a shortfall between assets and liabilities of some $55 billion. By
the first week of February 1995, the United States was ready with a
rescue package even larger than the one arranged, also under US
leadership, in 1982. This time, it was the IMF and the BIS, not the
banks, who were persuaded to contribute. The US put up $20 billion
by raiding the Exchange Stabilization Fund and the two international
bodies contributed $32 billion.[5] (Clinton had first proposed a
unilateral US $40 billion bailout but the Congress had baulked at this
so he had had to go to the IMF and BIS for help (Erdman 1996: 13;
Pauly 1997: 124).)

On both occasions, therefore, the peso had been forcibly devalued;
the government had had to give in to the market. Both times, the
United States had arranged a rescue package. Both times it was the
Mexican economy and Mexican people that suffered most.

But there were significant differences. From the point of view both
of the rescuer as well as the rescued, the second crisis was costlier and
more dangerous than the first. For the United States, the whole NAFTA
enterprise (and beyond it the dream of an even bigger single market,
covering the whole of the western hemisphere) was at risk. More than
that, as the distinguished French economist Michel Aglietta has argued,
the stability of the entire international financial system was at stake.
He pointed out that the financing gap facing Mexico in the first half
of 1995 was huge – $55 billion – with no prospect of raising money
from the markets. Ninety per cent of the debt was owed to non-official
investors, including the holders of *tesobonos*, foreign fund managers
and non-banks. If the international monetary authorities had stood by
and done nothing, the subsequent economic slump would have been
even worse. The Mexican government would have had no other choice
but to pay back *tesobonos* in pesos. The currency would have become
worthless. Banks and other firms would have gone bankrupt in their
hundreds, bringing the open economy predicated by the NAFTA
agreements to an abrupt end (Aglietta 1996: 12–14).

In the aftermath, the US Administration had committed a substantial
part of the monetary reserves over which it had direct authority. These
were funds that could be mobilised without the need to seek
permission of the Congress. Fortunately, the Mexican rescue brought a
much more rapid recovery than expected, so that the United States was
able to get most of its money back. If it had not, a second raid on the
Exchange Stabilization Fund would have been impossible. The result
was twofold. In the spring of 1997, the US Treasury contemplated

seeking agreement from the other rich countries to a New Arrangement to Borrow, much larger than the 1962 General Arrangement to Borrow (see Strange 1976: 105–16). But then, by the summer, when turmoil hit the Asian markets and their currencies, the US strategy shifted even more from the unilateral to the multilateral. That is to say, the United States decided to be the leader of the rescue parties, but to make sure that other governments and the IMF, the World Bank and the Asian Development Bank between them put up most of the funds. It was a sort of replay on the monetary front of US strategy during the Gulf War on the military front. Thus the chain of events which started with apparently local events in Mexico like the Chiapas rising, and with the rise in US interest rates, ended by saddling the United States with a new kind of dependency – the need to negotiate with the other G7 governments and with major international banks the provision of funds in defence of the international financial system.

But while American opinion rejoiced in the Mexican 'recovery', that recovery related only to a restoration of confidence in financial markets. It did not mean that life in Mexico was the same in 1997 as it had been in 1994. For the Mexican people, the consequences of the 1995 crisis were even worse than those of the earlier crisis. Badly hit were small banks and small and medium-sized businesses – some 8,000 firms were closed. Worst affected were poor people. Official figures spoke of cuts in real wages of 25–30 per cent. A parish priest I spoke to in the prosperous northern town of Monterrey, assured me his poor parishioners had had family incomes cut by half. What this meant in reality was no meat to eat, only the eternal beans and tortillas; no new clothes or shoes to wear – only second-hand or make-overs for the children. Even the bus fares to get to work had to be borrowed from friends or relations. And even better-off people often lost their mortgaged houses or cars if the debt had been financed in dollars. Respect for ruling elites – and especially the PRI – will not easily recover. A spontaneous protest movement grew rapidly. It called itself El Barzon, referring to the strap that held an ox under the yoke – as Mexicans felt themselves held in the yoke of foreign debt.

As Grieder comments:

> The case of Mexico illustrates, in the most horrendous terms, that developing nations make a kind of deal with the devil when they open themselves to the animal spirits of global capital. As liquidity sloshes about in the global financial system, seeking the highest returns, a nation may find itself inundated with 'hot money' from abroad that can ignite a giddy boom – or abruptly starved for credit when the foreign money decides, for whatever reason, to leave. (Grieder 1997: 263)

The players in the drama, too, were different. Instead of the big transnational banking interests, the chief players in the 1990s were the more mobile, less vulnerable insurance and pension fund managers and other portfolio investors. Although by 1995 there may have been some losses, on the whole these can be counted as winners from the arbitrage game, in that they made money while the brokerage game lasted but did not have to pay up afterwards, as the banks had done.

The contagion question

In the longer perspective and in the light of the 1997/8 Asian crises, the other question for the system as a whole was how far the contagion of lost confidence was apt to spread. A big difference between the two Mexican crises was the effect on other indebted countries in the international financial system. Why was there this difference and why later did contagion spread so rapidly in Asia?

In 1982, the Mexican collapse and devaluation had had an immediate (and much resented) effect on the Brazilian economy. Where in 1981 and up until August 1982 Brazil had been easily able to finance its borrowing with Eurodollar loans from the banks, after September this source of credit had completely dried up. Hungary had experienced the same financial drought when Poland was unable to service its foreign loans, mainly from German banks. In 1995, this contagion effect seemed at first to be the same. Portfolio investment flows into Latin America, especially into Brazil and Argentina, dried up and began to withdraw. Because Mexico was seen to be the cause, it became known as the Tequila effect. But as it turned out, the contagion, though sharply felt, was relatively short lived. That is to say, it did not spread fast and fatally to the whole financial system. To the extent it did spread, the damage was done to the debtors, not to the creditors, and was long term.

In Brazil, for instance, the central bank began to lose its $40 billion reserves as capital outflows added to a growing current account deficit. Too rapid, unsustainable, domestic expansion was caught unawares by the Tequila effect on foreign capital markets. A Brazilian economist commented that the Mexican crisis set off a small capital flight out of Brazil. Debts maturing early in 1995 could not be rolled over. And the unavailability of external financing dashed hopes of domestic monetary stabilisation based on a fixed exchange rate. The Brazilian real was devalued and President Cardoso found it necessary to raise interest rates and restrict credit. This effectively checked economic growth and opened new opportunities for arbitrage between US and Brazilian interest rates (Martone 1996: 61).

In Argentina, similarly, from 1991 to 1994, the government had managed dramatically to bring down inflation rates, build up reserves and start the economy growing. An Argentine economist commented that this expansion was brought to a halt by the combination of rising US interest rates and the Tequila effect (Bouzas 1996: 71). Impending elections compounded the effect of a quite modest capital flight and a run on bank deposits. Sticking faithfully to its anti-inflationary currency board strategy, the Menem government with the help of the IMF stopped the rot with a restrictive fiscal programme. But the harsh medicine also hurt the patient. The economy stagnated through 1995 and 1996. Real investment and output fell. Unemployment rose – though neither the stagnation nor the unemployment was as bad as in Mexico. The conclusion seemed to be, first, that the government had no option but to follow deflationary policies, given the pressures of the ultra-sensitive world financial system. But how quickly growth and relative prosperity would return after the contagion had eased depended not on Argentine responses so much as on the mood of global capital markets. Should they fail to supply external financing at reasonable cost, the automatic adjustment mechanisms of Menem's Convertibility Plan would keep the economy in recession or even take it into deflation for some time to come.

Before we consider the Asian situation, an earlier study of contagion is worth noting. Some research based on the experience of the 1980s by Sylvia Maxfield compared the policy responses of Brazil with those of Mexico in the 1982 debt crisis (Maxfield 1990). Her conclusion was that policy makers in debtor (and other) countries do not all react in the same way. Nor do they always just passively respond to market signals. Rather, national policies and national monetary institutions reflected different balances of power between economic interests. In Brazil, coffee and sugar exporters and later manufacturing interests dominated over financial interests, so that economic policies were marked by frequent devaluations backed up by capital controls. In Mexico, financial interests were strong and concentrated and favoured orthodox liberal policies of free exchange convertibility. Brazil therefore responded to the 1980s crisis and to the 1990s one with heterodox intervention, while Mexico from the 1920s to the 1990s reflected the strength of the bankers' alliance behind the central bank and opted repeatedly for orthodox neo-liberal responses to external pressures and crises. Maxfield's conclusion is in sharp contrast to IMF orthodoxy: 'unorthodox, capital-controlling policies can have benefits that may, for newly industrialising countries in a rapidly internationalized world, outweigh their social welfare costs' (Maxfield 1990: 192).

Her analysis was consistent with the explanation given by Jeff Frieden of the clash of interest in Mexico between those with liquid assets (e.g. US bonds or shares) and those with illiquid assets (e.g. fixed capital assets in Mexican land, factories and real estate). The latter would have preferred a more interventionist, even protectionist, economic strategy, while those with liquid assets wanted convertibility into dollars and tight deflationary policies at home in order to pacify foreign creditors. Class structures, in a word, and the nature of wealth, explained the differential definitions of national interest and the divergent preferences of policy makers faced with a credit crisis (Frieden 1991).

The Asian scene

If one instructive comparison can be made between the Mexican debt crises of 1982 and 1994/5, another might be made between the latter and the crisis in Thailand and other east Asian countries two and a half years later. The bottom-line question in both cases for many observers was whether either crisis threatened the stability of the global financial system or jeopardised the prosperity of its core countries. For most of the winter of 1997/8, the financial press and the academic pundits worried away at the question, like a dog with a bone. As on other questions, there was no consensus. Some argued that although Japan, as the major exporter to and investor in east Asia, might suffer, America and Europe would feel an unpleasant draught, but one that would not blow their economies off course. Others, foreseeing a scramble for export market shares by the stricken Asian industries, and cancellation of their orders for foreign aircraft, arms and construction projects, saw signs of slower but still inexorable contagion spreading across the Pacific and indeed the Atlantic oceans.

Once again, comparisons can help, if only by identifying, and separating, the common and the divergent factors. How did the crisis originate? What kinds of foreign capital were involved? Did the authorities in America, Japan and Europe react quickly enough, and similarly, or not? What, then, sets the limits of the contagion effects of national financial crises on the wider system?

One obvious common factor was the surge of foreign capital going into the country in the months before the crisis. That, in both cases, had more to do with external factors than with internal ones – specifically, the hungry search by international fund and pension managers for profitable places to put their money. At first, this seems to pay off because the inflow itself tends to create a boom in asset values. Share market indices rise, encouraging yet more inflow.

Jeffry Sachs' (1996) Brookings study drew what he called 'some basic economic lessons' from the experience of emerging markets.[6] One lesson was that players were deluded by the optical illusion that the strong currency that follows economic liberalisation was due to the liberalisation and not to the capital inflows chasing high rates of return. The effect of these inflows is to start a bubble in real estate prices and in non-traded goods and services. When the bubble bursts and share prices start falling, the currency starts to lose value in the markets. The other optical illusion was that the freedom given to local banks by deregulation was risk free, whereas the reality is that borrowing abroad and investing in the local bubble economy is vulnerable to the local currency's exchange rate. That rate is apt at first to be overvalued. Using a rough index based on the ratio of domestic price increases from 1900 to 1996 compared with price rises in a weighted basket of the countries' main trading partners, Sachs found the Malaysian ringgit, the Singapore dollar and the Thai baht had appreciated by 10 per cent, the Indonesian currency by 20 per cent, and the Philippines' by 30 per cent. These figures should have given warning of future vulnerability. So should have the fact that Thailand's foreign interest payments as a percentage of GNP were three times as big as Mexico's in 1994.

There was also the slowdown in the Asian tigers' export growth. In dollar terms the average in 1995 was almost 23 per cent; in 1996 it was only 5.6 per cent. That again was due more to external than to local factors. European and Japanese markets were sluggish and competition from low-cost exports from China was beginning to bite. The dollar, too, was part of the problem. In Mexico, it was the higher interest rates chosen by the Fed. In Thailand, it was the strong dollar which made the fixed link less sustainable.

The Sachs model of emerging markets vulnerable to new external risks and internal mismanagement naturally emphasises the common factors. But there were also some important differences. Mexico's political system actually encouraged capital flight. But the economy was less deeply in foreign debt than the tigers' and moreover had its oil output and potential as an underlying source of strength. These factors helped markets to bounce back comparatively quickly. Geopolitics also mattered. Mexico in NAFTA meant the United States could not afford to stand aside. The Japanese government was slower to realise that its banks and multinationals had such a strong interest in stopping the contagion from Thailand and Malaysia spreading to Indonesia, the Philippines, Hong Kong and South Korea. Yet the key deal was eventually struck in Tokyo under Japanese leadership. In both cases, the rescue was a collective one. And in both the IMF was given the

thankless task of pulling political chestnuts out of the economic fire –
notably for the corrupt Suharto regime in Indonesia and the *chaebol*-
dominated system in South Korea (see below).

Why were the warning signs ignored both in Mexico and in east
Asia? Western comment tended to put the blame on the Mexican and
then the Thai and other Asian governments. Certainly, the Bangkok
government waited too long before acting and mismanaged the floating
of the baht in early July. But as with the Mexican government in 1994,
the money managers, focusing on dollar exchange rates, had wrongly
dissuaded the Thai government from devaluing sooner. Also too little
and too late in the Thai case was the collective action by regional
central banks. Meeting in late July, their declaration of mutual support
failed to impress the markets. So did individual market intervention on
behalf of the baht and the rupiah. The big guns – Japan, China, the
United States – were silent for too long, so much so that there were
many Asians who firmly believed their troubles had been deliberately
engineered by the Americans.

The result was that when finally, in August, the IMF had to be
called in, the terms of the first $16 billion collective bailout were
tough. The foreign debt would be rolled over with funds from the IMF
itself, the Asian Development Bank and smaller contributions from
Australia, Hong Kong, Malaysia, Singapore, South Korea and Indonesia,
possibly backed up with a roll-over deal with Japanese banks. In
Thailand, General Chavalit's government would have to stop putting
public money into bad banks and the IMF would also try to force
political reform on the corrupt administration and an electoral system
based – like that of the United States or Japan – on bought votes.

Before the end of 1997, it had become clear that the size of the
funds needed to prevent total economic collapse of these Asian
currencies had been seriously underestimated. All told, something like
$100 billion was going to be needed – possibly even more. And that
might not be enough to stop a political backlash. Mahathir was not
alone in pointing at Soros and the foreign speculators as the prime
cause of Asian troubles. Thailand, so proud of its non-colonial past,
would not take kindly to IMF interference in local politics. A weak
government in South Korea was certain to hinder the IMF and the
creditors in their effort to get political as well as economic reform.
Meanwhile, there was the risk of fallout on the US strategy in the
WTO of forcing on Asian governments an agreement on liberalising
markets in financial services. Their resistance would, in turn, widen the
existing differences between Washington and Beijing.

As for the contagion question, the responses to the Mexican and
Asian debt crises suggest that the fear of contagion spreading from

debtors to the entire system certainly exists. Otherwise, why negotiate lavish collective rescue packages to prevent outright default? Sometimes, as with the Tequila effect in 1995, the risks of contagion proved exaggerated and the effects short lived. The rescue packages do work as antidotes to the virus that could attack the global financial system. They do not necessarily cure the carrier of the virus – the indebted country. The IMF empire expands but the inhabitants do not necessarily like or benefit from its technocratic intervention in their affairs.

The 1990s have certainly seen a general trend towards orthodoxy and conformity with the policy prescriptions given by the IMF. The tightening hold of liberal economics on political and professional opinion all over the world was surely one of the underlying changes marking that decade from the one before. The wisdom of the IMF's deflationary recipe, developed in the 1970s and early 1980s for Latin America, came under question only from economists like Sachs and Paul Krugman towards the end of 1997. India's experience with the IMF, for example, was typical of the shift in economic orthodoxy. From the 1940s on, India had chosen the import-substitution strategy for development, reinforced by protection of the domestic market and discouragement of foreign investors likely to compete with Indian firms in the domestic market. This strategy was turned around rather sharply in the early 1990s when an unforeseen balance of payments crisis threw it on the mercy of the IMF. But in face of the weak political system and the size of the country, the IMF could only nag. Six years later, the Indian government was still being scolded and lectured by the IMF. Executive Director Camdessus told newspapers in March 1997 that 'further fiscal consolidation' (i.e. higher taxes) was needed to lower the public sector deficit, that more state enterprises should be privatised and more trade liberalised.[7] But who is to say whether, if all this had been done, the predicament of India would have been significantly better? It may even have been worse. The slow pace of 'reform' (i.e. liberalisation) meant that foreign funds did not rate India highly as an emerging market. Little came in, so there was little to flood out as happened in Malaysia and the other east Asians.

The other notable escape from Asian contagion was Taiwan. True, its reserves of foreign exchange were second only to China's in size. But that is hardly a sufficient explanation, for Hong Kong too had large reserves but did not escape the contagion. Its savings rates were high (but lower than Korea's) and not that much higher than in other Asian societies. But on top of these factors, Taiwan was an exporter of capital – mainly to China – but it restricted capital inflows. It had also suffered a stock market crash in the early 1990s, so that there was no 'bubble' in share prices such as that in Thailand or Indonesia.

China also escaped the contagion. Not only did it still have exchange controls so that its currency was not fully convertible, but it had a big trade surplus and massive reserves, of over $100 billion. It had avoided dependence on short-term foreign borrowing to finance a deficit. That had been the common factor in Indonesia, Malaysia, Thailand, the Philippines and South Korea.[8] Ten years before, in the late 1980s, all of them had had substantial surpluses, but in 1997 all were hit by currency markets. The only weak point in China's preventive armour was in the psychology of its traders. If the belief spread that a devaluation of the yuan, to maintain a competitive edge in export pricing, was a possibility, the traders could weaken confidence in the currency by delaying the repatriation of their earnings abroad and paying promptly for imports. Years ago, Italy, for instance, and Britain suffered from traders playing this 'leads and lags' game.

All the evidence briefly rehearsed here goes to underline the immense complexity of the phenomenon of international debt. Internal factors sometimes combine with external ones – and sometimes work the other way. It is evident that the lifeboats sent out to rescue the debtors are only an emergency service, not a permanent solution. And while the IMF's empire may be growing, it would be wise as an institution to beware the hubris of its own experts.

In this connection, it would be salutary to recall a 1996 IMF study comparing episodes of current account imbalances in three Asian countries (Korea, Malaysia and Thailand) with three Latin American ones (Chile, Colombia and Mexico) during both debt crisis periods. Its authors found that only three episodes out of ten resulted in a currency crisis with the outside world.[9] They concluded that this 'depends in large part on key macroeconomic and structural features of the economy – in particular the level of savings and investment, the degree of openness, the level and flexibility of the exchange rate and the health of the financial system' (Milesi-Ferretti and Razin 1997). Predictably, the study emphasised the shortcomings of national financial systems and economies rather than any shortcomings or weaknesses in the international system. IMF researchers evidently are not encouraged to bite the hands that feed them.

What to do with the poorest debtors?

Generalisation about transnational indebtedness in the 1980s, moreover, has often obscured important differences in the experience of specific countries (Stopford and Strange 1991: 45–7). It is even less defensible in the late 1990s, especially when it comes to generalising about the poorest debtors as compared with the rest. These go by the acronym of HIPCs (highly indebted poor countries), or SILICs (severely indebted low-income countries), as distinguished from SIMICs (severely indebted middle-income countries). For African HIPCs, the cost of servicing debts to the multilateral organisations that are their main creditors is now greater than what they have to spend on health, education and basic nutrition (Oxfam 1996). It is now generally acknowledged by economists that the 'debt trap' for these poorest of debtors has been getting deeper; that it will continue to get worse if nothing more is done; and that this is in part because of their treatment by the multilateral organisations who are their chief creditors (International Monetary Fund 1996; Killick 1995; Mistry, 1996). Yet despite much publicity, efforts to find a solution have so far got nowhere. At best, the proposals put forward by the IMF and the World Bank can be described as tinkering with the problem.[10]

The facts are that transnational debt owed by HIPCs to multilateral organisations has grown faster since the first debt crisis than any other type of debt. It was $98 billion in 1982. By 1992, it was $304 billion. The cost of servicing this debt was $7 billion in 1980. By 1992, it was £36 billion. While the creditor states – led by the US Secretary of the Treasury – managed to agree on the Brady initiative to allow SIMICs to reschedule their foreign debt, agreement on a comparable way out of the vicious circle of poor country debt has been possible only in principle. A joint IMF/World Bank initiative launched in 1996 by the World Bank's President, Wolfensohn, and given lavish publicity by both sponsors, apparently encountered three insuperable difficulties when it came to translating principles into a practical scheme of debt relief. The first difficulty was definitional – how to define a 'poor' (therefore eligible) HIPC, and how much short of 100 per cent to wipe out. The second was distributional – how was the burden of 'forgiveness' to be shared out? Thirdly, how should it be financed? None of these questions was technical; all were political. True, some unilateral arrangements to wipe out debts of poor African and Caribbean states had already been taken by the British and French governments on their own account. Getting agreement among a collective of creditors was bound to prove much more difficult.

To make the escape sustainable, the economists calculated, it was not enough to wipe out the agreed 67 per cent of the total. It had to be 80 per cent or the cost of servicing the remaining 20 per cent would continue to overburden export earnings and capital inflow (if any), so that growth would be halted. Growth in these HIPCs had already slowed from an average 2 per cent per year over 1985–90 to an average 1 per cent over 1990–5. The World Bank argued that if the agreed enhanced Toronto terms for the relief of HIPC debt were implemented, incentives for foreign investment would improve, raising the chance of exporting to world markets and with it people's living standards.

But – as already pointed out – implementation meant political agreement on the definitional, tactical and distributional issues. British and French governments had their favourite candidates – Ivory Coast for France, Uganda for Britain. The Ivory Coast had comparatively strong exports, in relation to its debt, but its government revenues were low and the economy small. According to the Bank and the IMF, however, it did not qualify. By comparison, Uganda's export earnings – mainly from coffee – were substantial, yet vulnerable to price falls in the volatile world market. So the British wanted the escape route opened for Uganda earlier than the Bank and IMF had suggested. France objected.

The obvious fact is that every one of the twenty-one SILICs on the Toronto list can be included or excluded on one ground or another. And at least the same number could find reasons for being added to the list, many on the grounds that the fiscal burden of the debt on state revenues is unsupportable. If they were to be added, however, this would put up the cost of the whole scheme to the Bank and IMF to the point where the IMF would think it necessary to part with some of its gold reserves. This is bitterly opposed by Germany, supported by Japan and Italy.[11] Indeed, almost all the G10 governments share an unspoken fear that if the debts of the HIPCs were cancelled, it would be increasingly difficult to resist requests for similar treatment by other poor countries for whom debt servicing was a perpetual handicap in achieving higher economic growth.

There is the further fear – perhaps not even articulated – that forgiving debt is no guarantee that the problem of unsustainable debt is not going to be repeated. The nineteenth century was full of examples of debtors being rescued, only to need a second or third rescue in a few years' time. Portugal before the fall of the monarchy in 1911 was a prime case; the reason for the repeated rescues was political not economic – its special relationship to Britain, rather like Mexico's special relationship with the United States almost a century later. While it is neither very costly for France or Britain unilaterally to cancel loans to their respective African ex-colonies, a multilateral plan for doing the same thing to a whole group of countries opens a Pandora's box that the G10 governments would really rather keep tight shut. Hence the disagreements serve a deeper but unspoken purpose.

However, according to Percy Mistry, himself a former World Bank official, these disagreements not only delay the whole project, making the debt trap ever harder to escape, but the trap itself is of the creditors' own making. That is to say, the Bank and the Fund actually created a debt trap even worse than the one they purported to remedy. What happened was that the multilateral organisations in the aftermath of the debt crises of the 1980s lent debtor governments new money to pay off or reschedule private or bilateral debts. But the terms on which this money was lent was much harsher and the sanctions against non-payment much stricter than for the debts they took over. Then, between 1986 and 1988, the IMF started withdrawing funds from debtor countries, exacerbating the effect of commercial withdrawals. Similarly, the World Bank started taking more money from the debtors than it lent them for new or old projects. As with moneylenders of old, the unpaid interest, added to the capital, actually increased the amount of debt.

> The pyramiding of multilateral debt has hurt not just the developing countries. Its reciprocal but less visible effect has been to erode and compromise the financial strength and asset portfolio quality of key multilateral institutions which are central pillars of the official international financial system. (Mistry 1994: 15)

The reason why he says this is that both institutions are constitutionally accountable to their members, who are guarantors of their solvency – the World Bank through the capital markets from which it has to borrow the money it lends, the Fund through the collective guarantee of the availability of drawing rights (special and original) to its members. Together, the Fund and Bank have been jointly backed up with whatever funds may be available through the New Arrangement to Borrow, the nearest thing that the international financial system has to a lender of last resort in case one may be needed at any time in the future. But the whole point of the role of lender of last resort is that a national central bank can refuse its help, enforce very tough terms for it or even sack the managers and bring about bankruptcy and closure. Until the Asian crises in 1997, the IMF had not dared to play the role in full. When a state is indebted, the Fund cannot and will not go as far as bankrupting the country. With banks, the IMF is not experienced enough to take on the role everywhere. The role is difficult enough at all times, since each decision to support or to allow a bank to go under is circumstantial rather than subject to rational or preordained principles or guidelines. When it is compounded by political partialities reflected in basically political conflicts over the choice of different technical criteria, the prospects for progress look poor indeed.

On another occasion, Mistry suggested that thinking about reform of the Bretton Woods organisations – of which there has in the 1990s been a great deal – tends to start from the wrong end (Fischer and Reisen 1993; Williamson 1977). It is based, he said, on a stale view of the institutional framework inherited from the past rather than starting from the pragmatic question of what to do about HIPCs – in particular, about the multilateral indebtedness of the African states, which make up the largest number (Mistry 1994: 48). These remarks were made in response to a much-discussed paper by the eminent Princeton economist Peter Kenen, commissioned by the independent Dutch Forum on Debt and Development (Fondad) on international monetary reform and the developing countries. Both Mistry and the veteran Canadian development economist Gerald Helleiner criticised Kenen for being too cautious and conservative in his approach; both thought that 'tinkering' with the multilateral organisations was not enough and that the excuse that there was no interest among politicians and officials was one no independent academic should accept. Helleiner commented in verse:

> The poor complain.
> They always do.
> But that's just idle chatter.
> Our system brings rewards to all,
> at least to all that matter.

But this is just the point. The assumption is that Africa does not matter because no important economic interests are greatly affected. Who cares, it implies, if Liberia is in chronic turmoil, if Hutus and Tutsis are killing each other in tens of thousands? Who cares about Algerian massacres or if one-party governments and their autocratic rulers keep people in subjection and backwardness? Probably, in the short term, none of the rich or the powerful. In the longer term, however, perhaps they should be concerned, in their own long-term interest. Historically, the rich and powerful in all pre-revolutionary periods have been complacent and unmoved by the suffering of the poor. Remember Marie Antoinette's cynical 'Let the people eat cake!'. Remember the myopia of the ruling class in Tsarist Russia.

The difference is that, today, discontent leading to violence in Africa has repercussions outside the continent. Not only do aid workers, UN blue berets and foreigners trying to do business get caught in the crossfire and cannot always escape in time. Moreover, even before trouble starts, African revolutionaries and discontents do not stay at home. They emigrate. Already the cities of Europe as far north as

Stockholm are filling with unwelcome Turks, Moroccans and Algerians as well as black Africans – Nigerians, Senegalese and Congolese. Tinkering with the IMF and the World Bank is not going to stop them.

Mistry's suggested solution was a devolution of responsibility from the IMF and the World Bank to the regional development banks, the African Development Bank, the Asian Development Bank, the Inter-American Development Bank, and the EBRD (Mistry 1994, 1996). This, he thought, might make sense at a time when everywhere governments were busy building regional associations with their neighbours for preferential trade and other reasons. Neighbours, moreover, were more likely to understand and make allowance for cultural and social factors, and to empathise with the needs of very poor countries for the infrastructural investment in health and education, in transport and communications without which private capital was unlikely to play a part in long-term economic growth.

Perhaps these considerations led him to write a detailed and informed study of these institutions (Mistry 1995). Although it is clear that he would like the regional development banks to open up an escape route for HIPCs in Africa and elsewhere, his honest account of their evolution is not encouraging. It shows how the African Development Bank, since its establishment in 1965, has staggered from one self-serving expedient to another without ever either achieving long-term viability for itself or contributing anything substantially to the prospects for African people. Since 1983, its administrative costs – what the bank spends on its staff – have doubled. By the mid-1990s, the staff was about twice as large as it needed to be. It had allowed governments to get into a mire of arrears in their contributions. Its poor financial structure exposed it to serious currency risk – by borrowing funds denominated in dollars or yen, for example. And the response to that is to engage in sophisticated dealing in derivatives, which serves only to obscure, not to solve, its real problems.

The administration of the African Development Bank, in short, is no better than that of the Fund or the World Bank. In both, as Mistry (1995) has pointed out, over the years there has been a shift of decision-making power from the executive directors appointed by governments to the senior officials of the organisation. He notes correctly that this has been achieved by the 'mushroom theory of management', that is, a strategy of keeping the Executive Board in the dark and burying them in horse manure (actually, loads of mostly useless documentation). He argues that there are in fact a wide range of options and possible solutions but that their consideration by governments is hampered by the resistance of the bureaucracies. These bureaucrats need, he concludes, to become 'less defensive, less complacent, more open-minded and more concerned about finding a way out of the present situation with its attendant dangers – and less prone to tediously repeating self-serving justifications and rational-isations' (Mistry 1996: 71). Mistry may be right about what should be done. But the record he gives of what has been done – or left undone – either in Washington or in the African Development Bank holds out precious little hope for positive change.

Central and eastern Europe

If one of the big failures of the 1990s was the treatment of African debt, the other has surely been the treatment – or neglect – of the financial needs of post-socialist countries of east and central Europe, including Russia. Already in the early 1980s, both Hungary and Poland had been involved as debtors with the international financial system. Central banker Fekete, visiting the Council on Foreign Relations in New York in the aftermath of the 1982 Mexican/Polish debt crises, had complained bitterly that the markets had unjustly punished Hungary for Poland's over-exuberant borrowing, just as Brazil complained about being judged by Mexico's near default. Before the end of the decade and the fall of the Berlin Wall, both countries had nevertheless increased their involvement, commercial and financial, with the western market economy. Then, with the end of the Cold War, the shadow of Moscow and the Politburo over central and eastern Europe was gone. New opportunities beckoned to escape the stultifying hand of state economic planning and to take whatever help might be offered by the west.

The situation was not unlike that which existed after the end of World War II in western Europe. Economies long subject to state controls and the demands of government for armaments were suddenly in sore need of help with a difficult transition. Their own resources were slender and would soon be exhausted. In June 1947, Secretary of State Marshall had thrown away the speech he had written for Harvard University's commencement celebrations and called instead for a new initiative to put western Europe back on its economic feet with massive help from the United States. The Marshall Plan was born, welcomed in Britain, spurned by Moscow, and eventually passed through the US Congress as a necessary investment in keeping Europe – France and Italy especially – out of the hands of the communists.

That, of course, was the big difference. In 1990, there was no other superpower threatening to overrun eastern Europe if its 'postwar' transition stumbled. Otherwise, the experience of the European Recovery Program (ERP) between 1948 and 1952 was a classic demonstration of keynesian logic and the effectiveness of a large programme of foreign aid in boosting confidence and setting in motion the processes of economic reform. The Marshall Plan gave $13 billion in credit to western Europe, asking no repayment in dollars but only the agreed investment of counterpart funds in local currency. Other key features of the plan were that western European governments had to agree among themselves as to who should get how much of this largesse – or no one got anything. Secondly, they were each monitored by an Economic Cooperation Agency mission which offered free help from American industrialists on improving productivity. These missions also used their political leverage to force governments to liberalise trade relations with their neighbours and to privatise them by taking trade away from state officials and returning it to private enterprises. Most revolutionary of all the provisions of the Plan was the licence given to western Europe to save its scarce dollars for essentials by keeping controls over foreign exchange and by allowing the Europeans – contrary to liberal most favoured nation principles enshrined in the GATT – to discriminate in trade against tobacco and other commodities and manufactures exported from the United States. As noted earlier (chapter 5), revisionist historians have since argued that European economic recovery by the time Marshall spoke at Harvard was going well and that US aid was not needed (Milward 1984). They conveniently forgot that by then Europe's reserves of hard currency were running desperately short and that, without US credits, there would have been severe shortages of food and raw materials, not to mention the capital goods to re-equip industry and the economic infrastructure that only North America could still supply.

Why then, with such a detailed political and economic blueprint on how to manage a postwar economic reconstruction so readily at hand, did the western governments in 1990 not simply look back at the historical record and do for eastern Europe what the United States had done forty years before for western Europe? Here, surely, was a golden opportunity to prime the pump in a group of economies well endowed with an educated, skilled workforce, with leaders and people desperately keen to 'come home' and to become accepted in a community of European states that was building a single common market for anything they could produce. For it was not only postwar Europe which had benefited from the Marshall Plan. As left-wing critics later pointed out, the United States also gained (Block 1977). Where Henry Wallace had predicted and feared a postwar recession in America, it never happened. The ERP had opened up new business for US firms in

Europe, both as exporters and as foreign investors in offshore production.

But instead of a Marshall Plan for eastern Europe, the ex-socialist countries were given the EBRD, a pathetically small, self-serving regional development bank with its potentially helping hands tied tight behind its back. Instead of the 1990s equivalent of the $13 billion 1940s dollars – probably about $130 billion – the EBRD ended up merely with some $3.4 billion to lend or guarantee, or 30 per cent of its agreed capital base of $11.5 billion. Peanuts indeed. Instead of a flexible system of counterpart funds that could be used for public infrastructure like roads, bridges and ports, or to finance industrial re-equipment of municipal housing, the EBRD was bound, under orders from the United States, to dedicate 60 per cent of its loans to the private sector, leaving only 40 per cent for publicly funded infrastructure. Here was a development bank pretending that what was needed was a profit-making merchant bank.

Why the missed chance for an initiative? It would have not only accelerated the transition for the ex-socialist countries but would also have given a kick-start to western Europe's sluggish slow-growth economy by providing it with eager new consumers with purchasing power – just as the ERP had done for American industry in the postwar years. It was not because no one thought it a good idea. Max Kohnstam, an early founder of the EEC, several economists and economic commentators made the suggestion. A conference of east and west academics and journalists in Florence in February 1990 endorsed it. Why then was the chance missed?

Everyone shares the blame. Germany, whose economy stood most to gain from it, was self-absorbed in the problems and dilemmas of German unification; its short-sighted politicians showed little interest in helping their eastern and southern neighbours. The United States, led by President Bush, put up only 10 per cent of the money but adamantly insisted on the 60–40 rule. The British, who had benefited so much from Marshall aid and should have known better, went tamely along with the Americans and were determined only that the EBRD be set up in London. Mitterrand, for France, insisted that if that was to be so, the head of the bank must be French – and then appointed Jacques Attali, whose ignorance of development economics was equalled only by his administrative extravagance. The 'glistening bank' became a byword for wanton luxury and mismanagement. By the end of 1993, it had lent or guaranteed only $2 billion and concentrated its energies on getting income for itself by investing more than this in the markets – profits soon eaten up by its soaring administrative costs – and by charging fat front-end and wind-up fees to its debtors.

Conclusion

To sum up this long survey, unlike the 1980s, there was no general 'debt crisis' in the 1990s.[12] There were various kinds of debtors, each with rather different problems and prospects. There were the Mexicans, the other Latin Americans and there were the east Asians. There were also the HIPCs in Africa and the ex-socialist countries of central and eastern Europe, whose problems were not so much that they had debts that they could not repay as that they had not been given the right sort of credit in sufficient amounts for their needs.

For all of these debtors, and for many would-be debtors, the system seemed even further away from finding a long-term solution than it had been a decade earlier. In a market economy you could not stop – did not want to stop – the use of credit, the right to borrow. But when almost all the market economies were open to the world economy, and the system allowed debts to be incurred in any currency, private debts were easily translated into public ones. The collapse of share prices for private debtors became the collapse of the national currency, for which the government was responsible. The very size of the rescues necessary in 1998 compared with the 1980s showed how the problem had escalated. And meanwhile disagreement was growing about the two big questions. Who is to blame? What is to be done? On the one hand, the IMF, backed by conservative economists, was still insisting, 'Take the IMF medicine and you will soon mend'.[13] On the other, a growing number of economists, many from leading business schools, was protesting that the IMF was fighting yesterday's war, that deflation was the major risk and that either one big shock or a series of smaller shocks were very likely to end in a world depression. In short, not only were the prime causes contested, there was deep dispute over the gravity of the debt problems and the optimum response to them.

Notes

1   On this, see Prout (1976). Prout (now Sir Christopher and a former leader of British Conservatives in the European Parliament) commented on the totally different attitude of nations when they cease to become lenders and become creditors. 'As lenders [they] were behaving like highly speculative fringe bankers devoted entirely to profit considerations and mindless of asset security.... As creditors they establish elaborate procedures to salvage a financial disaster which need never have happened if even a fraction of the cooperation they demonstrated *ex post* the insolvency had been demonstrated *ex ante* the insolvency' (p. 389).

2   The debate is summarised in Strange (1986: 92–5).

3   Some important contributions to this literature were Maxfield (1990); Bouzas

(1996); Thurow (1996); Greider (1997); and a series of articles on the 1994/
5 crisis in *The Economist*.

4　There is an interesting comparison to be made here with Taiwan, whose
central bank, in 1987, imposed ceilings on banks' foreign liabilities after a
surge of hot money flooded into Taiwan from abroad. These were successively
eased and finally abolished ten years later (*Free China Journal*, 30 May
1997).

5　The Exchange Stabilization Fund was the result of a 1936 tripartite agreement
between the United States, Britain and France to give mutual support to each
other's currencies. Though not wholly successful, it is seen by historians as the
forerunner of the Bretton Woods fixed exchange rate system (Clarke 1973).

6　See also an updated summary in his article, 'Lessons from the Thais',
Financial Times, 30 July 1997.

7　IMF press summary, 6 March 1997.

8　Korea's trade deficit in 1997 was the highest at $19 billion. Thailand's next
at $10 billion, followed by Indonesia at $8 billion.

9　*IMF Survey*, 24 March 1997.

10　The phrase 'debt trap' was first coined by Cheryl Payer, a radical American
critic who wrote a rather hysterical book with that name in the mid-1970s
(Payer 1974). Payer argued fervently that 'The IMF has been the chosen
instrument for imposing imperialist financial discipline upon poor countries
under a facade of multilateralism and technical competence.' Substitute
'system-preserving' for 'imperialist' and the charge is more sustainable. See
also Delamaide (1984); and for the argument that the IMF was partly to
blame see George (1988).

11　*Financial Times*, 'Not much sign of relief', 16 April 1997.

12　It could be argued that, even in the 1980s, 'the debt crisis' was an
oversimplification. There were debtors who had borrowed heavily, like South
Korea, but whose chief creditor had saved them from the clutches of the IMF
or the Paris Club. There were debtors who had borrowed, but with
moderation and prudence, like Malaysia, whose export earnings from
commodities and manufactures gave confidence to foreign investors, who kept
up an inflow of capital from abroad. And there were others like India, whose
debts in relation to their current balances had not yet become a problem.

13　The title of an upbeat article by Michael Mussa and Graham Hacche, the
IMF's Chief Economist and its Assistant Director of Economic Studies,
respectively (*International Herald Tribune*, 17–18 January 1998). Paul
Krugman, Lester Thurow and others profoundly disagreed (*ibid.*). Thurow
likened the situation to the risk of earthquakes on California's San Andreas
geological fault line; there was no doubt that catastrophe would strike. The
only question was when – and where.

Chapter 7

Finance and crime

As noted in chapter 1, one of the big changes in international finance in recent years has been the greatly increased use of the system by organised crime. It would have hardly been possible to design a 'non-regime' that was better suited than the global banking system to the needs of drug dealers and other illicit traders who want to conceal from the police the origin of their large illegal profits. The business of money laundering could not have so prospered and grown without the facilities for swift and relatively invisible transnational movements of money. That much is common knowledge.

This chapter will consider, first, how and why this money laundering boom has come about so quickly; and, second, whether the collective efforts of governments to prevent the wholesale laundering of dirty money have been effective. Could they be made more effective? There are also other, more fundamental questions to be raised. Perhaps laundering illegal drug money is not really the most serious kind of lawbreaking to be made easier by the international financial system. There are other kinds of serious financial crime that have received much less public attention, but which may constitute much more serious threats to the viability of the world market economy. It will be argued that, from the point of view of damage and risk to public confidence in the international political economy, money laundering is much less serious an issue than, for example, tax evasion, private fraud or public embezzlement. Why these are overlooked or even tolerated is one of those questions that political economists are right to pose and that economists for the most part do not even consider.

Of course, crime is never an absolute concept. Different societies and cultures have very different attitudes to the same kind of conduct. Adultery in Saudi Arabia is a capital offence – at least for the women.

In western Europe, it is commonly accepted as morally reprehensible but regrettably unavoidable. Libel is a serious matter in Britain but much less so in the United States. In the past, in Australia or the American West, you could be hanged for stealing a horse, or even a sheep; not so today. In Dickens' time, defaulting on debt could land you in Marshalsea Prison, while employing small boys to sweep chimneys was considered perfectly normal. In the 1950s, in the Soviet Union and its east European allies even trading with foreigners could be punished with death. And on both sides in the Cold War, spying for a foreign government was seen as the worst kind of treason, though (in the west at least) spying on someone's wife or husband on the orders of a jealous partner was a recognised – and licensed – trade. So why have governments picked on money laundering, especially by drug dealers, as a crime to be prevented if possible by collective action?

In fact, drug dealers are thought to be responsible for rather less than half – perhaps only 40 per cent – of the money laundering done through international banks. The rest is accounted for by the profits from other kinds of illegal trading – in arms, for instance, or even nuclear materials, or increasingly in illegal immigrants and other forms of smuggling. Altogether, the current value of laundered money is thought to amount to as much as £400 billion a year (United Nations 1997).

Yet it is remarkable that the attention given to money laundering resulting from the trade in arms, nuclear materials or illegal immigrants has been far less marked than the attention given to the laundering of profits from trade in drugs. Throughout the 1980s and 1990s there was growing political attention – especially in the United States – to this particular kind of dirty money. In 1986, the US Congress passed the Money Laundering Control Act, making it a crime to engage in receiving illicitly obtained money. This was followed by another piece of legislation in 1992 and the Money Laundering Suppression Act in 1994. The chief motivation all along was to prevent the laundering of money made from the sale of drugs – a traffic which no amount of speechmaking nor the setting up of the Federal Drug Enforcement Agency appeared able to stop. Comparatively little attention was paid to the equally significant profits made out of the sale of arms, some part of which was also illegal, nor to the trade in immigrants made profitable by the high barriers to legal movements from poor to rich countries.

In targeting dirty money from drug sales, the US government also sought throughout to reinforce national policies with international agreements. The 1988 UN Convention Against Drug Trafficking was followed by a report in 1990 by the Financial Action Task Force (FATF), which made forty separate recommendations to governments for strong action against banks that accepted drug money. The FATF has been the chief body through which US agencies tried to get better compliance with its recommendations from Latin American and European governments. The assumption was commonly made that it was the laxity of the Latin American governments – particularly the Mexican one – that was the reason for the booming drug sales north of the border. In the spring of 1997, indeed, President Clinton was under strong pressure from the Congress to report to it that Mexico had not kept its part of the agreement to suppress the drug traffic. Only at the eleventh hour did he avoid imposing the sanctions some American politicians would have liked to see applied to its NAFTA partner. Meanwhile, the FATF's 1996 report had proposed that 'money laundering crimes be extended beyond the predicate offense of drug trafficking' to include money derived from any kind of criminal activity (Williams 1997: 14) and that the prohibition should extend to any laundering activity by non-banks as well as by banks. Yet Williams himself concludes that 'the global financial system provides many more opportunities than law enforcement can ever hope to forestall or block … law enforcement is playing a game of catch-up which it is almost certainly destined to lose' (Williams 1997: 1).

Eric Helleiner, a Canadian political economist, has been more optimistic, putting his faith in the information technologies that allow financial transactions to be traced through the three major transfer systems used by banks to move money from one jurisdiction to another (Helleiner 1995). These are the CHIPS, the Fedwire system in the United States and SWIFT, the inter-bank settlements system. In 1992, FATF did indeed ask SWIFT to broadcast a request to all its users to supply names and addresses of people other than banks who were making suspicious transfers through the system.

But while in theory this technical capability looks impressive, it does not follow that the law enforcement agencies can use them to catch up with the offenders. In practice, Helleiner's optimism is not convincing. In the real world of dirty money, people habitually use false names and firms invent a maze of shell companies to cover their tracks. The man from New York whose trail led the Federal Bureau of Investigation (FBI) to a Swiss bank branch in Nassau and to evidence eventually used in the trial of Mike Milken called himself only 'Mr Diamond'. The detective work was painstaking; it took months to track him down. So even if all the users of SWIFT or Fedwire complied with the FATF's request, the chances are that the information would be out of date by the time the enforcement agencies got hold of it.

Nor is information by itself sufficient for conviction – as any police officer knows only too well. What if the suspect named by the clearing house or bank protests that the money came from gambling or some other legal activity? How do you prove him to be lying? Where is the army of bank inspectors who are going to dredge through the veritable mountains of information in the slim hope of finding the one transfer that looks suspicious? They do not exist. There are not enough of them – as Williams argues – to catch up with the offenders. And even if they did, by the time they acted, the money could have been moved and relaundered several times over. This is the same problem in law enforcement that arises in some places with stolen cars or stolen jewellery; if there is an airport or a ferry port handy, up-to-date criminals will have the 'evidence' out of the country even before the loss has been reported to the police. If there is no hot pursuit of crime by the law enforcement agencies, the law can – and will – be disregarded with impunity.

Politicians and officials must be well aware of the facts of life in the real world. Why then should they go the trouble of passing new laws against money laundering and negotiating new intergovernmental declarations and agreements to act – in principle? Why the pantomime when those concerned know perfectly well that their laws and conventions will have little effect? The money laundries will carry on as usual.

The answer, of course, is to be found in the vulnerability of politicians to public protest, especially if the protests are taken up by the media. 'Don't just stand there! Do something!' is the cry, whether it is over the drug trade and the profits made from it, or over factory closures and lost jobs. The smart politician in office has learned that it is better to respond quickly with a 'tough new policy programme', a special inquiry, a new government agency and even, if it seems appropriate, with an international conference and a solemn agreement with other governments to take collective action. That was exactly the origin of the FATF. It was set up in 1989 by the Group of Seven industrialised countries. Recent history shows that such initiatives often emerge when dates have been set for ministerial summits long before anyone has thought of an agenda for the discussions. As the date approaches, ministers demand that their officials draft some grandiose initiative that will catch the international headlines.[1]

States and markets in money-laundering business

Why governments have been so ineffective in acting to stop money laundering can best be explained by considering the opposing strength of market forces. In the money-laundering business, there are three markets involved. They are all interrelated. One is the market for banking services. Second is the market for hallucinatory or mood-changing drugs. But the forgotten third is the market for tropical crops. The last is often overlooked in studies of transnational organised crime. But common sense tells us that it would not be so easy for the entrepreneurs in charge of processing and marketing the raw material for drugs to find farmers eager to grow coca, cannabis or opium if the prices the farmers could get from growing legitimate crops – sugar or coffee or cereals – were not so low and so uncertain. For the Colombian peasant, the Medellín drug cartel is a much better source of income than the wholesalers or cooperatives dealing in conventional crops who can offer just a fraction of the return on land and labour. Indeed, there are counties in rural Georgia in the United States where farmers have gone on television to explain why they elected as sheriff a sympathetic politician who they knew would turn a blind eye to the crops of cannabis which the farmers found far more profitable than growing tobacco. To them, both crops produced drugs for which there was a steady demand. Who were they to discriminate between those who killed themselves with tobacco and those who killed themselves with cannabis?[2] In short, a part of the problem of enforcement against illegal drugs is to be found in the weaknesses of commodity markets for primary products – and especially for primary products grown in the poor developing countries.

Recall that this element of inequality in the world market economy was one of the chief complaints brought against the rich countries by the so-called G77 governments of the Third World – as it was then known – in the 1960s. Out of their protests emerged the first UNCTAD in 1964. Out of UNCTAD in the 1970s came the proposal for a new international economic order. One of its features – had it ever been adopted – would have been an integrated programme for stabilising the prices of eighteen key commodities mainly produced and exported by LDCs. This programme supposed a system of intervention in commodity markets fundamentally comparable to the sort of managed support for farm prices practised by every one of the industrialised countries – but only within their own territorial frontiers. Yet the logic of managed market intervention accepted for these national economies (and by extension for the EU's CAP) was completely rejected by the governments of the industrialised countries. Their advisers – sound liberal economists – dismissed the whole idea of commodity stabilisation as no more than a sneaky but misguided attempt to raise prices artificially. Nothing happened. As Arghiri Emmanuel had always argued, poor people got poor prices for what their work produced because they were poor and therefore weak in bargaining power (Emmanuel 1969). In the 1970s, and after, the prices they got fell still further in relation to prices of manufactures and services produced by the industrialised world. As the World Bank noted, 'During the 1980s, prices for many primary commodities fell to their lowest level since World War II.... By 1989 average commodity prices were still 33 per cent lower than in 1980 ... the decline in the terms of trade during the 1980s has been most pronounced in sub-Saharan Africa *and Latin America*' (World Bank 1990: 13; quoted by Dicken 1992: 456; my italics). Little wonder that the *narcotrafficantes* in Central America have had no difficulty in finding a plentiful supply of the raw materials they needed to meet the North American demand for cocaine and heroin.

That demand was what had made the mafias rich. The story came out in Italy during the 'maxitrials' of mafia members in Palermo in 1994/5. Hitherto, the outside world had guessed much but really known very little about what went on within secret societies like Cosa Nostra or 'Ndrangheta. The solemn vows of *Omertá* (silence) made it very difficult to prove the complicity of any mafia member in any particular crime. It was only after 1993, when the Italian parliament made membership of such organisations a criminal offence, that some mafiosi had a strong incentive of self-protection to turn state's evidence against their fellow members (Paoli 1997). These *pentiti* (repentants) explained in court how the protection rackets they had run in rural Sicily had never made them rich. Wealth came only – and suddenly – when, for a while, the mafia acted as processing intermediaries between Asian suppliers and the drug-hungry markets of Europe and America. The business was even more profitable than the prewar business of supplying Americans with illegal alcohol had been for the Italian-American mafias in the 1930s (Strange 1996: 113–15). Soon, however, the logic of international production moved the drug processing closer to the raw material supply, where labour was cheaper and law enforcement weaker – in short, from Italy to Colombia. But while it lasted, the mafiosi got rich – and looked for ways to move their profits out of the reach of Italian tax collectors.

An essential condition for their new-found wealth was that the business was illegal – for producers, processors and consumers – and prices therefore could be kept high to compensate for the risks of being caught. The size of the market and the rapidity of its growth go far to explain the corresponding growth of money laundering as an aspect of the international financial system. Over the twenty years from the mid-1970s to the mid-1990s, UN and FATF calculations estimated that the heroin market recorded a twentyfold increase and the cocaine market a fiftyfold increase. The net profits probably ranged between $120 billion and \$150 billion every year (Strange 1996: 114). This was a lot of dirty money for the bankers to launder.

I do not propose to speculate on the reasons for this exploding demand in the rich countries for cocaine, heroin and the new synthetic drugs like ecstasy or crack. There is a large literature and I have no qualifications to judge whether the large demand is simply an economic phenomenon reflecting the greater affluence of new generations of young people, or whether there are deeper psychological, moral or sociological reasons to explain it. What is beyond doubt and disagreement is, first, that it is a development that greatly worries governments because of the link between drug use and violent crime; secondly, that their efforts to enforce prohibition of drug sales and use are generally rather ineffective; and thirdly, that these sales are highly profitable so long as the trade is made illegal and so long as the traders risk serious penalties if they are caught. The risk raises the price, as with other goods and services that states declare illegal. This is because the illegality adds to the trader's costs and also because the risks involved deter some potential competitors. Think of the price of illegal handguns, of illegal abortions or false passports. Hence the argument – which most societies still reject – that it would be better to legalise the whole drug business – both the dealing and the consumption. This would lower prices and so make the traffic less profitable.[3] The lower profitability of the traffic would lessen the demand for money laundering even if it did not much lower the demand for drugs – any more than abolition of the Volstead Act in the United States reduced the demand for alcohol.

The other market involved is that for banking services. Without this, it would be much more difficult to cover up the origins of profits from illegal trading, including drug trading. How and why does the international financial system offer such an easy cover-up for dirty money?

There are two answers to that question. One is to be found in recent international history and the other in the sociology of the professions. Recent political–economic history explains why some governments set their territory up as tax havens where money could be deposited easily but no tax would be payable on the interest earned. The historical sociologists explain why bankers have so strongly resisted official demands for transparency in their dealings with clients; why they have claimed to share with priests the right to confidentiality in relations with their customers. This is part of a larger debate concerning more fundamental issues of the socio-economic role of certain professions in capitalist society. Does the economic system need the sustaining support of moral authority derived from a precapitalist society? If and when that authority is undermined, can the system manage without it? These questions were raised some years ago by the distinguished political economist Albert Hirschman of Princeton. They were never answered by mainstream economists, but are still relevant.

Sociology tells us that most societies have honoured two basic professions – priests and warriors. Sometimes, the priests acted also as judges and administrators, as in Hindu culture. Sometimes, as in China, judges and administrators formed a separate profession of their own. It was only in about the fourteenth century in Christian Europe that bankers were added to the number of honoured professions. As trade and industrialisation grew in Europe, they were joined by other new professions. Industrial societies seemed to multiply the number of occupations claiming to be 'professions'. According to the sociologists, as occupational groups make this claim, they initiate changes in the class structures of societies, so that the hairdresser and the cook no longer belong in the category of artisans or trades people, but are 'professionals' and thus part of a social elite rather than part of the working class. Much sociological inquiry has then gone on to study people in the professions and how their political views and attitudes and their social relations were changed by the transition from worker to professional. These studies thus passed over the two more fundamental questions: first, whether the phenomenon of professions was a product of the division of labour in capitalist economies; and second, whether the professions performed a unique but necessary function in an industrialised society (Johnson 1972: 10).

Some twenty-five years ago, Terence Johnson (1972) argued that the conditions that originally gave rise to professionalism in society no longer characterised modern industrial societies. Professions had lost their exclusive social cachet along with their moral authority. They now had to be analysed in terms of the increasingly cosy relations that grew up in advanced economies between the professionals and their clients. As their independence came more and more into question, society had to decide whether the regulation of a profession could still be safely left to some collegial body, or whether the conduct of professionals, being increasingly subservient to the interests of the client, was no longer filling the same impartial and authoritative mediating role in the economy that had originally justified their social status. In consequence, their claim to a kind of sub-state self-government was no longer justifiable, so that they should be subject to regulation, supervision and disciplinary sanctions by some agency of the state, like everyone else.

This argument has some force and in recent years many governments have sought to impose more of their own rules on the professions. In the case of the bankers, those rules – as noted earlier – have been extended by making the banks legally responsible for reporting suspect transactions to the government. For all other transactions, the bankers still claim that their clients have a right to secrecy and confidentiality. The assumption is still that the state is dealing with professionals whose integrity is so assured that their relationship with customers carries no threat to the stability of society or of the financial system.[4] Common sense and recent experience tell us that this is not a safe assumption. Although governments have applied a stick in the shape of a threat of action against banks that knowingly launder dirty money, there is no corresponding carrot. What does a bank stand to gain by reporting to the government any suspicions it might have about a particular client's account? Nothing. And meanwhile other clients are more likely to shun this bank in favour of more tight-lipped (or unsuspicious) competitors. Until the system produces a system of bank-rating indicators comparable to the bond-rating agencies – Standard and Poor, and Moody's – and until the system finds a way to reward those with cleanest ratings, the declaration that money laundering is illegal is unlikely to be effective (Sinclair 1995).

The other assumption justifying bank secrecy for all other bank clients is that the broader interests of a market economy require that business executives can trust their bankers not to reveal anything concerning the state of their corporate or personal finances, neither to their competitors nor even to government. It has not so far been challenged. Indeed, the evolution of the financial system in recent years actually makes it more desirable than ever – to the customers – that banks reveal nothing to government or to the public about the finances of their clients. Most important financial operations – mergers, takeovers, divestment of affiliates – actually require secrecy until the strategic move is made. All the law can do is to declare illegal the practice of insider trading – the use of inside information in such cases for personal gain. The consensus in most financial markets is that proof is so difficult that most insider trading goes undetected and, indeed, that inside information is what makes the markets profitable.

Bank secrecy is particularly necessary in – and to – the tax havens that have proliferated around the world. If it were ever to be seriously challenged, it would be necessary to close down every tax haven in the world. Otherwise, all the business still transacted within the leading industrialised countries would simply move offshore to one or other tax haven. Much of it already has done so, in order to minimise the impact of corporate tax on profits, since profits declared to arise from transactions in the tax haven are by definition not susceptible. Why then have governments allowed this to happen? Why has the number of tax havens steadily grown over recent years, so that Gibraltar and Cyprus now join the Cayman Islands, the Bahamas, the Channel Islands and Liechtenstein as recognised refuges for untaxed profits? If most governments lose so much revenue through the tax havens, why do they not try to close them down?

It is not because they could not do so. If the Group of Seven were to announce that they would be publishing a blacklist of the known tax havens and another blacklist of the firms and individuals actively making use of tax havens, and would impose fines or other sanctions on them unless the accounts were closed within a specified time, there can be little doubt that most could not survive for very long. The reasons why this does not happen are, once again, political rather than technical.

In past times, when European empires were acquired, there were certain advantages to be gained from raising the flag over distant islands, especially Caribbean islands. Their harbours were valued refuges from the weather and from enemies, while native inhabitants were no serious threat to settlers. To start with, the passing sea trade between Spain and the New World was easy to stop and rob – which was why some became bases for pirates, others for privateers, others for naval forces. Caribbean islands were acquired by the Dutch, French, British and Danes. Helped by cheap labour from the slave trade, settlers could do well from raising plantation crops. The state gained a strategic outpost at low cost.

During World War II and after, all sorts of promises were made to Caribbean leaders about their future economic development. But little was done. Dependence on export crops like sugar or bananas offered no escape from poverty. Shutting official eyes to the longer-term consequences of creating tax havens was the easy way out. It was one way in which the newly independent governments of the islands could readily raise a little revenue and the economy could earn some foreign exchange. Air transport and communication with the United States was easy enough to bring in the customers. And diversification of the services offered brought not only banks but insurance companies. Bermuda was the first of several tax havens to offer big multinationals very accommodating rules for their captive insurance affiliates. These affiliates saved the parent the expense of insuring ships, cars, factories and so on with independent insurance firms. In this way they gained the advantages of internalising the cash flow on all kinds of corporate insurance by diverting the premiums to their captive insurance companies registered in a friendly tax haven (Haufler 1997a: 103; Haufler 1997b).

Since about the mid-1970s, new competition in the tax haven game has come from various places, mostly in Europe. Some, like the

Channel Islands, the Isle of Man, Monaco, Andorra or Liechtenstein, were the result of historical accident. But others have been deliberately developed by governments. Three new tax havens – Malta, Gibraltar and Cyprus – are all former British naval and air bases which once provided necessary services to the Royal Navy. As times changed, the US Sixth Fleet took over security in the Mediterranean and the Royal Navy, in its own vernacular, 'scarpered'.[5] The locals had to find other sources of income.

But not all are abandoned orphans of empire. Ireland is one example of an *arriviste* tax haven. Its government began by encouraging British writers and artists to change their domicile by offering to impose no taxes on literary earnings. Then in 1990 it initiated an international financial services centre on an old derelict dockland site up the Liffy River from Dublin. The government put funds into the development and its infrastructure and persuaded the EC to sanction tax write-offs and a low 10 per cent corporation tax until the year 2005. For the EC it was an easy way to add to regional subsidies, of which Ireland was already a substantial beneficiary.

Luxembourg, Liechtenstein and Switzerland also share some of the characteristics of the tax havens.[6] All three offer secrecy and low taxes to foreign clients. All three are a source of irritation and resentment, especially for Germany as German firms set up holding companies and register them in Zurich or Luxembourg, where tax rates are lower and requirements of disclosure much less demanding. The German Finance Ministry claims to lose billions of Deutschmarks in tax revenue every year as a result. Under pressure, both states now require banks to know the identity of clients and to report them to the authorities unless they are sure of the legitimacy of their dealings. Auditors have to pass their reports to a banking commission and insider trading is illegal.[7] But there are many firms run by financial operators every bit as devious and sophisticated as Robert Maxwell or Sir James Goldsmith – and not all of them stay inside the law on money laundering. Should they be caught, the host government will plead ignorance. For all the legal commitments to exercise 'due diligence', the practical definition of what is required of them remains a grey area (Johns 1983).

Conclusions

Focusing on the tax havens makes clear that laundering drug money is only one of several financial services performed in these places. Nor, I would argue, is it the most serious charge against them from the point of view of the viability of modern capitalism. The other three functions are: first, to cover up the proceeds of private fraud and financial crime; second, to assist legitimate business in avoiding national tax rules; and last, to make public embezzlement – stealing from the public purse – much too easy for corrupt politicians and officials. All three of these functions carry more serious threats than laundering drug money.

As pointed out at the beginning of this chapter, laundering of drug profits was the symptomatic result of conditions in three markets – drugs, alternative crops and financial services. It was also pointed out that there was much to be learned from the proceedings of Italian maxitrials of leading mafiosi. One thing that came out very clearly indeed from these proceedings was that laundering money served the mafias in two ways: it helped them avoid both tax and prosecution, and it also made their new wealth respectable. All the evidence suggested that the mafia families were changing as they got rich. As their need for financial management and optimal investment made it necessary to recruit professional advisers, they were less and less based on blood relations. The laundered money was being invested in the construction business and in service enterprises like dry-cleaning, travel agencies and garages and car repair firms. There was nothing new here. From the earliest times, robber barons, pirates, thieves and confidence tricksters – unless they were caught and punished – all ended up wanting to become pillars of society. They married their sons and daughters to the aristocracy or at least into worthy bourgeois families. Three generations on and no one knew or cared about how they had got there.

Much the same might be said of the private cheats and fraudsters who have existed in all credit-based systems for the past two or three hundred years. Some got caught. But others escaped and became respectable members of the wealthy classes. Clarence Hatry went to prison in Britain between the wars. Robert Sindona went to prison in the United States and then Italy in the 1970s. Bernie Cornfield's fraudulent IOS scheme came to grief in the 1960s, but he got away. Nobody caught the Albanians who robbed thousands of their compatriots in the 1990s with a classic Ponzi bubble scheme for robbing the gullible of their savings.

Far more serious from the point of view of the global financial system is, first, the wholesale leakage of tax revenues from governments already hard put to meet rising administrative and welfare costs; and, second, the open invitations given by the tax havens to public embezzlement – that is, to the misappropriation by corrupt politicians of public money from foreign aid donors and creditors and from state enterprises.

If governments are getting weaker in relation to markets, it is also true that they are getting poorer. Their inability to satisfy the demands of citizens – for better welfare and health services, for more investment in modernising water supplies, drains, ports and railways – is partly their own fault. If they were better at cutting back on expensive defence spending like the Stealth bomber in the United States or the Euro-fighter in Europe, they would have more to spend on other things. If they were better able to cut back the costly but ineffectual agencies like the Central Intelligence Agency or the FBI and their counterparts in France or Britain that mushroomed during the Cold War, the tax problem would not be so acute. It might be thought that the prevention of wholesale tax evasion through the tax havens was a common problem in which the advantages of collective action would be apparent to all governments, great and small. But it does not seem so. Some will have found temporary relief by selling off state enterprises – though privatisation is only a temporary and unrepeatable remedy. Others – like the United States in 1997 – will have found that accelerated economic growth has unexpectedly swollen tax revenues, easing the pressures on the fiscal deficit. As with the failure of indebted countries to present a common front to their creditors, the difficulty lies in the inequality of pain and therefore the unequal incentive for negotiating common action. Yet the costs of inaction, when added up, so greatly outweigh the marginal differences between national interests that the inaction must be judged irrational. Agreement among the leading countries' governments to apply common rules on corporate earnings worldwide – what the Californians once tried as a unitary tax on presumed corporate earnings within California as a share of their global profits – would go far to easing the fiscal problems of most advanced states. It is astonishing that so little constructive thinking has gone into how this might work.[8]

As for the robber heads of state who make use of tax havens to steal from their citizens, the list is a very long one. Only a few have become notorious for the fortunes they managed to take out of their (mostly poor) countries and to hide away in foreign banks, often via one or more of the tax havens. The Shah of Iran was one of the first to be noticed. When he fell from power, his family was found to control funds and real estate in the United States and Europe that should by rights have belonged to the people of Iran. President Marcos of the Philippines and Imelda Marcos, his wife, were found to be millionaires several times over. President Mobutu of Zaire, arap Moi of Kenya, Bokassa of the Central African Republic, Saddam Hussein of Iraq were other super-robbers of the public purse. The Suharto family in Indonesia surpassed most of these in the vast list of businesses and state monopolies acquired by the long-lived president. Even Fidel Castro is reputed to have amassed a private fortune out of a country where most people live in great poverty.

In many cases, the source of these ill-gotten fortunes has been foreign aid, the credits extended by international organisations and by foreign governments as well as by private banks and financial markets. Why have none of these official bodies complained? Once more, the answer lies in politics and the nature of the international political system based on the principle of territorial sovereignty. To demand accountability from the head of any other state opens a door that every other head of state in the entire system would rather see kept fast shut. The alternative for recipients of official foreign aid would be the imposition of independent auditing on the use made of the foreign funds. And even that would not be thief proof. Since money is fungible, the aid could be applied to public expenditure while public revenues from within the country were diverted to personal bank accounts in Switzerland or some other conveniently silent tax haven.

Nor does the political system easily allow aid donors to impose moral or social conditions on foreign governments. The Americans – who at the time exercised hegemonic power over Latin America – tried in President Kennedy's time to make their aid conditional on serious efforts by Latin American governments to redress social inequalities and to spread the wealth. The programme was called, grandiloquently, the Alliance for Progress. And it soon became apparent, as flagrant violations of these political promises became known, that the United States could not, in practice, withdraw its aid from Argentina or Brazil, no matter what their governments did. The United States did not want to be blamed for punishing poor Latin Americans for the sins of their rulers. It also needed the support of those rulers in other conflicts within the international political system.

The logical conclusion must be either that all foreign aid by governments (or by the international organisations that act as their agents) must cease, or else that the opportunities for public embezzlement will continue to arise in countries that receive such financial assistance, whether in grants or loans. There have always been some critics of the practice. Most notably, Peter Bauer long argued that aid was economically counterproductive as well as socially and politically corrupting (Bauer 1993). His complaint was mainly that aid 'pauperised' the developing countries, making them poor beggars and so perpetually dependent on handouts, without enabling them to escape the dependence. A study of foreign aid in Bangladesh concluded that after years of comparatively generous foreign grants and loans, the economic condition of the country – its GNP per head, its balance of payments, its fiscal deficit – was actually worse than it had been at the beginning. Moreover, the political and social consequences had been highly corrupting. For the rich Bangladeshis, 'Aid was the only game in town' (Thompson 1991). Making the most of the opportunities it offered, the rich became richer as the poor stayed poor, so that the income gap actually widened. Bangladesh has not been the only developing country to experience such a widening gap.

More recently, the IMF has tried to put pressure on the government of Kenya to stop the notoriously corrupt practices of the government of Daniel arap Moi. Since Moi is already losing support from his own people and is unlikely to survive promised elections for long, IMF threats to suspend the standby credits Kenya needs may appear effective. But will the IMF apply the same standards when it deals with Russia or Korea?

To sum up, the political consequences of tax havens are much more serious than their usefulness to drug dealers. Their use by corporations to minimise liability for corporate taxation and their use by heads of state to rob their own people bring contempt and ridicule on both governments and on the private enterprise system.

Notes

1   Much the same process can be seen with international sanctions or when firms 'downsize' (i.e. cut down) their workforce, either by substituting robots for men and women or by shifting operations to places where labour is cheaper. Public protest moves politicians to action. But the action is more symbolic of goodwill than effective in putting right the wrong or giving workers back their jobs. By the time this becomes obvious, smart politicians know that they will have moved on to another department – or perhaps be out of office and able to join in the chorus of protest.

2   It is widely believed that cannabis, unlike nicotine, is harmless and non-addictive. There is some recent research, however, which suggests that the long-term incidence of cancer in habitual cannabis smokers may be greater than that in habitual tobacco smokers (personal interview with Professor H. Ashton, Newcastle University, 18 December 1996).

3   Martin Wolf in the *Financial Times* has argued that there are strong economic arguments for legalising the sale of drugs, because the costs of prohibition (including crime prevention, legal enforcement and imprisonment) are much heavier than the social costs of drug use and almost tripled between 1988 and 1993, while drug use certainly continued to increase (*Financial Times*, 22 July, 29 July and 12 August 1997). He concluded that prohibition penalised consumers and that the only victors in the war against drugs were the gangsters. The debate on the policy issue continues (*The Economist*, 15 and 22 August 1997; Ruggiew and South 1995).

4   That assumption is even more doubtful in those banking systems where banks have substantial interests and/or links with major transnational corporations.

The German universal banking system is one such system, the Japanese another (Story and Walter 1997; see also McCahery 1997).

5   The word – meaning to disappear, go away – derived from Scapa Flow, the Scottish inlet where the German Navy was scuttled after World War I according to the provisions of the Versailles Treaty.

6   Liechtenstein's currency is the Swiss franc and has been since the 1920s; Luxembourg's is the Belgian franc. In each case the larger neighbour acts as lender of last resort to the banks.

7   As recently as 1986 only three member states of the EC prohibited insider trading. And even in the United States, which led the move to ban it, the SEC was in a weak bargaining position when it came to enforcing legislation, both at home and, even more, abroad (McCahery 1997: 63–71).

8   There are notable exceptions. Professor James Tobin proposed a universal tax on foreign exchange transactions – the well known Tobin tax. But the purpose was more to damp down the volume of trading on the foreign exchanges than to raise revenue. More recently Professor Howard Wachtel of American University has proposed a Tobin tax, a unitary tax on corporate profits and, more controversially, a tax on foreign investment (see chapter 10 and also Strange 1996: 60–5). Here, surely, is a fruitful field for interdisciplinary work between lawyers, economists and political economists.

Chapter 8

Managing mad money –
national systems

There are two reasons for regulating the behaviour of international financial dealers and the conduct of international financial markets. One is to moderate and restrain greed. The other is to moderate and restrain fear. Greed and fear are the two human emotions most evident in the day-to-day behaviour of the international financial system today. Mad money is the result. Either dealers are drawn by greed to take too big risks with their own or, more often, with other people's money; or they are overcome by fear that the risks they have taken will catch them out. In their rush to escape the consequences of greed, they may start a chain reaction, an avalanche of panic that carries away the innocent along with the guilty.

These common-sense truths tend to be hidden in the growing literature on financial regulation. It is mostly written by economists rather than historians. Some are academics. Some work for international organisations. Most of them have a professional bias towards rational explanations for rational behaviour. They are uncomfortable when faced by irrational emotions like greed and fear and the often irrational behaviour that follows. Moreover, they are often grossly ignorant of the financial histories of even their own countries, let alone others, and of the elementary facts of life concerning international organisations.

To simplify a little, at the time of writing there are two opposed schools of thought about what has to be done to ensure greater stability and safety in the international financial system. One assumes – or hopes against hope – that bankers and other financial actors in the markets are rational enough to moderate their own greed and quell their own fears so that they can be trusted to use the technical information and risk-evaluating methods available to them to discipline themselves. This, crudely put, is the conclusion prevailing at the BIS.

139

The other school – more likely to be found in the IMF – puts faith in intergovernmental cooperation to reproduce at the international level the kind of regulatory mechanisms developed within states and used by them until recently to exert discipline over national banking and financial systems. Some contemporary academic writers go further in this direction and produce fanciful and grandiose schemes for codes and rules to govern all banks in all countries.

In the next chapter I shall show why both schools – and the academic draughtsmen of utopian blueprints – are wrong. There is no evidence to be found in national histories or in international history to support these views. Indeed, far from helping to solve the problems, they may actually be misleading the rest of us into thinking that is easier and less dangerous than it really is. The next chapter will make this argument with the help of a brief review of the history of international organisations bearing direct or indirect responsibility for the stability and viability of finance. While the organisations themselves are at pains to declare that they are making progress, the evidence – as implicitly suggested at various points earlier in this book – is that progressive liberalisation is eroding the remaining bulwarks of national systems of control faster than they can be replaced by new international systems.

The logical sequence therefore will be first to explain how the national systems of financial regulation came into being and how they were shaped by the political ideas and motivations prevailing in national societies. It is these political – even philosophical – ideas which make the national regulatory systems so very different from one another. This is the everyday stuff of comparative politics and political economy but it does not seem to be at all well understood. This is possibly because of the intellectual domination of American social science – especially economics – where it is often assumed that the rest of the world has patterned its mechanisms of government on those of the United States – or if they have not already done so, they soon will. The reality is that this is far from the case. The national stories will show, first, the very wide variation between the regulatory systems and the institutions set up to administer them. And secondly they will show the important part played by domestic and foreign politics, so that for agreement to have been reached on a working system, deals had to be made and bargains struck between public and private interests and between political opponents.

Some of this will be familiar stuff to many international and national political economists and historians. They are welcome to skip over them and pass to the next chapter which will describe in more detail the specific danger areas in the financial system. Banking supervisors and financial commentators are well aware of them, and of the difficulties in finding ways to avoid them.

The conclusion to be drawn will not surprise students of international relations. The prospect is for a compromise between the BIS and the IMF approaches. The synthesis will mean that there will be agreement between governments on a code of best practice for banks, but at the same time some extension of the responsibilities of the IMF into areas hitherto considered to belong to national governments. It will look good but in reality there will be many banks that are unwilling or unable to meet the best-practice code. And there will be many countries where the power of the IMF to enforce compliance by threatening to withdraw its lender-of-last-resort support will be seen to be hollow. The danger will continue to lie in the gaps – what Alain Minc (1993) has called the *zones grises* – between the two approaches to the problem. As on other issues of general concern – disarmament, human rights, protection of the global environment – governments find it comparatively easy to draw up an agreement in principle on what needs to be done but extremely difficult to translate that agreement into political reality. In my opinion it is more important here to find out how these national systems of financial regulation came to be set up in the first place than to know the constitutional details of which national authorities and institutions are supposed do what in relation to banks, non-banks and financial markets. The historical record will reveal much more clearly the mixed motives and the confused ideas of governments in setting up and running these systems and the wide variation in how they have worked and changed in practice. Between the extreme of total state control over credit (as practised in the former Soviet Union) and the much looser, more delegated regulatory system developed in the United States, there are national systems that are closer to the state-planned model and others closer to the American one. In short, there is no single model that fits all the developed national economies, let alone the so-called emerging market economies. The question therefore is whether it would be possible to negotiate a compromise, synthesising the different national systems into one standard one; or whether it is possible for other forms of regulation to change and conform slowly to the dominant US model. Or, if neither of these is feasible, whether the system can manage without state intervention on the basis of self-discipline.

Financial regulation in the United States

Since it is probably the best known and politically the most dominant system, let us look first at the history of financial regulation in the United States.

The first puzzle is why the United States waited so long to set up a national system of control over banks and financial markets. Germany, by contrast, had no sooner achieved a united state in 1870 than it set about creating a central bank. The Bank of England boasts a history of 300 years. The Federal Reserve System in the United States dates only from 1913. For nearly a century the US economy had managed without it.[1] Despite a civil war and a rather anarchic system of banking, especially in the west, it had survived and grown from being a small peripheral agricultural economy to a great manufacturing one spanning an entire continent. By 1913 it had passed from being a debtor to a creditor country in the world economy and had joined the inner circle of great powers.

But in fact neither great-power status nor economic development was behind the belated institution of a central bank. Instead there were two reasons: war and a financial panic. The war was the Spanish–American War of 1898, for which the Congress immediately appropriated $50 million for national defence, giving President Teddy Roosevelt full discretion in spending it. Federal taxes were raised and $200 million in war bonds issued. By 1901, the final defence costs amounted to over $800 million. In line with its past practice in paying off government debt incurred in the Civil War in the 1860s, US policy aimed at refunding its war debt by issuing new, long-term, 2 per cent bonds. To do so, the growing number of banks were given tax and other incentives to hold the new government debt first in the Currency Act of 1900 and later in the Federal Reserve Act of 1913.[2]

In the meantime, the economy had experienced the financial panic of 1907. A bubble of speculation, inflated by railroad construction and rapid credit creation by trust companies in competition with banks, finally burst, with many bankruptcies and a collapse of confidence. The state's role in ensuring financial stability was added to the political agenda – as usual, after, not before, a crisis. The government responded by setting up a National Monetary Commission to ponder the various reform proposals suggested to the Congress. After three years, it reported and put its plan forward in a report in 1912. What emerged in the Act of 1913 was a three-way political compromise between Republicans and Democrats, between public and private interests, and between the claims of federal and state governments.

To simplify a somewhat complex picture, the original Republican plan proposed by Senator Aldrich and supported by Wall Street banks had favoured central control. The Democrats, led by Senator Glass, favoured a more decentralised system, giving power if not to every state in the Union at least to twelve banking districts, each with a kind of regional central bank. Instead of the Federal Reserve Board elected by the banks, as proposed by the Republicans, Democrats wanted a board largely appointed by the President and therefore politically accountable. The compromise was a decentralised system of district reserve banks but which allowed the member banks to elect two-thirds of their members. They were to clear cheques, provide discount services and hold local reserves.

The compromise between public and private interests introduced an unusual voluntary element into the regulatory system. State-chartered banks were given the choice of staying out of the Federal Reserve System and foregoing the security it offered, or going in but abiding by its rules and depositing part of their reserves with the regional central bank. Most national systems give banks no such option.

The other part of the public–private deal was that the government used the incentives for banks to join the system to pursue its own interests in managing a growing public debt – and one which was fated to grow enormously in World War I. After 1915, the Federal Reserve Board could command member banks to buy government bonds up to a total of $25 million a year. It also levied a tax on bank profits over 6 per cent to help public finances.

Subsequent history shows that the compromise between conflicting interests and purposes was only temporary. All through the interwar period, political controversy raged around the decision-making processes of the Federal Reserve System and its policies. After the Wall Street crash, its reputation and influence declined. Its interest rate policies were blamed – perhaps unduly – for the boom and bust. The New Dealers who came in with Roosevelt in 1933 thought it was too subservient to the banks and their interests. It was time for a change. The result was the Banking Act of 1935. Its declared purpose was to make the Federal Reserve System an instrument of national economic management and to ensure that it served the general and not vested interests. The balance of power in the system was shifted from the regional banks to the Federal Reserve Board and especially its chairman. He was given power to alter discount rates – Republican critics called it a change to fiat money – and took the control of open market operations from a committee of the reserve banks to a committee answerable to the Board.

The last change was not just technical. Besides setting the reserves that private banks must deposit with the central bank as a kind of insurance premium, and besides the power to fix discount rates, open market operations are a third weapon of central banks' regulatory power. These can be effective when, first, government debt is an important element in the financial markets and, secondly, where there is a functioning market for credit instruments. It works by affecting the level of bank reserves, which in turn affects banks' propensity to lend. By buying its own Treasury bills or selling more of them to the reserve banks, the central bank can force the reserve banks to increase their reserves and limit lending, or it can allow them to reduce their reserves and increase their lending.[3] This is the theory of open market operations as practised in the United States. But it works best if the volume of credit in the economy depends mainly on the behaviour of national banks. Obviously, it won't work so well if there are large inflows (or outflows) of funds from outside, or if other non-bank enterprises outside the Federal Reserve System are taking credit business away from the banks.

In the 1930s, when capital mobility across the exchanges was low and banks were still dominant in the credit-creating business, the conduct of open market operations was a big political issue. Unfortunately for the theorists, the 1935 Act failed to provide guidelines on operating strategy and the trade-off between full employment, stable prices and the country's external balance of payments. As Jane D'Arista commented:

> The result has been that the Federal Reserve continues to contribute to economic instability ... as the Federal Reserve System has evolved over the decades since 1935. Conflicting views of its function would seem to have been perpetuated rather than resolved. (D'Arista 1994: 193)

One reason is that since 1935, the personality of the head of the Federal Reserve Board has varied widely, and so has his dependence or independence of the government of the day. Alan Greenspan (1987–97), for example, has been much more independent – and therefore influential – than Arthur Burns, who presided over the Fed when the Vietnam War made a nonsense of price stability in the United States. Greenspan's predecessor, Paul Volcker, had a strong personality and an independent mind but could change US monetary policy in 1981 only in concert with the Administration's policies. When, instead of Carter, he had the backing of Reagan as President, it was possible to make the switch to an anti-inflationary monetary policy that restricted the supply and raised the price of credit (Mayer 1997).

These two factors – the ongoing political struggles within and around the Fed, and the personality and reputation of its chairman – cast serious doubts over the notion of central banks as reliable, consistent, politically neutral institutions independent of elected governments. And especially questionable is the independence of the most influential of all central banks – that of the United States.

The American regulatory system, moreover, is additionally peculiar in the way in which responsibility is shared, in a rather messy way, between the Federal Reserve Board, the Comptroller of the Currency, the FDIC and the SEC. A brief word about each will explain – not the outcome – the supposed relation between these regulators.

The Comptroller of the Currency – as the archaic name suggests – dates back to the early days of the republic. Then, the office controlled the printing of currency and the chartering of national banks. Now as then, the Comptroller is a political appointee and this makes the impact of the office somewhat unpredictable (Reagan, for example, appointed a lawyer for Texas banks who surely contributed to the banks' later disasters in real-estate loans by allowing them to undervalue their losses on the grounds that in five to seven years the property values might bounce back – see Mayer 1997: 405). According to Mayer, the Comptroller 'probably exerts greater influence on the banks' than the Fed. But the division of responsibility between them is fuzzy. Banks operate all kinds of affiliates. Their holding companies are regulated by the Fed, the banks themselves by the Comptroller.

The FDIC was a New Deal creation, set up in 1933 against strong opposition from the big city banks. Its purpose was to operate an insurance fund that would compensate small customers of banks if they went bust. It works by buying up the assets of a failed bank and getting another bank to take them over. Its costs are covered by the fees it charges to banks for making them look safe to the customers. The FDIC was briefly active (and, with government funding, enlarged) in the 1980s in connection with the S&L fiasco. Although a junior partner to the Fed and the Treasury's Comptroller, it would be difficult for any US President to do away with it.[4] Whether its example should be followed by Asian countries is debatable. The insurance inevitably introduces a risk of moral hazard – tempting the bank managers to take imprudent risks.

Last but not least, there is the SEC. Also set up in the New Deal to oversee the conduct of stock exchanges, it controls the accounting procedures that must be used by banks when they buy and sell shares or bonds for their clients. It is a key player in the International Organisation of Securities Commissions (IOSCO) – the informal transnational organisation set up by stock exchange regulators in the mid-1980s (see chapter 9). In the American system, the SEC creates one more area of uncertain responsibility. Its chairman may disagree profoundly with the Fed or the Comptroller when it comes to saving a distressed bank or letting it go under – as happened over Continental Illinois in the 1970s. And the chairman may take a radically different view on accounting practices – as Richard Breeden did with Greenspan in the early 1990s.

What does all this add up to for the future management of the global financial system? First, the American system of financial regulation is not necessarily a model for other countries, or for the global system. It is very idiosyncratic, reflecting social and political attitudes highly specific to the United States. It has also been highly dynamic, changing substantially according to popular mood or the personalities of key actors. It has worked – so far – for the United States, but not necessarily because it is a good system. Partly, the US system can get away with multiple flaws and all sorts of bitter internal political conflicts because the US economy is so large and fundamentally so strong that losses and slowdowns are not – or so far have not been – catastrophic. Americans can live with U-turns in policy, volatile swings in fortune, misguided or ineffectual regulators. It does not follow that other countries and the international system are similarly resilient.

Moreover, US policies, in all fields, not only the financial, are essentially domestic. Decisions have been taken in response to national moods, national problems and national interests. US governments have not so far been good at taking into consideration how their own actions affect others. Whether and how this may change as the fortunes of American banks and firms become more and more dependent on events and conditions in the world economy – Asia, for instance – and not just on the US economy is one of the key issues of the next century. In the meantime, and as a consequence of the same forces of global-isation, US governments have lost a measure of control over their own economy. Growing use of the US dollar as monetary reserve and means of international exchange means that total foreign government hold-ings of US government securities have come to exceed the Federal Reserve's own holdings. The price of US Treasury bills can be changed by the decisions of foreign central banks to buy or sell dollar assets. The values of shares in US firms may be affected by the decisions (taken for whatever reason) of their foreign owners. These movements can either frustrate or amplify US monetary policies. Since the late 1970s, the US government has also come to depend on foreign, especially Japanese, savings and investments to finance both its trade and its fiscal deficit.

Japanese dirigisme

This close symbiosis between the United States and Japan makes their respective systems of financial regulation a matter of mutual concern.

Yet the two systems could hardly be more different – always excepting a totally state-planned and controlled system such as that of the former Soviet Union. Until quite recently, while the American system was one in which credit was created and traded by private enterprise subject to partial, intermittent and indirect intervention by government, the Japanese was a dirigiste system in which the state controlled the creation and price of credit, while gradually allowing private interests a chance to profit from the managed markets. While the controlling power of the Japanese state today is not what it used to be and big changes have taken place, much of the former machinery still exists. Past Anglo-American attempts to apply common regulatory rules to Japan – like the Basle capital–assets ratios – either did not work or had negative results. It may be that neither a complete transition to a US-type regulatory system nor a halfway synthesis of the two is workable.

To appreciate why this is so, we have to look back, once again, into postwar history. As the occupying power in the late 1940s, the US authorities realised that the risks to social and political stability of opening Japan either to foreign trade or to foreign capital were too great. Economic chaos would have resulted. Instead of a secure forward base in the Cold War, Japan would have been a potential political liability (see chapter 3). So when Japanese governments took over in the 1950s, the Americans made no objection to the strict exchange controls, bans on foreign investment, controls over imports and managed finance that Japanese elites believed would reconcile private interests, political and economic, with the perceived national interest.

For the first twenty years, the system worked smoothly and successfully. The government, through the MOF and the Bank of Japan, rationed credit and the Ministry of Trade and Industry (MITI), aided by the Longterm Credit Bank and other state agencies, helped direct it to export industries, which gradually turned the postwar deficits into growing trade surpluses. Interest rates were kept low and credit was cheap.

The other secret of success has been called 'compartmentalisation' (Reading 1992: 151). This is a euphemism for licensed cartels, protected from competition with newcomers by rules which forbade firms to do any business other than their own. For example, banks were not allowed to underwrite or trade in securities while stockbrokers were not allowed to take deposits and act like banks. Such rules made for rigged markets and guaranteed safe monopoly profits. At the same time, cosy *keiretsu* relations grew up between big manufacturing and trading firms and the banks, once again limiting competition and securing a steady source of comfortable profit. The stability of the system was further assured by the political system, in which some of these profits were diverted to support politicians in the dominant LDP.

Change came in the 1970s, from inside and outside Japan. At home, the public debt which had been unusually low, especially by comparison with the United States, grew in the space of ten years from under Y100 billion and under 10 per cent of GNP in 1972 to over Y1,000 billion and over 40 per cent of GNP in 1982 (Hamada and Horiuchi 1987: 227). At first the authorities tried to fix the prices and restrict the market in the new public bonds. But bit by bit, and especially after 1983, the restrictions were dropped and banks began to deal freely in them. The high savings and low interest rates in Japan combined with low savings and relatively high interest rates in America increasingly tempted the big Japanese banks to go abroad to London and New York in search of profitable arbitrage, especially in the bond markets. By 1986, Japanese banks were the biggest lenders in the international financial markets. In going abroad, they weakened the control of the government over the financial system, escaped the 'Chinese walls' compartmentalising financial dealings and possibly added to the volatility of exchange rates.[5]

In the 1990s, the erosion of government control over the national financial system has continued – but slowly. Although one liberalisation tends to lead to another, there has been stubborn resistance to change in and out of the bureaucracy – even after 1990 and the collapse of the bubble economy.[6] Some of the government agencies like the Ministry of Trade and Industry or the Ministry of Posts and Telecommunications – which controls the large postal savings system – see their former power and influence under threat. The old guard in the LDP and its supporting rural and land-owning constituents also see their interests threatened. In the private sector, the banks have been slow to reveal either the losses incurred with non-performing loans or the true state of their hidden reserves.

People at first believed official assurances that there would be a quick recovery. But when this failed year after year to materialise there were conflicting reactions. To conservatives – especially when their political or financial interests were at stake – it proved that liberalisation on the American model had gone too far and too fast. To the growing number of reformers it showed that further radical change – political as much as financial – was inescapable. As in other countries, Japanese financial interests have tended to be ambivalent. They want the freedom to make bigger profits at home as well as abroad. But they do not always welcome foreign competition. And when in trouble, as over the bankrupt *jusen* real-estate holding companies in 1995, or in the aftermath of the east Asian turmoil in

1997, they want the government to come to their rescue with public money.

The French system

Even the briefest account of the French and German systems of national financial regulation will serve to reinforce many of the points already made, especially perhaps concerning the damage done to prudential supervision by the globalisation of finance. Of the two, the French experience has been closest to the Japanese. As in Japan, French postwar strategy produced fast economic growth – second only to Japan in the years 1960–73. It managed a rapid exodus of people from agriculture to industry, rising real wages and a prosperous middle class. More subtly than in Japan, the government used powerful levers to influence trade, investment and finance. Nationalisation put large sectors – railways, electric power, steel, aircraft, shipyards – under direct government control. French economic planners had tight control over credit granted to public and private sectors.

The key agency in allocating credit for investment was the Conseil National de Crédit. It was backed by the Ministry of Finance, the Bank of France and the Trésor and assisted by the Commissariat du Plan. As in Japan, strong Chinese walls compartmentalised commercial banks and savings banks, limiting competition. Membership in corporatist bodies like the Association Française de Banques and the Fédération Française des Sociétés d'Assurance was compulsory and controlled.[7] Any financial institution with surplus funds was legally obliged to deposit them with the Trésor. If they lent above their deposits, they had to borrow at rates fixed by the government. Indeed, up to 1958 as much as 80 per cent of all French investment was made through another government body, the Caisse des Dépôts et Consignations. Linked to what Story and Walter (1997: 192) describe as a 'maze of state corporatist networks' were such institutions as the Crédit Agricole, the farmers' bank with origins in the 1840s, which in the 1970s became the largest bank in the world, and the Banque Française de Commerce Extérieure, which with COFACE (Compagne Française d'Assurance pour le Commerce Extérieur) monopolised the financing of French export trade and subsidised export credit.

This well organised, keynesian corporatist system in which, with the aid of indicative planning, the financial system was supposed to serve the national interest was much admired by Andrew Shonfield and others in the 1960s. Even in the 1970s, the low growth and delayed recovery after the oil price shock was blamed on external factors, not on the national political economy (Matthews 1982). The first serious setback came only in the early 1980s, when international financial markets decided that French Euro-currency borrowing was unsustainable, forcing a devaluation of the franc. It was the first of several setbacks.

Despite the ding-dong political struggle between Gaullists and socialists through the 1980s and 1990s, which among other things first nationalised French banks, then privatised them, there was a certain continuity of French policy in matters of finance. Its distinguishing feature was a sort of desperate nationalism – a determination to keep up with London as a financial market, to dominate the EC's expanding bureaucracy, and to resist German economic hegemony. All these efforts – like the parallel defence of the French language and culture – were doomed to fail. As Story and Walter (1997: 216) remarked, 'Inexorably, internationalisation pulled the French economy into the slipstream of the Anglo-American financial markets'.

There was a price on each of the national goals. To challenge London's financial dominance, in 1986, France set up a futures market, MATIF, complete with computerised dealing. And the Paris stock exchange, hitherto somewhat moribund, was revived with brokers' commissions no longer fixed and stamp duty abolished. The first laid French banks and firms wide open to speculative dealing. The second allowed foreign investors to buy shares in French firms, so that they came to own up to a third of French equities and bonds. French firms, in their turn, began to invest heavily outside the country, especially in the United States and to deal financially in London or Luxembourg rather than Paris. As in Japan, it was easier to unravel the old system of regulation than to put another in its place.

The appointment of Jacques Delors, a former finance minister, as President of the European Commission in Brussels, with another French civil servant, Emile Noël, as its Secretary General also backfired. The Commission began increasingly to propose regulatory directives on banking and insurance to apply in all member states. The need for these became more evident with the renewed push for the Single European Market in the mid-1980s and the Maastricht Treaty's endorsement of monetary union as a common goal. The time came for first Noël then Delors to resign, but the directives from Brussels remained.[8]

French resistance to German economic hegemony took various forms (see chapter 4). One was the vain attempt to make one of the oldest leading French banks, Crédit Lyonnais, into a national champion – and potentially a European champion – but still under state control. This was consistent with the backing given to Thomson in electronics, to Air France in air transport, to Aerospatiale, Dassault in aerospace. It was to be achieved by wholesale foreign acquisitions in Germany, Italy, Spain and Belgium to make Crédit Lyonnais both bigger and more European. These were expensive and risky. The end result was a loss of market confidence, a downgrading by Moody of Crédit Lyonnais's bonds and eventually a massive bailout by the French government.

On the wider issue of European monetary policy, French demands that the European Central Bank should be politically accountable met with German resistance, and at the time of writing the issue has not been resolved. At home, the *franc fort* policy had tied French economic management to the fiercely deflationary strategies of the Bundesbank. Whether the connection was made or not, rising unemployment and government budget cuts brought a loss of popular confidence in politicians' honesty and in government promises to cut taxes and create new jobs. The regulatory system shared authority between the Banque de France and various government agencies with no real clarity as to who, in the last resort, was really in charge.

Regulation in Germany

If France was a bit like Japan in financial regulation, Germany was a bit like the United States: a federal state in which authority was shared between the central government and the provincial *Länder*; a banking system with many small, local banks and just three very large ones – Commerzbank, Deutschebank and Dresdnerbank; a mixed system of public regulation and regulation at a sub-state level by trade associations governing the private banks, savings banks and insurance business. For most of the postwar years, the delicate balance was maintained by overall support for a neo-corporatist *sozialmarkt* philosophy and by the credit popularly given to the central bank for the strength and stability of the Deutschmark.[9]

Yet the story of slow disintegration of national financial regulation under the impact of global competition in financial services, and of other external factors, political as well as economic, is not fundamentally so different that a very detailed account is necessary. I shall be content with trying to identify the main points of the story and referring interested readers to others better qualified to tell it.[10]

Global competition for market shares, as elsewhere, forced German banks to go abroad for more profitable business. By the 1980s, domestic business, once their bread and butter, had declined and the big banks entered investment banking, bought foreign subsidiaries and built up operations in New York, London and the Far East. At the same time, Frankfurt had opened its bond market to foreign competition – a step initiated by the Bundesbank in the mid-1980s to stop the drain of German savings to the United States. By 1990, half the members of the Frankfurt stock exchange were foreign banks and over half of new issues were bought by foreigners.

Meanwhile, social and economic change greatly increased German savings rates as the prosperous middle class grew older and more concerned about the return on capital. This helped break down the Chinese walls that had kept banking separate from insurance, causing dilemmas for the regulatory authorities. The European Single Market rules further eroded the exemptions banks and insurance firms had once enjoyed from national anti-cartel laws. Majority voting on matters relating to the Single European Market undermined national authority over both.

German unification in 1990 dealt another blow to the Bundesbank's power. Against Bundesbank advice, Chancellor Kohl had insisted on a one-to-one exchange rate between East German and West German marks. This inevitably put up the costs of unification. The Finance Ministry proposed to allow investment trusts to deal in money markets, thus allowing the government access to a new source of credit. The Bundesbank objected that there were no reserve requirements on money market funds so that this would weaken its control over the money supply and thus inflation. In the end, in 1993, it had to give way by reducing reserve requirements and then in 1994 allowing the government to use money market funds (Story and Walter 1997: 180).

As in Japan, the German political culture valued consensus and consultation. As Story and Walter (1997: 185) conclude, this 'ensured that change came slowly and as a function of the multiple interests to be reconciled in negotiations.... Reforms were partial and always incomplete.' They also quote Walter Nolling, a former member of the Bundesbank Council, 'It is no exaggeration to speak of an abdication of the democracies in the face of anonymous, uncontrolled market forces'.

British eccentricity

Thanks to the City, London is still one of the three great cities of the modern world (Sassen 1991). Yet of all the leading developed countries in the world economy, the government in Britain had traditionally played a less direct regulatory role than any other. Indeed, some historians have argued that it was not the British government that ruled the City so much as the City that ruled the British government.

The old British empire, so this argument goes, may have been won by naval power, but it was maintained and extended by British finance capital, which even exerted a dominant extraterritorial influence in Latin America, the Ottoman empire and Middle East and Far East (Cain and Hopkins 1993; de Cecco 1974; Ingham 1984). I myself argued that British postwar policy, at home and abroad, was prisoner to the belief that the country's political status and prestige depended on the Commonwealth, that the Commonwealth was held together by the reserve role of sterling and that too much priority was given for too long to the balance of payments and the sterling exchange rate (Strange 1971). The fatal alternation of stop–go signals to the private sector hardly encouraged investment and long-term corporate strategies. To a large extent, British policy was captive to the interests of the City (Hutton 1995).

But as with the other countries, there have been major changes in the way the City is regulated. Little remains today of the old, informal, cosy system of self-regulation under the watchful eye of the Old Lady (of Threadneedle Street – i.e. the Bank of England). That system depended less on law than the US system or the German and more on implicit bargains between the government and a series of select clubs of what Cain and Hopkins (1993) call 'gentlemanly capitalists'. As elsewhere, Chinese walls enclosed each club, limiting competition from outsiders and exchanging a measure – often deliberately indeterminate – of support from government for compliance with official monetary and financial strategies.

Briefly, there were half a dozen or more of these clubs – cartels, to be blunt – the clearing banks; the discount houses; the overseas banks; the merchant banks; the savings banks; building societies; stockbrokers and stockjobbers; Lloyd's underwriters, brokers and 'names' (i.e. investors). Also part of the City were specialised markets like the Baltic Exchange for shipping, the London Metal Exchange, and since 1984 the financial futures market, LIFFE.

The clearing banks were the commercial high-street banks. But as a result of mergers before and after World War II, only four major ones remained: Barclays, Midland, Lloyds and Nat West. It was mostly through them that the Treasury operated its monetary controls. In return, they foreswore competition on the price of loans to customers, competed only feebly on services, did no short-term dealing but had privileged use of the London Clearing House for cheques and deposits.

The discount houses specialised in short-term bills and credits and were the intermediaries through which the Bank of England operated its open market operations to supply or withdraw reserves from the clearing banks. Before 1914, the discount houses also traded in private bills of exchange issued by the merchant banks or accepting houses. The latter thereafter turned more to what Americans would call investment banking and fund management.

The overseas banks also changed as decolonisation deprived them of their *chasses gardées* in Africa, the Middle East and elsewhere; with Bank of England permission, they switched in the 1960s to Eurodollar dealing (Strange 1971).

Each of the City's professional clubs, including Lloyd's and the stock exchange, was allowed – like the legal and medical professions in Britain – to use its own methods to discipline members who offended against written or unwritten rules. Once 'hammered' on the stock exchange, stockbrokers for example were banned from share dealing for life. The separation of jobbers and brokers meant that it was difficult for brokers to push shares on unsuspecting investors, who bought only indirectly, through the jobbers.

By the late 1990s, almost nothing remained of this informal system of control. Instead of a cosy circle of financial clubs presided over by a silently watchful central bank that only occasionally intervened (and then more by nods and winks than commands), the City was being ostensibly governed by a veritable maze of government statutes and agencies. The limits of what was allowed and what was forbidden were far from clear and so was the division of responsibility among the regulators. Financial scandal and crime were seldom out of the headlines, yet long-established legal principles put strict limits on the state's powers of criminal prosecution. The 'gentlemanly capitalists' were either long gone or remained only as figureheads. Action in the markets was in the hands of greedy young Turks with a command of financial technology beyond the comprehension of an older generation – and probably quite beyond the control of the regulators. The Bank of England to outward appearance was more independent than ever of Whitehall and Westminster, and its statutory power much enhanced. But the reality of its regulatory control over a financial centre more wide open than ever to a larger and more unruly world was highly doubtful.

How and why had this happened? In a nutshell, because of competition, of two kinds: transnational competition between the City and Wall Street, and between American and Japanese and British banks; and domestic competition between the insiders who belonged to the cosy clubs and new interlopers who didn't, but were eager to share in the profits. In economic theory and the textbooks, competition among producers who sell goods or services is supposed to bring down prices to the buyers and users. It therefore makes the system more efficient. This dogma is easier to defend in manufacturing than in services – though even there the prevalence of 'private protection' and price fixing among the producers has been systematically ignored by most economists (see Strange 1996: ch. 11). In banking and financial services, experience abundantly shows that when competitive pressures increase, managers rarely cut their prices. Rather, they are tempted to take bigger risks in order to stay in business. The old cartel arrangements common to almost all national financial systems in the past had at least guaranteed them a secure and comfortable living. Once deprived of that security, the law and morals of the jungle took over. A kind of madness ruled.

Part of the metamorphosis of the eccentric British system has an international explanation. Competition came first from America and later from Japan and others. To simplify the story a little, US banks followed their corporate clients to London as these invested heavily in postwar Europe.[11] The licence so nonchalantly granted them by the US and British governments to operate in London in dollars, not sterling, made this foreign business much more profitable than their taxed and regulated business at home.[12] By the late 1970s, it had grown so large that New York was feeling the pinch. The result was a change in US law in 1981 that allowed the same sort of profitable offshore business to be conducted at home in New York. Conversely, London came under pressure from 1975 to deregulate share markets in order to match the American abolition of fixed commissions for share dealing.

The other part of the competition story was domestic. Within Britain, the clearing banks came under competitive pressure in the early 1970s from so-called 'secondary' banks. Less closely regulated and monitored than the clearing banks, these took risks in the property market and in 1973 got into such bad trouble that the Bank of England felt it had to launch what it called a 'lifeboat' to rescue them – but made the clearing banks pay the cost of it. That was only one part of the story of growing competition. The end of British exchange controls over capital in 1979 gave British financial operators still greater freedom to go abroad in search of better profits. Barings was only one of many, but exceptionally lax and complacent in its management. Meanwhile, on all sorts of fronts, everyone was trying to poach other people's business: the clearing banks on the merchant banks, the non-banks on the banks; the banks on the building societies.[13]

Successive governments, Tory and Labour, responded with a string of new statutes – 1973, 1974, 1977, 1979 and yet more in the 1980s. The famous 'Big Bang' of 1986 was only one in a series of political bargains in which, in return for deregulation, governments insisted on statutory reforms. To prepare for it, the Financial Services Act had set up the Securities Investment Board (SIB) as a new watchdog. Beneath the SIB, in a second tier, there were to be seven separate self-regulatory organisations. They would be responsible for seeing the rules were kept. To cut a long story short, the SIB had neither the necessary resources nor the strong sanctions to prevent and punish financial wrongdoing. By 1997, it was decided to replace it with a super-SIB, amalgamating the regulatory offices under one roof. These had proliferated in the 1990s, involving the Department of Trade and Industry, the Serious Fraud Office under the Home Office and the Securities and Futures Securities Association Authority – not to mention the Internal Revenue Service and various mixed bodies like Lloyd's that relied on auditors to blow the referee's whistle on their clients.

The picture was further complicated by the overlapping roles of these national bodies with the European Commission in Brussels and the BIS (see chapter 9). It seemed as though the British wish to reconcile 'liberalisation' (i.e. deregulation) of financial services and adequate regulation of profit-seeking private enterprise was producing only more and more cooks to spoil the broth. Yet where Britain was already headed, other European countries, and Japan, were likely to follow. The City of London being bigger, more open and involved in more kinds of complex financial dealing than others is encountering ahead of the rest the regulatory problems implicit in a political system of national governments faced with an integrated transnational financial system.

Notes

1   Two early attempts to have some sort of central bank had both failed. The First Bank of the United States, set up by Alexander Hamilton in 1791, ran into populist opposition, so that its charter was not renewed in 1811. The Second Bank of the United States, chartered in 1816, had its charter renewal vetoed by President Andrew Jackson, who shared a general American distrust of banks and strong central government. It was Jefferson who once remarked that there was only one thing worse than a standing army – and that was a bank.

2   The number of US depository banks grew fast in the early 1900s. Fewer than 500 in 1900, by 1913 there were more than three times as many (Dewey 1918).

3   The full explanation is a bit more complex. When it wants to tighten credit, the Fed sells more Treasury bills to the reserve banks, debiting their reserves and forcing them to cut back on lending and raise interest rates. When it wants to expand credit in the economy, the Fed conversely buys in its Treasury bills, and pays for them with a cheque that can be cashed only by a member reserve bank. When its reserve account is so credited, its larger reserves allow it to lend more liberally. The enlarged supply of credit lowers interest rates. I am indebted for this clear exposition to Jane D'Arista.

4 Amending legislation in 1991 had the effect of making bank auditors liable if they did not reveal potential weakness in a client bank. Indirectly, this increases the role of the major accountancy firms in maintaining a viable financial system (see chapter 9).

5 On the internationalisation of finance in Japan, and the policy issues involved, see Shinkai (1988). Other sources are Murphy (1996) and Reading (1992).

6 As Shinkai (1988) prophetically observed, 'We can expect a fairly long period of trial and error in the process of domestic liberalization.'

7 Actually, there were only five major insurance firms (Story and Walter 1997: 190).

8 Notably, perhaps, the EU's Capital Adequacy and Own Funds Directive.

9 This respect was undimmed either by awareness of the chequered history of central banking in Germany nor by the correlation in the 1990s between Bundesbank policies, the strong mark, the exodus of German manufacturing to cheaper locations abroad and rising unemployment at home (see Marsh 1992).

10 For a full account, see Story and Walter (1997: ch. 6) and Edwards and Fischer (1993).

11 Vernon's product cycle theory explained that by doing so US firms with an innovative product or cost advantage could continue to reap oligopolistic profits by being the first to export and then to produce their goods in Europe (Vernon 1971). His neat and conventionally acceptable explanation overlooked the necessary political condition for this to happen, which was the open door to US foreign direct investment in Europe (but not Japan).

12 How quickly sharp operators like Robert Sindona were to see this is well brought out by the story of the rise and fall of the Franklin National Bank in 1974. Joan Spero has told how dilatory and complacent the Bank of England was in investigating what Sindona's bank was up to in London (Spero 1979; see also chapter 9).

13 For details on this, see Story and Walter (1997: ch. 8); also Hall (1987), Moran (1984) and Deane and Pringle (1994).

Chapter 9

Our international guardians

With national regulators caught – as the last chapter related – in the midst of change brought on by forces of financial innovation and integration beyond their control, attention shifts to the possibilities of internationally negotiated systems of control.

Finance is not, of course, the only policy area where social and economic problems have outgrown the limits of state authority. Global warming, forestry management, enforcing competition over monopolies, property rights and the political rights of dissidents are some of the others. But financial regulation is certainly one of the most urgent. As noted in chapter 2, two very different international institutions have been engaged in it for some years now – the BIS and the IMF. What does their record, and that of other intergovernmental institutions, tell us about their potential for taking over from the national regulators?

The central bankers' bank

Although the BIS dates back to 1930, it really got involved with the management of private banking only in the 1970s. Two dramatic bank failures in 1974 spotlighted the problems. One, already mentioned, was the Franklin National Bank in New York with big Euro-currency trading in London. These speculative operations had fallen between the two stools of British and American bank supervisors. Rightly or wrongly, but to maintain confidence, both decided on an expensive rescue operation in which the FDIC put up $2 billion and a syndicate of European banks took over the business – while the owner, Robert Sindona, was eventually gaoled for fraud and larceny (Spero 1979).

158

The other failure, of Bankhaus Herstatt, was more accidental than criminal, although it too came about through currency speculation. Rather than have Herstatt default on millions of dollars of deals falling due in New York on 26 June 1974, the German bank supervisors abruptly closed it down at 3.30 p.m. German time. The Bundesbank stopped clearing trades done by Herstatt. Its US agent, Chase Manhattan Bank, refused to honour Herstatt's debts, sending panic warnings to the New York foreign exchange market. Daily clearings dropped in three days from $60 billion to $36 billion. The interbank market virtually closed its doors to many small banks. Big arguments ensued over whose fault it was and who was to pay the creditors. The Bundesbank was criticised for acting too slowly and in disregard of the time difference with New York markets. It acted to compensate the depositors, but the damage to the interbank market was less easy to repair (Deane and Pringle 1994: 153–5).

The result the following September was a statement by the Group of Ten central bankers that they were aware of the lender-of-last-resort problem and had decided to set up a committee, which came to be known (after its first chairman, Peter Cooke) as the Cooke Committee or, more formally, the Basle Committee on Banking Supervision. The first Basle Concordat purporting to settle the question of who was responsible for what was negotiated and agreed in 1975.[1] As Joan Spero shrewdly observed, although this was a big step forward, 'Because of national differences and the competitive dynamic of international banking, international management remains limited to informal consultative processes' (Spero 1979: 191).

And so it proved. The principle of the 1975 Concordat looked simple enough. When banks operated abroad, the authorities in their home base were responsible for their overall conduct. Their foreign operations were the responsibility of the 'host' authorities. Each should exchange relevant information with the other. Fine. Except that, in practice, there were grey areas where each thought the other was in charge. There were also countries whose regulatory requirements on banks allowed them to withhold important information from the regulators. And there were the tax havens, inviting banks to find the loopholes in the Concordat.

One such was the Banco Ambrosiano. In 1982, the body of its president was found hanging beneath Blackfriars Bridge in London. The bank had uncovered debts of $1.3 billion. Most of these were incurred by its holding company registered in Luxembourg, so that while the Bank of Italy came to the rescue of the parent bank, it argued that responsibility for the holding company's debts lay not with Italy but Luxembourg. But Luxembourg had a monetary union with

Belgium and had no central bank of its own. The Cooke Committee's response was a revised Concordat in 1983. This made parent banks responsible for supervising holding companies, whether at home or abroad, which might, as in Ambrosiano's case, own other banks and insurance firms. If the parent's central bank thought these were not properly supervised, it should close them down (Deane and Pringle 1984: 157–8; Gurwin 1983).

Peter Cooke had declared Ambrosiano a 'wholly exceptional case'. So it was: banking disasters usually are. And despite the amended Concordat, it was not the last. The fraudulent and corrupt Pakistani-owned Bank of Commerce and Credit International, operating out of Luxembourg, registered for tax purposes in the Cayman Islands, had escaped supervision for years. The story came out only in 1991, when it was abruptly closed (Kochan and Whittington 1991). Other costly disasters were dealt with by national governments – Continental Illinois in the United States in 1984;[2] a German bank, SMH, that over-lent against the rules to a risky construction business the previous year and was kept afloat until sold to Lloyds Bank; the subsidiaries of Johnson Matthey rescued by the Bank of England. These and other examples showed up the growing gaps in central bank supervision. Banks were driven even in the 1980s by growing competition to branch into new and risky business, to engage in 'off-balance-sheet' activities that earned fat fees but not through regular banking business, and one way or another to get round or ignore the regulations.

But it was not these which moved the BIS into a new phase in its guardian role. Instead of getting agreement between central banks as to their respective responsibilities, it moved towards agreement on common rules that should apply to the banks under their control. This was the essence of the 1988 Concordat, which agreed capital adequacy standards to ensure that all banks should have reserves sufficient for their assets (i.e. loans) in case these should lose value. The initiative for the change came not from Basle but from the US Congress. Beginning in 1983, the Fed was under political pressure from US banks to make sure, through international agreement, that they were not unfairly handicapped in competitive international business. Foreign banks, it was argued, should be made to observe the same rules on capital adequacy as US banks. This political pressure, which eventually resulted in a new Basle Agreement in 1988, overrode the doubts of many practising bankers that national regulations could be made to converge on what a bank could count as its 'capital'. The agreement in Basle was preceded by bilateral agreements: Paul Volcker first got support from Britain and then from a reluctant Japan.

The Japanese system, as described in the previous chapter, provided much more solid support from the state than the somewhat unpredictable US system. To increase their reserves to meet the 8–1 Basle standard meant that Japanese banks had to cut back on their lending while putting more profits aside to increase their capital. Although it was not always declared openly, many Japanese thought the 1988 Concordat was little more than a clever American ploy to get their own back on Japanese banks for the success of Japanese export industries in world markets. Some even thought it contributed to the bursting of the bubble economy in 1990 and the subsequent long recession in Japan. It certainly did not improve political relations between the two countries (see chapter 3).

For the next eight years, the Cooke Committee did all it reasonably could to reconcile the contradictions between bank practice and national regulation concerning capital adequacy. Was it to apply to all banks, or only those that traded internationally? How was a bank's capital to be rated and defined? These were only two of many problems of interpretation.

> The Basle Committee is continuously trying to refine its capital rules and to iron out anomalies, to close loopholes and to extend their coverage to capture trading and other risks as well as credit risk. The banks respond in age-old fashion: they devise ways to circumvent or minimise the impact of the rules. With the help of lawyers, they can repackage some of their assets into channels that escape or at least reduce the reserves that must be set against them by Basle rules. They can also deliberately direct their new lending to categories ranked low in risk. (Deane and Pringle 1994: 164)

By 1996, the BIS had virtually thrown in the towel on capital adequacy rules. It abandoned, in effect, the whole idea of agreed common standards of banking supervision. This virtual U-turn is not easily perceived by reading its annual reports, which naturally concentrate on the institution's positive achievements. The BIS general manager, Andrew Crockett, however, in an unofficial study has explained why a policy that had been developing for twenty years was finally abandoned (Crockett 1997). No regulatory system, he observed, was perfect, and applying standard rules to banks in very divergent national banking systems encountered all sorts of difficulties and dilemmas. Classification of a bank's assets into categories with different capital requirements, as the BIS had tried with its two-tier categories of capital assets, had proved arbitrary and could even be counterproductive. Much depended on the borrower – small or large – and on the degree of diversification of a bank's lending. Worldwide standards were very hard to agree and even harder to enforce. Common capital adequacy standards, by implication, were not to be depended on.

Henceforward, therefore, the BIS would depend on its powers of persuasion, especially over the regulators in countries in Asia and Latin America that had not so far belonged to its exclusive club. By expanding its membership it hoped to get support for the *25 Core Principles of Effective Banking Supervision*, published in April 1997. The hope was that central banks, in their country's national interest, would recommend these core principles to the banks in their care. By persuading them of the value of enhanced disclosure requirements and by getting financial intermediaries to mark their portfolios to market (i.e. to price them at current market values), banks, non-banks and other financial actors would acquire the knowledge, expertise and incentive to put their own limits on the risks they ran, according to the kind of business they did, the counterparties they dealt with and the strength of their reserves (Crockett 1997). It remained to be seen, of course, whether enlightened self-interest would overcome the pursuit of profit in such a highly competitive business as banking – especially in emerging markets.[3]

To some extent, circumstances beyond its control were in any case forcing the BIS willy-nilly to change its previously rather Euro-centric image. The EU, in setting up the European Monetary Institution – the precursor to a European central bank – in Frankfurt, had effectively moved out of the Basle office which had been its base since the early 1970s. The move gave the BIS an opportunity to expand not only its membership but in another direction altogether – that of insurance. Here was another market which hitherto had been regulated nationally but which, thanks mainly to pressure from the United States, was becoming international as states allowed foreign insurers to compete with local ones.

There are also technical matters on which the BIS can act as a useful promoter and source of technical advice. For example, in 1990, the Group of Ten central banks agreed minimum standards for interbank settlements and these have gradually been adopted. With the help of advances in the necessary electronic technology, by 1996 the Group of Ten's Committee on Payment and Settlement Systems was able to propose some further improvements to trading in foreign exchange, derivatives and securities. Traditionally, clearing between banks was left to the end of each working day. As the Herstatt case had shown long ago, time zone differences could create problems between the time at which the buyer settled its account and the time at which the seller received the funds. One failure to settle on time could conceivably start a chain of others, putting the system in jeopardy. It is now likely that electronic technology will bring to most of the world's financial centres a system of real-time gross settlement, by which all interbank transfers will take place automatically and at once.

What all this added up to was that the BIS was still needed, as a forum, as a sophisticated central data resource for central banks and others, and increasingly as a means by which fragile banking systems in emerging markets could be brought into the consultative circle. When crises struck – as they certainly would – the hot-lines constantly open between regulators linked to the BIS were one way in which the speed of response to markets could be matched – or nearly so – by the speed of political decision making.[4]

The IMF – how many lifeboats?

By the late 1990s, while the BIS was effectively abdicating regulatory authority to the banks themselves, the IMF was increasingly acting as the world's lender of last resort. It was launching and equipping financial lifeboats to a number of Asian as well as Latin American countries, confident that it could always find the necessary funding. In the summer of 1997, the United States made it clear that this was what it wanted, rather than let the Asian countries manage their own system of mutual support. It may be that in the long run this was not a wise decision. It might have been better to leave it to the Asians, so that when their combined resources were overwhelmed – as they probably would have been – by the markets, some hedge funds and others would have been unable to get their money back. The international financial system could have survived such a *de facto* default just as it had survived the *de facto* defaults of the Ottoman and Chinese empires and of the USSR after the 1917 revolution.

For it was one thing for the IMF to act with the World Bank in Africa as a neo-colonial overseer of national policies supposedly aiming at structural adjustment. The funds involved were relatively small and the risks to the Fund and the World Bank were consequently easily manageable. If the structural adjustment programmes seldom achieved their goals, it was mostly the Africans who suffered. Sending large lifeboats to Asia was quite another matter. Once launched, the donor inevitably lost political leverage. The support funds were committed but the power of IMF missions to change the way the Asian economies were politically managed was open to question. Louis Pauly's thoughtful study of the evolution of multilateral surveillance over national economies, from the League of Nations to the IMF, reveals a

deep scepticism about the IMF's role (Pauly 1997: chs 6 and 7).[5] It may
– for a while – command the financial resources but whether it has the
human resources and the political leverage to make its deals in east
Asia stick is far more doubtful. Indeed, there is a chilling analogy here
with the US experience in Vietnam in the 1960s. The IMF may have
been pushed by the US Treasury into biting off more than it can chew,
just as the US military was pushed by Presidents Kennedy and Bush
into doing the same. The military had the necessary financial and
technological resources. But – like the IMF missions in Korea or
Thailand – it lacked the necessary political legitimacy. To see how this
has come about, an historical perspective on the evolution of the IMF's
role in international finance is necessary and instructive.

The IMF likes to present itself as an organisation set up with wise
forethought in the 1940s and whose development since then has
followed a consistent path. Continuity, it suggests, has marked its
expanding importance in the world market economy. That is not
exactly true. It is an institution that has happened to be there, available
to do different things at different times. Its role today is not at all what
it was supposed to be at Bretton Woods. But as the Belgian trotskyist
Ernest Mandel remarked, 'If the IMF hadn't existed, it would have had
to be invented' (Strange 1986: 94). Its history in this context is
important only for the clues it can offer to its actual and potential role
today and tomorrow. The question is whether it is adequate to the
demands being made upon it, or whether constraints that emerged in
the past will still limit its effectiveness. To be brief, it has passed
through three incarnations, interspersed with periods in which it
existed thanks only to inertia – and an income (from banking)
independent of its member states. For the first decade after 1947, it
was inactive, waiting in the wings for the convertibility of European
currencies in 1958 to inaugurate the fixed exchange rate system devised
at Bretton Woods. That system was abandoned by the United States in
August 1971, when Nixon broke the link with gold and allowed the
dollar to float (i.e. sink against the yen and the mark). It was formally
buried in favour of generally floating rates in 1973, putting the IMF
in another limbo in which it had no real role. Its purpose had been to
provide short-term financing for countries experiencing balance-of-
payments problems that jeopardised their fixed exchange rates. If there
were no fixed rates, the drawing rights on the IMF should not be
needed and its oversight of their use had no justification.

But international institutions do not easily leave the world stage. In
the IMF's case, the problems arising for the LDCs brought its second
incarnation. These arose first after 1974 from the oil price rise and
then after 1981 from the rise in interest rates triggering the debt crisis

of the 1980s.[6] HIPCs, unable to pay the interest on their foreign debts, let alone the capital, went for help (when all else failed) to the IMF. The IMF's help went not to those most in need, nor to those with the best record of observing IMF rules – but to those whose predicament was most likely to jeopardise the stability of the international system (Pauly 1997: 115).

The third incarnation for the IMF overlaps with the second but has more far-reaching implications. It is as launcher and skipper of financial lifeboats to governments – like that of Thailand or South Korea – whose troubled banks are spreading contagion to stock markets abroad as well as at home. Although this is the role that thrust the IMF more than ever into the international limelight in the late 1990s, it is one that dates back to the early 1960s. It was then that the ground rules were hammered out on when, and on what terms, the IMF could acquire the funds necessary for it to act as global lender of last resort.

Bargaining about the ground rules was preparatory to an innovation in 1962 called the General Arrangement to Borrow (GAB – *not* General Agreement to Borrow). It was mainly between the United States and France, backed by the Dutch and Belgians. They were the protagonists; the IMF itself played little part, although it was the beneficiary inasmuch as its contributed resources – the members' quotas of gold, hard currency and national currencies – were almost doubled by the GAB, although only under negotiated conditions. The idea that the IMF could intermediate – like a real bank, by borrowing funds that it could lend where necessary – came from one of the great creative minds in matters of international finance, This was Ed Bernstein, first Research Director at the IMF and a major loss to it when he resigned in the late 1950s. In 1959, in a Harvard seminar, he broached the idea of the IMF using borrowed money, perhaps by issuing bonds like the US government (Strange 1976: 107). Over the next year or so, the IMF's limited resources came to be a hot issue on account of Britain drawing on it so heavily that, by 1961, the IMF's cupboard, like Mother Hubbard's, was pretty well bare.

Sterling was the first line of defence for the dollar, so US negotiators quickly began bargaining with the reluctant French about the terms on which the other rich countries would agree to replenish it. General de Gaulle and his advisers in Paris already believed the Bretton Woods system and the IMF gave the United States, as the world's major reserve currency country, an exorbitant privilege over others. It was only after a good deal of haggling that they agreed to subscribe to a pool of currencies on which the IMF could draw, but only if the Europeans collectively decided it was necessary. Before that, under the

IMF's articles of agreement, only the United States had had the power of veto over IMF decisions. This delicate bargain, expressed informally in an exchange of letters between the Governor of the Bank of France and the IMF, not only put limits on US control of IMF operations, but it also diffused power from Washington to Paris, to the other signatories of the GAB – henceforward called the Group of Ten and their working parties in the Paris-based OECD (Strange 1976: 105–17, 121–4).

After the Mexican rescue in 1995, it was evident that the GAB was both inadequate to needs and politically obsolete inasmuch as it was a US–European deal rather than a global one.[7] A New Arrangement to Borrow was going to be needed. But how big would it have to be? On paper, the IMF had resources of some $200 billion. But at least half of this was in currencies no one wanted. Most of the other half was committed to Asian bailouts. Would the US government be able to persuade the Congress to agree to increased quotas so that it had resources enough for future lifeboats? What if India and Brazil both needed help at the same time? Sometimes – as in the Thai case – the IMF is asked only to top up bilateral contributions from regional neighbours. But there is no certainty these will always be forthcoming without a New Arrangement to Borrow. As in 1962, those who contribute to it might demand an individual or collective right of veto. How could this be arranged? At the time of writing, such broad questions were still under consideration in Washington, and presumably in Tokyo and the European capitals. Meanwhile, each lifeboat had to be designed *ad hoc* and launched quickly in crisis conditions.

The initial ASEAN proposals for rescues for Thailand and Indonesia showed that there was some political support for regional lifeboats – an Asian solution for a problem brought to Asia by fickle western investors and wicked western speculators like George Soros – that at least was the view at first taken by Malaysia's Mahathir. For Thailand, the IMF's contribution of $4 billion to the first $17 billion package was more a token of support and approval. But the size of South Korea's crisis swung opinion away from regional rescues. Only the IMF, swayed as it was by US strategic as well as financial concerns, could be expected to find a lifeboat large enough. In 1983, it was Japan that had unilaterally decided to help Seoul avoid having to go to the IMF. A $3 billion loan sufficed. This time, Korea was asking for $20 billion and even this soon proved not to be enough.

Thus, while the problems of and demands on the IMF have multiplied, the basic political constraints on its role have not. The consent and cooperation of national governments to any New Arrangement to Borrow or to any extension of the IMF's powers as lender of last resort are as necessary today as they were in 1962. In essence, the ground rules have not changed. And they are important because the IMF, as lender of last resort, is not like a national central bank which is backed by the power of the state to command, to create credit ('print money' so to speak) and to punish or close down recalcitrant private enterprises. As Pauly's historical analysis of the IMF's efforts at multilateral surveillance showed, even when its members gave it money – increased quotas, special drawing rights, enhanced facilities of various kinds – they did not – could not – give it power to control either the fiscal policies of states or the conduct of banks and markets (Pauly 1997). Pauly makes the useful distinction between *accountability* – the obligation on all its members to consult and explain, implicit in the whole concept of multilateral surveillance – and the *responsibility* which each of the members by virtue of the international political system owes only to its own citizens (Pauly 1997: 141). The record of IMF missions to some of the weakest, most incompetent, divided or corrupt governments amply demonstrates the point. In Zaire, in Kenya, in Egypt or in Russia, the IMF can advise and propose. But in the final analysis it is only the country's political leaders who dispose. Moreover, history shows that the governments of the IMF's leading members are easily distracted from the problems of the international financial system by their domestic difficulties. When these are acute, as in America in 1933 or Japan in 1997, or indeed Germany in 1990, international cooperation tends to be put on the back burner.

The IMF also suffers from other limitations on its role as guardian. It is accustomed to dealing with governments, with finance ministry officials who often share professional and ideological mind sets with staff missions and are therefore inclined to cooperate. Take the IMF's involvement with Britain in the 1970s, for instance. Both the Treasury and the Bank of England welcomed the conditions that the IMF imposed in return for support of sterling – limits on domestic credit expansion and public spending. Though neither were welcome to some Labour ministers, Chancellor of the Exchequer Denis Healey was able to insist that the government at least tried to comply. But supervising banks and securities houses is a very different kettle of fish, as fraud squads and any national regulatory officials would readily agree. Yet that is precisely what the conditions imposed by Asian lifeboats ask the IMF to do – to impose conditions and demand disclosure of information on non-performing loans granted to political cronies and on commitments to invest in lavish state projects, as in Malaysia.

Consider some of the changes in financial systems that the IMF missions will be asked to deal with. To begin with, banks everywhere have become much more vulnerable than in the past to competition from non-banks (see chapter 2). As their protecting Chinese walls crumbled and non-banks took deposits and business from them, they have been tempted to engage in riskier trading. At the same time, bank supervisors in many countries, led by the United States, lowered the standards applicable to banks, for the sake of equally regulating banks and securities businesses (Dale 1994: 175). The analytical question is whether, when banks go into the securities business, they are any different to non-banks. The old assumption was that banks are more vital to the general economy and therefore need closer support and supervision. The issue then is whether this is still so (Dale 1994: 192–3). There follows a strategic and political issue, which is whether to relax the rules for banks in the interest of fairness or tighten the rules for securities firms for the sake of safety. Is the IMF really qualified to take what is essentially this highly political decision?

Secondly, banks are vulnerable to their managers and to their employees. Rogue traders like Nick Leeson, indulging in complex derivative trading, can bring down a bank like Barings. Now that the BIS has effectively concluded that banks must monitor their own business, the analytical question is whether managers are competent to do so – and whether, as suggested by the 1995 case of Daiwa in the United States, either they or their state regulators are willing to do so. The issue is whether the hands-off strategy will work or whether to look for some more radical alternative. Doubt arises first over the ability of internal bank supervisors to keep up with accelerating technological change in finance (see chapter 2); second, with the willingness of bank managers in emerging markets like Thailand or China to exercise the same prudential control as might be expected of an American or European bank. One of the conditions of IMF rescue funds is financial reform. But whether in practice IMF missions have the expertise and the coercive power to enforce adequate disclosure by Asian banks seems highly questionable.

As to rogue traders or dishonest or dissembling managers, modern societies have few alternatives to imprisonment on criminal charges. Even if this can be made to stick against cunning defence lawyers, Mike Milken's experience in gaol is not much of a deterrent to others. The Victorian sanction of public shame and social isolation requires a shared morality that is inconceivable in today's world. Perhaps only a financial catastrophe causing widespread suffering and loss could bring about a change of opinion on how society should treat financial crime. The tax haven issue will be a good test of how far political attitudes are, or are not, changing (see chapter 7).

Other international bodies

Another part of the problem of shifting erstwhile national regulatory responsibilities on to the international bureaucracies is that there are too many of them. Too many cooks spoil the broth – and especially so if each is cooking from a different recipe book. For example, the WTO has been charged – on US insistence – with seeking international agreement on the liberalisation of financial services. What this does, as experience in Brazil and other countries has shown, is to increase competition and with it risk taking. Not everyone agrees that the efficiency gains from increased competition outweigh the security risks in the operation of deregulated financial markets (Key 1998).

The EU's concern with creating a single market in financial services as a necessary complement to the single European currency adds further complications. It also highlights the political obstacles in the path of coordination of banking regulation between states – what Story and Walter (1997) describe without exaggeration as 'the battle of the systems'. They describe how the rhythm of British policy came, early on, to be driven by crucial decisions reached not in Europe but in the United States. London in the 1960s, as recounted in the last chapter, became the market for Euro-currencies and later, after the lifting of exchange controls in 1979, the leading market for Euro-securities, which was one of the growth businesses of the 1980s. As much as half the shares traded in London came to be foreign, mostly German and Japanese. The Big Bang of deregulation in 1986 was not simply the expression of Conservative ideology. By it, Britain hoped to join New York and Tokyo as the third leg in global financial trading (Story and Walter 1997). The strong trader in financial services, as in other things, is always the free trader, as Friedrich List argued in the last century (List 1841). The British found allies against French and Italian protection in the European Commission, and in the Dutch, in Luxembourg of course, and in German banks and the government. The Commission's Second Banking Directive – agreed finally in 1989 – had two aims: to help Europe keep up with the United States and Japan in financial services, and to provide the financial foundation for the Single Market. But in the convoluted bargaining that went on throughout the 1990s over its interpretation, allies on one issue became opponents on others. There was no stable political background to the regulatory argument. As on many other issues in Europe, the shared vision of a united Europe coexisted with strong national rivalries and conflicts of economic interest. This produced anomalies and uncertainties, grey areas of overlapping authority between the BIS and the EU, and yet another reason why a worldwide system of financial regulation remained a forlorn dream.[8]

BIS, IMF, IBRD, EU – the alphabet soup of international bureaucracies is even thicker than that. The OECD is another minor but not negligible player. In the 1960s, when the Bretton Woods fixed exchange rate system was under pressure from the markets, the OECD occupied more of the limelight than either the BIS or the IMF. Its Working Party 3 was where Europeans and Americans met to discuss balance-of-payments problems arising between them and how to deal with them.[9] Since 1972, however, Working Party 3 faded from the picture but the OECD has had its Financial Markets Committee and since 1980 a Group of Banking Experts.

Nor is that all. There are semi-official and non-official organisations each with their own ideas and concerns. One is IOSCO. Originally an inter-American network between the US SEC and its counterparts not only national but provincial, as in Canada, it was enlarged in 1986 and established with a small secretariat. Its declared aims are to exchange information among regulators, establish standards and monitor their implementation, and provide mutual assistance to those ends. It reflects the same sort of shared professional concerns that made the International Association of Bond Dealers draw up their own rules regarding settlement times, contract forms and so on when governments failed to regulate the growing global business in bond trading. But, of course, unless backed by the authority of national governments, its recommendations count for little. And, as Geoffrey Underhill has pointed out, IOSCO has been the means for private interests to dominate public purpose:

> The closed nature of the policy communities and the growing dependence of regulators and supervisors on private market interests has meant that regulatory standards are increasingly aligned to the preferences of the largest global market players.... There is in fact in the global financial order an ongoing tension between the need for efficient crisis management and preventive regulation and the need for more open consideration of the financial policy options open to states ... [there is] the old dilemma concerning a sustainable balance between particularistic interests and wider public concerns. (Underhill 1997: 43)

Another unofficial organisation, rather more pretentious, is the so-called Group of Thirty. This started in New York in the 1980s as a think-tank but got the ready support of former central bankers and distinguished economists. Recently, one of its working parties, jointly chaired by a former US Comptroller of the Currency and the nominal head of a major British bank, came out with a report making a virtue of the BIS's necessity. Far from the retreat from common banking standards being a setback, this report argued that self-supervision by banks was actually more efficient. The markets would make it so. 'The speed and complexity of innovation in the markets, the supervisors' inevitable position behind the curve and their real handicaps in competing for talented staff all argue for private institutions to take on the responsibility' (Heimann and Alexander 1997). In case anyone might think this sounded like asking the poachers to take on the conservation of game birds, the rather specious argument was that a large bank, known to be strictly self-regulated, would gain a competitive advantage over more easygoing competitors. The more probable reason for this sudden enthusiasm for self-regulation was that large internationally active banks found that regulators were often uninformed and wasted everybody's time. Risk management was their business.

Ideas from the experts?

So it seems that the international institutions have not got all the answers – because they have largely given up, like the BIS, or because they probably lack the expertise and resources, like the IMF, or because they are split by internal conflicts, like the EU, or just because they are falling over each other in a disorganised free-for-all.

What about the experts, the academic social scientists and public policy people – have they come up with any bright ideas? Bright, perhaps but also, in many cases, specious or naively silly ones. Out of a great number, I will select only two. It is enough to show how easy it is, for economists especially, to confuse what should be with what could be, and how even experts who ought to know better can mislead the reader into thinking there are simple technical or institutional solutions to difficult political problems of financial regulation. One is the proposal for a universal international banking standard. Another is the proposal for international arrangements for the management of bankrupt states with insufficient resources to service or repay foreign debts, whether to private or public sources of credit.[10]

Professor Morris Goldstein of the Washington-based Institute for International Economics has proposed an ambitious scheme. His suggested international banking standard would – if implemented – have the agreement of developed and developing country governments and would set standards for accounting, put limits on state banks and government interference, and offer deposit insurance to bank customers on the US model, thus going far beyond the range of bank supervisors in most countries. Like the Federal Reserve System, Goldstein's international banking standard would operate a two-tier system, but it would be governments not banks who signed up. Yet it would be banks who would be supposed to keep the rules. Who would see that they did so? Goldstein proposes a combination of the IMF and the World Bank (Goldstein 1997). Although the author protests he does not see his international banking standard as a panacea or a sufficient solution to lax and corrupt banking practice, he nevertheless urges governments to 'get on with the job as a matter of urgency'. They have not done so, and for three good reasons. There is not sufficient agreement on the nature of the problem, nor on how a safe financial system ought to work, nor on how agreement in principle could be administered in practice (Kapstein 1992).

In short, the Goldstein proposal has all the logical flaws of international plans for disarmament or the protection of human rights against abuse. There is a problem (states fight wars with arms; banks run imprudent risks). There is an 'obvious' solution (get rid of the arms by international agreement; set international standards for banks to observe). It also, incidentally, somehow assumes that the solutions that work in the United States, like deposit insurance paid for by all banks and the taxpayer, can be made to work all over the world. And it ignores the experience of Asian societies that government direction and management of credit have had rather good results on the whole and perhaps should not be lightly abandoned, and certainly not before regulatory institutions to control the banks have been set up.

Another naive idea is for an international bankruptcy court to arbitrate between creditors when a sovereign debtor cannot honour its debts. The notion was first broached by Jeffry Sachs in 1995 but has been taken up at the Institute for International Economics by John Williamson and more recently by Marcus Miller (Miller and Zhang 1997). Now the essence of bankruptcy since the nineteenth century has been to interpose legal authority between the debtor and creditors by giving power to an appointed receiver over the debtor's assets. In other words, there has to be a legitimate political power backed by the state. The purpose, as Miller says, is to prevent an unseemly grab by creditors for the debtor's remaining assets, in order that either another enterprise can take over the business or that it can be wound up and dissolved in an orderly fashion. There is no analogy with the plight of an insolvent sovereign state, although there have been plenty of such cases in history – Tsarist Russia, the Ottoman empire, the Manchu regime in China, and many, many others more recently. How have other states reacted and why? The only cases in which insolvent sovereign debtors have been, in effect, 'put into receivership' have been small, poor, weak states and/or ones in which great powers have had a strong strategic interest. Examples would include Caribbean republics submitted to customs house takeovers by the US Marines in the 1900s, Egypt in the 1880s taken into Anglo-French condominium, Germany and Japan under occupation after 1945. None of these was done by international agreement. Even the administration of Austria or Hungary by the League of Nations in the 1920s was arranged bilaterally and again for strategic reasons by the British and French (Pauly 1997: 52–6). And there were many more cases in recent times when the motivation behind the treatment of sovereign insolvency has not been to restrain the creditors from acting like vultures, but to safeguard the system by preserving the fiction that the debtor was not in fact insolvent and would not continue forever to default on its debts. Neither the legal framework nor the political will for an international bankruptcy court exists and no amount of fancy algebra based on the false analogy with corporate debt can get over this fundamental truth.

An alternative suggestion, for a bondholder's council charged with negotiating the reconstruction of sovereign debt, is more plausible (Eichengreen and Portes 1996).[11] But politically it is unlikely to win acceptance for the obvious reason that the political motivations of the governments of major creditors are neither predictable nor consistent. This was so in Palmerston's time and is still true today. Thus each rescheduling deal since the 1950s has had to be individually negotiated among the creditors. The Paris Club and the London Club are the furthest states have been prepared to go to institutionalise the handling of sovereign debt (see chapter 6; also Prout 1976).

To go on examining similar academic blueprints for new institutions would be a time-consuming and barren exercise. The historian would be reminded of all those long-forgotten schemes, drawn up mostly by idealistic lawyers in the 1930s, for reforming the League of Nations so as to transform it into a real guarantor of international peace. Guaranteeing international financial peace and stability is a similarly worthy objective. But in the 1990s, as in the 1930s, a great many utopian dreams are apt to hinder more than they help. By encouraging people to dream about the ideal world, they distract them from doing what can be done in the real world.

That cannot so easily be said of James Tobin's proposed turnover tax on foreign exchange transactions (Tobin 1990). The idea has attracted interest if not much political support (Grunberg 1996). The aim would be to discourage those speculative transactions made possible by futures trading without discouraging productive foreign direct investment. There is no doubt that the volume of foreign exchange deals that are actually necessary for purposes of trade or investment are completely dwarfed by those made in the hope of speculative profit. One doubt is whether the would-be profiteers are likely to be deterred by a tax of just a few per cent on their deals. The other is whether, without reinstating exchange controls, the authorities could in practice collect the tax in view of the advanced technologies now available for short-term financial trading.[12]

Another radical notion would be to get multilateral agreement on a modern, updated version of Henry Simon's concept of 'narrow banks'. His *Economic Policy for a Free Society* (1948) suggested that only 'narrow banks' should be licensed to take deposits and pay out on customers' accounts. They would hold reserves equal to 100 per cent of their loan liabilities and could make only very safe investments. The notion was regarded favourably by Milton Friedman, James Tobin and James Pierce (Crockett 1997: 30). Crockett explains that the idea of narrow banks has not found favour because depositors would get a very inferior rate of interest to what they could get from other commercial banks. Yet it corresponds in practice to Japan's Post Office Savings Bank and to some kinds of national savings banks. In a period of rising financial turmoil, it seems possible that popular preferences might shift against high interest rates and in favour of greater security. At that point, an old idea, like the Tobin tax, might be taken down off the shelf, dusted off and looked at afresh.

There is also the concept of deposit insurance as a means of maintaining confidence in the financial system in times of trouble. At present, this is organised on a national basis, either informally in an *ad hoc* manner, as in Japan, or through a state-sponsored institution like the US FDIC. In either case, governments have to find the funds to back it up. In view of the problems of financial contagion, as experienced in recent years, a multilaterally funded and managed deposit insurance institution for all small bank customers throughout the world might seem the logical solution. But its financing and management, and protection against fraud, would present so many problems that this does not seem a practical idea.

Crockett (1997) also discusses the contribution of enhanced disclosure standards, making banks reveal more about their trading, so that prudent customers can have enough information to avoid dealing with banks that take undue risks. He concludes, correctly in my view, that this is not a sufficient strategy for greater stability. Experience in fields like smoking or drink driving suggests that making information available to people does not ensure that they act on it. The information that banks might be made to reveal, moreover, is likely to be out of date. Customers would find it very hard – and extremely time consuming – to monitor risk day by day and week by week. The Baring's story alone shows that even the management of the bank, with access to information on Leeson's dealings in Japanese derivatives, did not act on it until it was too late.

There are very few examples so far of preventive action by states to insulate private or public actors from contagious volatility. Deposit insurance has been mentioned. There have also been efforts to protect public authorities from the risks of volatile markets. For example, the House of Lords, acting as court of appeal, ruled in 1991 that the treasurers of British local government could not invest in interest rate swap agreements. In view of the losses subsequently incurred by California's Orange County managers, this was a wise decision. It was probably taken because so many local authorities in Britain had earlier incurred large losses, which they could not afford, by borrowing on Euro-currency markets on the rash assumption that exchange rates would not change. Ben Steil comments, however, that the decision caused big losses to over seventy British and foreign banks which had been making profits out of the trading (Steil *et al.* 1996).

Another device, introduced in some national markets after the 1987 stock market slide, was the so-called circuit breakers. These automatically suspended dealing when, by agreed measures, prices moved too far and too fast. In some circumstances, this cooling-off period can have a calming effect; in others, some argue that it can be counterproductive, merely building up the pressure like steam in a boiler.

The fact is that in the late 1990s circumstances change too fast where the governance of international finance is concerned. In the early 1990s, it might have been still possible to believe, with Ethan Kapstein, that a two-tier framework for governing global financial markets had been developed in which the regulatory systems of nation states at the lower level were complemented by international cooperation – as through the IMF and the BIS – at the upper level.

> States have pursued international agreements as part of an ongoing effort to reconcile their prudential and competitive concerns; in the absence of such cooperation a regulatory 'race to the bottom' might occur. At the same time, given that central banks remain national in character, regulatory and supervisory agreements are ultimately founded upon the principle of home country control of domestic financial institutions. (Kapstein 1994: 177–8)

This chapter and the previous one suggest that this is no longer true. Kapstein's argument rests on the proposition that 'banks are not extranational actors, but highly regulated firms which must identify the piece of territory they call home'. The evidence tells another story. It is that while they identify with home when they need support, they also seek to escape national regulatory authority whenever there is a chance of profit.[13]

Financial innovation, liberalisation and the sharpened competition between banks and other private enterprises that goes with them have thus upset the delicate balance that Kapstein discerned between interstate and national controls.

A study by the Brookings Institution was much more cautious about the effectiveness of international regulation and the potential for harmonisation of national regulatory systems. Richard Herring and Robert Litan concluded that such harmonisation will not occur 'any time soon' and that the best way to avoid systemic risk without stifling innovation and competition may be 'to place greater emphasis on discipline by the market rather than by regulation' – in effect Andrew Crockett's conclusion (Herring and Litan 1995: 11). Interestingly, they have a good word to say about the concept of narrow banking, mentioned earlier, as a possible solution to the problem of financial conglomerates.

A reliance on the discipline of market forces, whether reluctant or enthusiastic, certainly seems to be the dominant theme in expert opinion at the time of writing. Writing early in 1997, Michel Aglietta, a former radical commentator, discerned the development over the previous five years of a 'market-friendly' approach, taking the place of 'heavy-handed regulation'. Its two core principles, in his view, were that state authorities should recognise the internal control systems developed by private institutions like banks or securities houses; and that for their part the internal supervisors should enforce corrective action in good time, before there is any danger of insolvency. This, he thought, would enable the central bank or other national lender of last resort to move away from the 'too big to fail' syndrome of the past, which had compromised its authority and given rise to problems of moral hazard (Aglietta 1997).[14] Central banks, he argued, would then be free to resume the important role of standing ready to provide liquidity in times of crisis. Put this touching faith beside the record of Crédit Lyonnais in recent years and it looks to me like a triumph of hope over experience.

We even hear the same confidence in market-enforced discipline from Japan. Commenting on Herring and Litan's study, Yasuhiro Maezawa from the Bank of Japan agreed with them that market mechanisms were better than rule making to monitor and discipline banks. Regulators, Maezawa rightly observed, often lagged behind market developments (Herring and Litan 1995: 153 and 161).

Conclusion

This rather brief and necessarily selective survey of current opinion, official and academic, will, I hope, give the reader a fair general picture of how far developments in recent years have changed ideas, analyses and policies. (Not nearly enough, in my view.) It remains, in a final chapter, to say something more about the basic political conflicts in theories of the international political economy that underlie the expert judgements, and to look ahead to the prospects before us. I cannot pretend to know where we are headed, but I can perhaps sketch some of the alternative scenarios that may be imagined. Readers will have to decide for themselves which of these sounds the most plausible.

Notes

1 A typically European concept. Concordats was the name given in the 1920s to informal agreements between Mussolini and the Pope on the respective authority of the Vatican and the Italian state in matters of education, taxation and so on. Like executive agreements in the United States, these Concordats were not to be treated as treaties between governments, yet the parties saw them as binding.

2 It was an expensive rescue, costing $6 billion, in which effectively the government had to nationalise a bank that had allowed an Oklahoma subsidiary to get vastly overextended in oil-related business. The manager's habits – which included coming to work in a Mickey Mouse mask – escaped the notice of the Chicago management.

3 The *Financial Times* has commented editorially that there may be no more than thirty banks in the whole world with the sophistication and discipline to construct and effectively apply credit risk models. That leaves many banks untouched by international standards.

4 Whether the technology available to markets has not run ahead of the capacity of governments or international organisations to respond quickly enough is a good question raised by Javier Santiso (1997).

5 Pauly's conclusion, reflected in the title *Who Elected the Bankers?*, is that unless there is the political collaboration between the major economies necessary and sufficient to maintain 'reasonable economic stability and widening prosperity', the IMF is headed for trouble. 'Even the citizens of leading states will rightly begin asking why they must defer to decisions over which they are losing control, and why the political authorities responsible to them are becoming impotent. At that point, the retreat from global markets will begin' (Pauly 1997: 143).

6 This is an oversimplification. Under US pressure, the IMF had always been available to support sterling and to help Britain out of payments crises (as in 1960, in 1968 and again in 1976). The IMF package given to the Callaghan Labour government in 1968 was an important early test of how effective IMF conditionality and surveillance of national government really was.

7 Surprising though it may seem, Japan was a signatory of the 1962 agreement

even though it was not yet a member of OECD and had at first been excluded from the GATT. European attitudes to Asians had not changed much since the 1920s.

8 The full but complex story of the political economy of recent European efforts to reform/regulate its financial enterprises is told by Story and Walter (1997: chs 9, 10, pp. 250–306).

9 Readers may wonder what happened to Working Parties 1 and 2. Thereby hangs a clue to subsequent history. Working Party 1 was set up to deal with the problem of short-term capital movements. As we know, it is these which have been the destabilising force in the crises of the 1990s, in Mexico, in Thailand and in Korea. It had support neither from the United States nor Britain. It was never appointed. It never met.

10 Although this relates more to international debt questions than to bank regulation, it is indirectly related, since if a state risked being made legally bankrupt it would have a strong incentive to so regulate its banks and financial markets that they did not put it in that danger.

11 See Eichengreen and Portes (1996: 35–7). Their conclusion is quite clear: a bankruptcy court is a 'quite unrealistic' idea.

12 Digital money would certainly make it much easier to evade the Tobin tax (see chapter 2).

13 The argument also claims to be supported by similar and comparable two-tier governance over oil tanker pollution and telecommunications. Neither case holds up: regulation of oil tanker operations is not by flag states reinforced by intergovernmental agreement, but port states' authority, reinforced by the marine insurers' terms. And in the global market for telecommunications services, market competition, as in finance, has recently undermined both the authority of the state and the force of international agreement through the International Telecommunication Union (see Hills 1994).

14 See also Aglietta's longer text, *Macroeconomie financière* (1995). Both contrast somewhat both in tone and conclusions with his earlier works, *Regulation et crises du capitalisme* (1976) and (with A. Orlean), *La Violence de la monnaie* (1982).

Chapter 10

So what?

The only honest answer to the question is that we do not – cannot – know the future. We should not be fooled by those who pretend they can tell what it holds in store. All we can do is to reflect upon the recent – and the more distant – past and try to see some of the general trends that have marked the past decade or so. Beyond that, we also can try to figure out some broad scenarios – possible directions in which the future might develop. That is what the planning units of the big firms already do, to guide the bosses' strategic decisions – the choice between alternative technologies, between alternative locations of production or product development, about alternative strategies for financing them. These are choices they must make – which they cannot put off making, yet which still have to be made in an uncertain environment.

Similarly, to be aware of these scenarios may help us to interpret current events and policy choices by politicians or business leaders. It could help us decide whether this or that piece of news either shortens or lengthens the odds on one broad scenario rather than another. It could also be our only real weapon against giving in to completely passive determinism. Are we going to say, 'What's going to happen is going to happen. Nothing I can do or say is going to stop it. Nobody has any influence whatever on the destiny of the world economy'? If we succumb to that sort of dismal fatalism, we deserve whatever unpleasant fate does lie in store.

For the sake of clarity, let me suggest just five simple conclusions that I believe can be safely drawn from the foregoing account of what has happened to affect money, finance and governments since the mid-1980s.

The first is that 'finance calls the tune', as Cerny put it (Cerny 1993: 4). The real economy of manufacturing, services like entertainment,

179

tourism, transport, mining, farming and retailing – all of it dances to the fast or slow rhythms of financial markets. Already in the 1980s, Peter Drucker, the grandfather of management analysis, saw that finance was the 'driving force', 'the fly-wheel' for the rest of the market economy. Since 1989, that market economy has expanded over the ex-socialist world. It has widened its embrace to take in remote villages and indigenous people like the Amazon Indians who had hitherto been relatively untouched by 'globalisation'.

The second is that governments of states have less control over their economies and societies than they had ten, twenty or thirty years ago. This is still disputed by realist writers in politics and by liberal writers in economics; both are biased in their view of what is by their ideological perspectives of what ought to be.[1] But both are wrong. Chapter 2 showed how the organisation of credit in the world economy has been revolutionised by new ways of marketing credit, new credit instruments and new kinds of financial dealing like derivatives. Governments have had no control over these innovations. They could not be officially patented to stop others copying. Yet states had once asserted rights to control and regulate innovation, even to forbid the export of technology beyond their frontiers.

Taxation, as related in chapter 7, is another big area where states have lost control, where their spending power is beyond their own control, determined by the whims of foreign bondholders and by the agility of their business leaders in using tax havens to pay less. A striking example is Rupert Murdoch, whose News International, incorporated in his native Australia, was making most of its 1997 profit from television, films and broadcasting in the United States. Murdoch's company paid less than 8 per cent of its profit in taxes, compared with an average more than twice as much paid by his rivals, Walt Disney, Time Warner and Viacom.[2]

Organised crime, as also related in chapter 7, is another significant area of retreat by nation states. Whether we take drug trafficking or illegal immigration, we see the forces of both markets overwhelming the efforts, however strenuous, of national police and customs officials. What they catch is just a fraction of what gets through.

Nor is this all. We have seen constraints tightening over state policy making for the economy: not only interest and inflation rates but also employment levels and the financing of national welfare, health and education. All run up against limits set by international finance. In many countries, if not yet the United States, those financial limits are getting tighter, more constraining not less.

The third conclusion concerns mergers and acquisitions. Financial inventiveness has made possible a spate of mergers and acquisitions (see chapter 2, on KKR and other junk bond dealers). Globalisation in the form of increased foreign and local competition has made the survival of firms more hazardous. Although not every merger turns out as profitable as expected, it is the larger enterprises that are less at risk from their competitors. Alliances, permanent or temporary, are part of corporate armouries for survival. This means that the pace of economic concentration in big business has substantially accelerated. We see this in cars, aircraft, pharmaceuticals, insurance, accounting and banking – to name only some important sectors of international business. A side-effect is the dilution of the national identity of business enterprise. The global firm, incorporating local partners, allied with others across technologies, massaging its corporate image as a good citizen of a dozen important national markets, is less beholden to its home government. And this could not have happened without the means to finance takeovers and to grow.

The fourth concerns moral contamination. There has always been some moral ambiguity about financial dealing. The essence of profit in financial business is often information not available to others. Insider trading is everywhere condemned – and everywhere practised. Moreover, the need of big firms for large amounts of credit, whether for investment and development or for a takeover – has opened wide new opportunities for big profits for investment banks and others who can arrange the finance. Big profits, ever more actively competed for in the market, have led to big salaries and extravagant bonuses for the dealers in New York, London and Tokyo. The latter can be many times as large as formal salaries. Cheques for $1 million or so are at the bottom of the upper range; even for the lesser stars, hundreds of thousands come to be seen as the norm. This happens even in years, like 1997, when the media is full of news about the losers.

The point here is not so much that these bonus cheques are obscenely large by normal standards of effort and reward. It is that they have reinforced and accelerated the growth of the links between finance and politics. Firms that have access to large amounts of credit and that make such large profits can afford to bribe politicians and officials as well as to reward employees. Bribery and corruption in politics are not at all new. It is the scale and extent of it that have risen, along with the domination of finance over the real economy. Sleaze, as it has come to be called, in politics is not confined to Asia, the Arab states and the corrupt autocracies of Africa and Latin America. It is a concern of governments in Washington, Tokyo, London and Paris.

The fifth conclusion is that there are widening income gaps. I do not mean only the income gaps between the financial dealers and their office cleaners who creep in at night when the lights go out. It is more than that. There is a widening gap between the resources available to big business and to small and medium enterprises. Everyone has been concerned about this gap for decades past. Nothing much has been done to close it. Unequal access to credit is certainly a feature of the international financial system (see chapter 6). This inequality is not the whole story. But it is a big part of it. And the social consequences – the emergence of an underclass, of homeless people, illiterates and other dropouts from all the national societies of rich countries – are common problems for them all. The alienation of what the French aptly call *les exclus* is made greater by the increasing concentration of wealth at the other end of the social scale. Flagrant conspicuous consumption by the very rich – pop stars, tycoons, financiers, sports stars – is not in itself the problem. But it can become one when growth slows, jobs disappear and times for ordinary people suddenly become very hard. The desperation of the 1930s could be just a small foretaste of social reactions in the twenty-first century.

If I had to give even broader answers to the 'So what?' question, I would pick three ways in which old gaps in power and wealth have widened in recent years. The first would be the above point about rich and poor. It applies between societies as well as within them.

Second would be the widening gap between big business and small business. Big business is favoured by the innovations in finance; small business generally is not. Big business has an increasing influence on state policies and uses it to serve its own interests. Small business becomes increasingly disfranchised in national and international political processes. Critical theorists have predicated the emergence of a transnational capitalist class. I would rather call it a business civilisation, since it is not, as yet, fully class conscious, any more than we can see clearly the nature of the 'global state' they see emerging.

Third, the gap in power and influence between states is also widening. Many more poor, weak, mini-states are getting formal recognition and membership of the UN. Meanwhile, the global reach of the United States is more and more evident. The popular idea of the 1980s was of competition in the triad – between the three power centres of North America, Europe and Japan. Both Japan and Europe are less impressive as power centres today than they were at the end of the 1980s. The supposed decline of US hegemony never was more than a myth and is even more of one today than it used to be.

The open question that remains is about people's ideas and beliefs. That is always the key to political and therefore economic change. The key questions in international political economy are still the crucial ones. Who wins and who loses? Who benefits and who pays? Who gets new opportunities and who is made to run new risks? How people answer those key questions will determine all sorts of future choices. The last two decades of the twentieth century saw the shift from state power to market power, the apparent worldwide victory of neo-liberal ideas in economics over keynesian ones. It is an open question whether that tide is about to turn, or not.

Some scenarios

The one most generally feared is the crash of 1999, 2000, or even 2003. It has been a theme of scare thrillers for at least twenty years. Paul Erdman's *The Crash of '79* was the first but by no means the last. And by late 1997, even quite sober commentators in the financial press, reflecting on the financial typhoon that hit Asian markets that year, were starting to hedge their bets and to say that though the crash might not happen, it *could* happen.

What exactly did they have in mind? As retrospective reviews of 1929 and of 1987 and 1997 all show, the sudden collapse of stock markets almost always follows an 'unnatural' or at least an unsustainable boom – a bubble of some sort that cannot go on rising indefinitely. But 1987 and 1997 also suggested that such bursting bubbles did not necessarily cause permanent damage to the real economy. The question, therefore, if a repeat of the 1929–39 scenario is to be taken seriously, is whether there are conceivable circumstances in which another stock market fall *would* damage the real economy.

There are. They involve an unhappy coincidence of financial and political factors. The financial scenario would have to include large disruptions in the pattern of capital flows in and out of major economies. (Trade flows, as we know now, are secondary in affecting exchange rates between currencies.) The political scenario would have to include conditions in which governments were, for one reason or another, frozen in indecision or too slow to react and therefore failed to act to restore confidence.[3] The combination then sets off a domino effect of fear undermining confidence in the market economy and its ability to maintain credit and therefore purchasing power. Oversupply results from lack of demand.

The sort of payments disruptions that could happen in future would be those between major players – the United States, Japan, China, Russia and the EU. It is possible – although, at the time of writing, rather unlikely – that there could be a massive repatriation of Japanese funds invested abroad and especially in the United States. The survival of the Japanese enterprise would demand liquid funds to avoid insolvency or submersion in another bank or firm. At present, the costs of such repatriation are high and the perceived need for them is not compelling. But that could change. The dollar–yen exchange rate is notoriously volatile.

It is also just possible that when the euro is successfully launched it will become – as many Europeans fondly hope – a rival to the dollar. Funds may therefore shift from the United States into Europe. This, when combined with an outflow westwards to Japan, would so weaken the dollar that US authorities would have to raise interest rates to check it. This could set off a rerun of the early 1980s, when debtors were saddled with far greater burdens of interest than they ever contemplated. Another dim possibility is that the United States would take extreme measures to stop the flow. Recall the US freezing of Iranian, and later Libyan, assets. They were not expropriated, but they could not be taken out of the country. Governments are still capable of forcibly exchanging one kind of transferable, convertible government debt into another with lower interest rates and less mobility. It happened between the wars and although the risks are high, it might be that the US authorities under domestic political pressure would take a chance, convinced that the United States still represented for foreign investors a comparatively safe haven from turmoil and financial chaos.

Build into this scenario trouble from Russia and China. Neither is politically stable. Russia and several other former Soviet states depend on uncertain flows of foreign capital to finance deficits in trade. The IMF's control over an economy still in terrible disarray is doubtful and its financial and human resources are already overstretched. As for China, the boot is on the other foot in that its surplus with the United States is large and rising. Yet its market for American imports is still closed; US firms' branded goods sell in China, on sufferance, but only if made in China.

None of these circumstances would necessarily be fatal to the real world economy. Political factors – both international and, more likely, domestic – could make them so were the two to coincide. In the winter of 1932/3, a US Administration in protracted transition between Hoover and Roosevelt was supposed to be in charge of a faltering economy. By March, when Roosevelt took office, it was arguably almost too late to stop the panic and save the banking system. Another week or two and it might well have been too late. The scenarios of some recent films in which an unscrupulous bureaucracy substitutes an unprepared double for a dead President, or in which the President leaves the White House to lead a defensive raid against invading aliens, are fanciful and far fetched. But accidents and assassinations do happen. Everyone still agrees that US leadership is a *sine qua non* of global economic stability. In a period in which alternative political leadership from the Japanese or the Europeans is patently negated by internal divisions, it is all the more needed. But can it be guaranteed?

The second scenario is less dramatic and for that reason may seem more plausible. It was suggested on the concluding page of *Casino Capitalism*.

> By New Year's Eve on December 31, 1999 … the social consequences of playing Snakes and Ladders with people's lives will have been made only too plain. Only those financial gamblers that still survive in the great office blocks towering over the city centres of the capitalist world will be raising their glasses. For the rest, the American Century will be coming to a mournful and miserable close. (Strange 1986: 193)

In other words, not a crash but a whimper: the deflationary bias of monetarist economic strategies, reinforced by a shrinkage of credit resulting from multiple bank failures or takeovers, will land the world production and trade structures in a vicious circle of falling demand that cannot be overcome by rescue lifeboats or financial innovation. The suggestion at the end of *Casino Capitalism* was that if chronic depression were to stifle the animal spirits of international business, the United States would be the last to suffer. It would be able to enjoy the privileged immunities of its dominant position, military, political and economic. 'It will be able,' I suggested, 'to use its bargaining power as military protector, or as interventionist meddler, or as major trading partner to get its own way and to make others undergo the painful adjustments' (Strange 1986: 193). In the end though, American multinationals could not stay rich for long in an impoverished world. American export and service industries would starve without their foreign customers. Unemployment, falling real wages, would eventually start to hurt politically.

The response generally expected to a prolonged world economic recession is a reversion to economic nationalism and trade protection. Trade blocs, and trade wars, will result, says the conventional liberal economics wisdom. I am sceptical. The only really effective trade bloc to function in the 1930s was something the Germans called the Sperrmark area – the savings mark zone. Devised by the ingenious Hjalmar Schacht at the central bank, it offered debt-struck Balkan countries their one chance of selling primary products that no one else wanted, even at give-away prices. The Germans would buy them – but the condition was that the proceeds would go into a special counter-trading account in 'Sperrmarks' that could be drawn on only for purchases from Germany. Castigated later by Al Hirschman as opening the doors of south-east Europe to the German army, the Sperrmark experiment has been generally ignored. The point of mentioning it here is that it worked because the discriminatory trade concession was backed by Nazi Germany's very tough exchange controls. By comparison, the Ottawa system of trade preferences between Britain and its Commonwealth associates had little effect. Neither British industry nor Commonwealth food producers really benefited. 'Empire free trade' without exchange controls as backup was a political slogan and an economic myth. Paradoxically, it *was* a reality twenty years later, in the 1950s. Then the United States, in the Marshall Plan days, allowed the British to use discriminatory exchange controls to favour sterling area trade over dollar-denominated trade. That ended with convertibility in 1958. But it did work.

Notwithstanding this historical evidence, would not self-defeating beggar-my-neighbour trade policies still be the outcome of a chronic world depression in the 2000s? Very possibly they would. Clinton's failure in 1997 to get a fast-track trade-bargaining deal from the Congress suggests that more and sharper protectionist responses from both the United States and from Europe may lie ahead. But it does not follow that protectionism would be the cause of continuing depression. Rather, it would be a symptom, a knee-jerk response to the depression. If depression becomes chronic, the reason for it – as it was between the two world wars – would be found in finance, not in trade. Recovery would be difficult in the 2000s, as in the 1930s, because financial markets would have shrunk to a shadow, investors would have lost confidence in the future and governments would have tended to discriminate against foreign investments that could hurt fragile national balances of payment and therefore currencies. Recall the investment equalisation tax the United States put on foreign lending in an attempt to keep capital at home. In 1963, it was only of the order of 1 per cent of the investment. What if a new measure imposed a tax of 10 or even 5 per cent?

But are there not more optimistic scenarios to contemplate? And how realistic are they? First, among the greens and in the environmental movement, there is much talk of 'sustainable development'. What this means is that the goal of society should be a world political economy that escapes its dependence on fossil fuels yet continues to produce goods and services sufficient for the needs of a world population that is bound by the momentum of demography to go on growing for two, three or more decades before stabilising. Technically, such a world economy is perfectly feasible. Politically it comes up against powerful interests and unresolved conflicts of interest. As the 1997 Kyoto climate conference showed, developing countries, led by China, strongly resist the demands of developed countries for common standards of pollution control. 'You are asking us, who are poor, to stop doing most of the things that helped you in the past to grow rich. Wait till we are as rich as you before you ask for common standards of environmental protection.' That conflict is not easily resolved in the foreseeable future. And neither diplomatic pressure nor a market-based solution of transferable licences to pollute is going to resolve it. First, the conviction has to grow that the strategy has to be progressive, in that it should take 50 or 60 per cent of the incomes of the rich but only 5 or 10 per cent from those of the poor. And that may take time.

An opposite kind of dream would take us back to the past instead of forwards to a sustainable future. I referred in *Casino Capitalism* to the conclusion reached by the late Fred Hirsch and by a senior IMF economist, Jacques Polak, that a return to national economies, nationally regulated and managed, was the only way out, since international decision making was beyond the capacity of nationally accountable governments (Strange 1986: 189). Hirsch called it 'controlled disintegration'; Polak called it 'decentralised decisionmaking'. Both add up to turning the clock back to a time of strict exchange controls, state intervention in investment and production, and the closing – in effect – of international financial markets and the channels that link them together. Now, it may come to that – but only after an experience of such economic pain that people would accept drastic remedies. History does suggest that human beings find it easier to recreate the past – or to try to – than they do to imagine the future. When the Soviet Union was attacked by Hitler in 1941, Stalin found that an appeal to old-fashioned Russian nationalism worked better than the dream of a socialist future; history, not ideology, moved his people to resist Hitler as they had Napoleon. But today, the question is whether the genie can be put back in the bottle. Is it practicable, given the technology of communication, to turn the clock back in financial markets?

That would seem to be the necessary condition or prelude to realising another utopian dream of post-capitalist capitalism. Robert Heilbroner, the distinguished Professor of Economics at the New School for Social Research in New York, also found prediction impossible and opted, like me, for discussing alternative scenarios. His dream was of what he described as 'participatory capitalism', a world 'in which widely-shared decisionmaking by discussion and vote displaces decisionmaking by self-interest alone, or by persons privileged by wealth or position to make unilateral determinations' (Heilbroner 1992: 117). It sounds good but difficult to organise even at the national level, let alone the global. If the UN assembly is any guide, discussion would be endless, decisions would be rare. And certainly a degree of political devolution, even perhaps to the level of towns or provinces, would be necessary before such a system could take shape. When Sidney and Beatrice Webb wrote about the Soviet Union in the starry-eyed 1930s, there was much description in it of the hierarchy of local soviets, from the apartment buildings to the factory, to the republic and so on. That was what they read in the 1936 constitution of the USSR. The reality was rather different: the dictatorship of the Politburo under tight control of Stalin and the KGB.

In fact, Heilbroner's vision follows in the steps of Joseph Schumpeter, who wrote of the transition of capitalism to a socialist, or socialised, form (Schumpeter 1961). Schumpeter was Austrian and it is not hard to see a connection between his ideas and the neo-corporatist system of economic management of which postwar Austrian governments came to be model protagonists. Nor is it hard to see why his ideas have had a special appeal in Japan, where an Asian version of neo-corporatist economic management was practised. The system, as sociologists have long pointed out, depended on a triad of government, business and organised labour in which none was dominant. Globalisation, though, has significantly enhanced the power of big business and reduced the power of organised labour, except perhaps in public service and a few special jobs like lorry drivers. A Schumpeterian scenario seems less convincing for the twenty-first century than it did for postwar Europe.

So what, again? Is the only conceivable scenario for the future yet more of the same? More inequality, more volatility and nasty surprises, more unchecked pollution as attention fixes on finance? Is there no chance at all of doing more than hoping for the best but expecting and preparing for the worst?

That, surely, is the task for the future for officials, for journalists and especially for academics. They have more time than the journalists and more freedom than the officials to think about the feasible options of what might be done. In earlier chapters, there were two or three ideas briefly mentioned that would be worth closer examination. There are probably more that I have not thought about.

One was the notion that the tax havens should be closed down. That does not seem too hard to do and would surely appeal to many voters in the United States, Japan and Europe. It was pointed out in chapter 7 that there are more of them every year and that their business is growing. That surely contributes to social inequality. Britain's Labour government was embarrassed in 1997 to have to defend, in the same question time in Parliament, a decision to cut welfare for some single parents and the freedom of a Labour minister to salt away a tax-free fortune in the Caribbean.

What would be needed would be agreement by governments of the Group of Ten (or even Seven or Three) on the objective – perhaps closure in three or five years' time – and on the means to do so – perhaps a blacklist of non-conforming banks engaged in transfers from taxed jurisdictions to the untaxed havens. This strategy was developed by the United States to discipline firms into conforming with restrictions on trading with the Soviet Union. It was later applied – against strong protests – to certain firms engaged in business with Cuba.[4]

Another reform that is not totally beyond the realm of the possible was mentioned in chapter 6 – cancellation of the debts of HIPCs. Most of this debt is owed to foreign governments or international organisations. Unlike Japanese banks, they do not need to pretend to be richer than they are by keeping these debts on their balance sheets. Neither have anything to fear from acknowledging that these are bad debts that will never be repaid. Not only are they non-performing, but they never will be anything else. Cancellation might be a first step to a more thoroughgoing revision of the IMF/World Bank oversight of sub-Saharan economies.

In the previous chapter, mention was made of the old concept of narrow banking – of making a category of fully regulated, fully supported large banks that in return for their guaranteed security would be barred from risk-bearing business, including acting on behalf of clients in global financial markets. There are probably not more than forty or fifty banks whose failure would rock the markets. They are 'too big to fail', but at the moment their freedom to do risky deals creates the problem of moral hazard that is so often mentioned in the literature – that is, their too-big-to-fail status actually encourages them to take more risk than they might have done without the status. Some of those banks might prefer independence and some might elect to split in two, leaving the narrow bank the smaller of the divided whole. That smaller limb could certainly be asked to accept Goldstein's international banking standard. Because collective action has been practised in debt and currency crisis situations over recent years, a collective supervision by a new institution would be a formidable but not impossible task. That new institution could be some sort of joint venture between the BIS, IOSCO and the International Financial Institute, representing the banks, with that part of the IMF that would be asked to develop greater expertise in dealing with banks. Some exploratory thinking along these lines would surely be constructive.

Another positive suggestion has come from George Soros. He proposed setting up an international credit insurance corporation (ICIC) as a sister organisation to the IMF, rather as the International Finance

Corporation is sister to the World Bank. The ICIC would charge fees (like insurance premiums) for guaranteeing loans to borrowing countries – but only up to a ceiling based on information about total borrowing and resources. Refusal to insure beyond the ceiling would warn creditors that, from then on, the risks were theirs. There would be no bailout. Capital for ICIC would be SDRs voted to it by the IMF Executive Board.[5] The idea amounts to a sort of lender-of-last-resort facility with limited liability. The trouble would start, however, when creditor and debtor governments began to argue over the relative height of diverse ceilings and when markets disagreed with the ratings given on the basis of past performance to diverse debtors. So what seems at first sight to be a neat technical solution turns out to encounter big political pitfalls. As Soros says, though, it may be an acceptable idea only when creditors and debtors alike are seriously scared.

Lastly, we have the power of national courts to consider. So far, financial regulation has mostly involved a combination of Chinese walls, with rules governing those within the walls. But the walls have crumbled and the integration of markets has made the rules hard to enforce. But there is also the power of the state to hold some contracts enforceable and others – such as those requiring criminal activity, for instance – unenforceable. This is a weapon that leading governments like that of the United States could use if they wished against the most bizarre and sophisticated kinds of derivatives. As mentioned in chapter 2, it is the fancy new ones that generate most profit. To make such contracts not illegal but legally unenforceable would shift the risk concerned back from the market to the risk taker – possibly giving rise to second and more prudent thoughts.

At the end of the day, of course, we are talking about relative values and social preferences – the preference, for example, for more equity and more stability over the maximisation of wealth creation, and a preference for the quality of economic growth rather than its quantity. That is what the debates in international political economy and in theoretical economics ultimately boil down to. The conflicts between monetarism and market economics on one side and keynesian intervention on the other are not technical but political. And political choices are formed by people's experience. Our problem in the next century is that the traditional authority of the nation state is not up to the job of managing mad international money, yet its leaders are instinctively reluctant to entrust that job to unelected, unaccountable (and often arrogant and myopic) bureaucrats. We have to invent a new kind of polity but we cannot yet imagine how it might work. Perhaps, therefore, money has to become really very much more mad and bad before the experience changes preferences and policies.

Notes

1 One example of false logic in this debate is the proposition that because state spending has risen since 1960, state power has also increased. The figures are certainly dramatic: the average for advanced economies was 15 per cent of GNP in 1913, about 27 per cent in 1960 and 45 per cent in 1996 (*The Economist*, Schools Brief, 6 December 1997: 124–5). But the inference is false. Spending more, selling off the nation's capital assets, running into debt are all signs of weakness and desperation, not of strength.

2 'A global reach keeps tax man at bay', *International Herald Tribune*, 8 December 1997.

3 A French political economist, Santiso (1997), has suggested that there is a widening time-lag, ever since the Mexican crisis of 1994/5, between events in financial markets and the responses of governments, and that financial technology may explain this.

4 The Helms–Burton decision specified firms that benefited from Castro's nationalisation of assets formerly owned by US interests. It was criticised, though so far in vain, by Canada, the Europeans and Latin Americans on the grounds that the decision to blacklist these firms – even denying US visas to their directors – was an unacceptable exercise of extraterritorial authority.

5 'Avoiding a breakdown', *Financial Times*, 31 December 1997.

Bibliography

Aglietta, M., 1976, *Regulation et crises du dapitalisme*, Paris, Calmannlevy.

Aglietta, M., 1995, *Macroeconomie Financiere*, Paris, La Decouverte.

Aglietta, M., 1996, *Financial Market Failures and Systemic Risk*, CEPII Working Paper 96-101, Paris, Centre d'Etudes Prospectives et d'Information Internationales.

Aglietta, M., 1997, 'La crise bancaire en France et dans le monde', *CEPII Newsletter*, 1(7).

Aglietta, M. and Orlean, A., 1982, *La Violence de la monnaie*, Paris, PUF.

Anders, G., 1992, *Merchants of Debt: KKR and the mortgaging of American business*, London, Cape.

Arndt, H., 1944, *The Economic Lessons of the 1930s*, London, Oxford University Press.

Ashley, R. K. and Walker, R. B. J., 1990, 'Reading dissidence/writing the discipline: crisis and questions of sovereignty in international studies', *International Studies Quarterly*, 34(3), pp. 367–416.

Bank for International Settlements, 1996, *Sixty-Sixth Annual Report*, Basle, BIS.

Bauer, P., 1993, *Development Aid: end it or mend it*, San Francisco, ICS Press.

Bernstein, M., 1987, *The Great Depression: delayed recovery and economic change in America 1929–39*, Cambridge, Cambridge University Press.

Block, F., 1977, *The Origins of International Economic Disorder*, Berkeley, University of California Press.

Bouzas, R., 1996, in Roett, R. and Rienner, L., eds, *The Mexican Peso Crisis: international perspectives*, Boulder, Colorado, Lynne Rienner Publishers.

Bowe, M. and Dean, J. L., 1997, *Has the Market Solved the Sovereign Debt Crisis?*, Princeton Studies in International Finance No. 83.

Brunner, K., ed., 1981, *The Great Depression Revisited*, Boston, Martinus Nijhoff.

Burrough, B. and Helyar, J., 1990, *Barbarians at the Gate: the fall of RJR Nabisco*, London, Cape.

Cain, P. J. and Hopkins, A. G., 1993, *British Imperialism: crisis and deconstruction, 1914–1990*, vol. 2, London, Longman.

Calleo, D., 1982, *The Imperious Economy*, Cambridge, Harvard University Press.

Calleo, D. and Strange, S., 1984, 'Money and world politics', in Strange, S., ed., *Paths to International Political Economy*, London, Allen and Unwin, pp. 91–125.

Camps, M., 1967, *European Unification in the Sixties*, London, Oxford University Press.

Carr, E. H., 1961, *What is History?*, Harmondsworth, Penguin.

Cerny, P. G., ed., 1993, *Finance and World Politics: markets, regimes and states in the post-hegemonic era*, Aldershot, E. Elgar.

Clarke, S., 1973, *The Reconstruction of the International Monetary System: the attempts of 1922 and 1933*, Princeton Studies in International Finance No. 33.

Cohen, B. J., 1998, *The Geography of Money*, Stanford, University of California Press.

Cohen, S. and Zysman, J., 1987, *Manufacturing Matters: the myth of the post-industrial economy*, New York, Basic Books.

Corbridge, S., Thrift, N. and Martin, R., 1994, *Money, Power, and Space*, Oxford, Blackwell.

Cornford, A., 1995, 'Risks and derivative markets', *UNCTAD Review*, pp. 346–69.

Crichton, M., 1993, *Rising Sun*, London, Arrow.

Crockett, A., 1997, *The Theory and Practice of Financial Stability*, Princeton Essays in International Finance No. 203.

D'Arista, J., 1994, *The Evolution of US Finance. Volume II: Restructuring Institutions and Markets*, New York, M. E. Sharpe.

Dale, R., 1994, 'International banking regulations', in Steil, B., ed., *International Financial Market Regulation*, New York, John Wiley, pp. 167–96.

de Cecco, M., 1974, *Money and Empire: the international gold standard, 1890–1914*, Oxford, Blackwell.

Deane, M. and Pringle, R., 1984, *Economic Cooperation from the Inside*, New York, Group of Thirty.

Deane, M. and Pringle, R., 1994, *The Central Banks*, London, Hamish Hamilton.

Delamaide, D., 1984, *Debt Shock*, London, Weidenfeld and Nicolson.

Dewey, D. R., 1918, *Financial History of the United States*, New York, Longman.

Dicken, P., 1992, *Global Shift: the internationalization of economic activity*, 2nd edn, London, Chapman.

Diebold, W., 1959, *The Schuman Plan: a study in economic co-operation, 1950–1959*, Oxford, Praeger.

Drucker, P., 1989, *The New Realities: in government and politics, in economy and business, in society and in world view*, New York, Harper Row.

Dunning, J. H., 1993, *The Globalization of Business: the challenge of the 1990s*, London, Routledge.

Eatwell, J., 1996, *International Financial Liberalization: the impact on world development*, United Nations Development Program Discussion Paper, New York, United Nations.

Edwards, J. and Fischer, K., 1993, *Banks, Finance and Investment in Germany*, Cambridge, Cambridge University Press.

Eichengreen, B. and Wyplosz, C., 1993, *The Unstable EMS*, CEPR Discussion Paper 817, London, Centre for Economic Policy Research.

Eichengreen, R. and Portes, R., 1996, 'Managing the next Mexico', in Kenen, P., ed., *From Halifax to Lyons: what has been done about crisis management?*, Princeton Essays in International Finance No. 200, pp. 35–7.

Emmanuel, A., 1972, *Unequal Exchange: a study of imperialism of trade*, New York, Monthly Review Press.

Emminger, O., 1997, *The D-Mark Conflict Between Internal and External Equilibrium, 1948–1975*, Princeton Essays in International Finance No. 122.

Emmott, B., 1989, *The Sun also Sets*, London, Simon and Schuster.

Enkyo, S., 1989, 'Financial innovation and international safeguards', unpublished PhD thesis, University of London.

Erdman, P., 1996, *Tug of War: today's global currency crisis*, New York, St. Martin's Press.

Fallows, J., 1994, *Looking at the Sun*, New York, Pantheon.

Feddersen, H., 1986, 'The management of floating exchange rates: a case of the Dmark–Dollar rate 1973–1983', unpublished PhD thesis, European University Institute, Florence.

Feis, H., 1954, *Europe the World's Banker 1870–1914*, New York, Kelly.

Fiorentini, G. and Peltzman, S., 1995, *The Economics of Organized Crime*, London, Cambridge University Press.

Fischer, B. and Reisen, H., eds, 1993, *Financial Opening: policy issues and experiences in developing countries*, Paris, OECD.

Freeman, C., 1983, *Long Waves in the World Economy*, London, Butterworth.

Freeman, C. and Soete, L., 1997, *Economics of Industrial Innovation*, London, Pinter.

Frieden, J., 1991, 'Invested interests: the politics of national economic policies in a world of global finance', *International Organization*, 45 (4), pp. 425–51.

Friedman, M. and Schwarz, A., 1963, *Monetary History of the United States, 1867–1960*, Princeton, Princeton University Press.

Funabashi, Y., 1988, *Managing the Dollar: from the Plaza to the Louvre*, Washington, DC, Institute for International Economics.

Galbraith, J. K., 1955, *The Great Crash 1929*, London, Hamilton.

Gardner, R., 1956, *Sterling–Dollar Diplomacy: Anglo-American collaboration in reconstruction of multilateral trade*, Oxford, Clarendon Press.

Gelber, H., 1997, *Sovereignty Through Interdependence*, London, Kluwer Law International.

George, S., 1988, *A Fate Worse than Debt: a radical new analyses of the Third World debt crisis*, London, Penguin.

Germain, R., 1997, *The International Organization of Credit: states and global finance in the world economy*, Cambridge, Cambridge University Press.

Goldstein, M., 1997, *The Case for an International Banking Standard*, paper presented in London, July 1997, based on an eponymous monograph for the Institute of International Economics, April 1997.

Greider, W., 1987, *Secrets of the Temple: how the Federal Reserve runs the country*, New York, Simon and Schuster.

Greider, W., 1997, *One World, Ready or Not: the manic logic of global capitalism*, New York, Simon and Schuster.

Gros, D. and Thygesen, N., 1988, *The EMS: achievements, currents issues and directions for the future*, CEPS Papers No. 35, Brussels, Centre for European Policy Studies.

Grunberg, I., 1994, 'The Persian Gulf War and the myth of lost hegemony', in Morgan, R., Lorentzen, J., Leander A. and Guzzini, S. (eds), *New Diplomacy in the Post-Cold War World: essays for Susan Strange*, New York, St. Martin's Press.

Grunberg, I., 1996, *Rival States, Rival Firms: how do people fit in?: the global unemployment challenge*, United Nations Development Programme Discussion Paper, New York, United Nations.

Gurwin, L., 1983, *The Calvi Affair: death of a banker*, London, Macmillan.

Guttman, B. and Meehan, P., 1975, *The Great Inflation: Germany 1919–1923*, Farnborough, Saxon House.

Hall, M., 1987, *The City Revolution: causes and consequences*, London, Macmillan.

Hamada, K. and Horiuchi, A., 1987, 'The political economy of the financial market', in Yamamura, K. and Yasuba, Y., eds, *The Political Economy of Japan: the domestic transformation*, vol. 1, Stanford, Stanford University Press, pp. 223–60.

Hamelink, C. J., 1983, *Finance and Information: a study of converging interests*, Norwood, Ablex Publishing Corporation.

Haufler, V., 1997a, 'Financial deregulation and the transformation of international risks insurance', in Underhill, G., ed., *The New World Order in International Finance*, New York, St. Martin's Press, pp. 76–100.

Haufler, V., 1997b, *Dangerous Commerce: insurance and the management of international risk*, New York, Cornell University Press.

Helleiner, E., 1995, 'Explaining the globalization of financial markets: bringing states back in', *Review of International Political Economy*, 2(2).

Heimann, J. and Lord Alexander, 1997, 'Global institutions, national supervision, and systemic risk', *Financial Stability Review*, 3 (3), pp. 82–91.

Herring, R. and Litan, R., 1995, *Financial Regulation in the Global Economy*, Washington, DC, Brookings Institution.

Hills, J., 1994, 'Dependency theory and its relevance today: international institutions in telecommunications and structural power', *Review of International Studies*, 20 (2), pp. 169–86.

Hirschman, A. O., 'Rival interpretations of market society: civilizing, destructive of feeble?', *Journal of Economic Literature*, December.

Hirst, P. Q. and Thompson, G., 1996, *Globalization in Question: the international economy and the possibilities of governance*, Cambridge, Polity Press.

Hutton, W., 1995, *The State We're in*, London, Jonathan Cape.

Ingham, G., 1984, *Capitalism Divided? The city and industry in British social development*, Basingstoke, Macmillan.

International Monetary Fund, 1995, *Capital Account Convertibility: review of experience and implications for IMF policies*, Washington, DC, IMF.

International Monetary Fund, 1996, *International Capital Markets: developments, prospects, and key policy issues*, Washington, DC, IMF.

Ito, T. and Folkerts-Landau, D., 1996, *International Capital Markets: developments, prospects and key policy issues*, Washington, DC, IMF.

Jervis, R., 1976, *Perception and Misperception in International Politics*, Princeton, Princeton University Press.

Johns, R. A., 1983, *Tax Havens and Offshore Finance: a study of transnational economic development*, London, Frances Pinter.

Johnson, C., 1982, *MITI and the Japanese Miracle: the growth of industrial policy, 1925–1975*, Stanford, Stanford University Press.

Johnson, T. J., 1972, *Professions and Power*, London, Macmillan.

Kapstein, E., 1994, *Governing the Global Economy: international finance and the state*, Cambridge, Harvard University Press.

Kenen, P., 1995, *Economic and Monetary Union in Europe: moving beyond Maastricht*, Cambridge, Cambridge University Press.

Kenwood, A. and Lougheed, A., 1983, *The Growth of the International Economy, 1820–1980*, London, Allen and Unwin.

Keohane, R. and Milner, H., 1996, *Internationalization and Domestic Politics*, Cambridge, Cambridge University Press.

Key, S. L., 1998, *Financial Services in the Uruguay Round and the*

WTO, Group of Thirty Working Paper No. 54, Washington, DC, G30.

Keynes, S. M., 1926, *The End of Laissez-Faire*, London, Hogarth Press.

Keynes, S. M., 1936, *The General Theory of Employment, Interest, and Money*, London, Macmillan.

Killick, T., 1995, *IMF Programmes in Developing Countries: design and impact*, London, Routledge.

Kindleberger, C., 1973, *The World in Depression, 1929–1939*, Berkeley, University of California Press.

Kindleberger, C., 1987, *International Capital Movements*, Cambridge, Cambridge University Press.

Kindleberger, C., 1990, *Manias, Panics and Crashes: a history of financial crises*, London, Macmillan.

Kobrin, S., 1997, 'Electronic cash and the end of national markets', *Foreign Policy*, 107.

Kochan, N. and Whittington, B., 1991, *Bankrupt: the BCCI fraud*, London, Gollancz.

Lascelles, D., 1997, *EMU – A Fairy Tale*, London, Centre for the Study of Financial Innovation.

Lewis, W. A., 1949, *Economic Survey, 1919–1939*, London, Allen and Unwin.

List, F., 1841, *The National System of Political Economy* (1904 translation), New York, Longman.

Marsh, D., 1992, *The Bundesbank: the bank that rules Europe*, London, Heinemann.

Martin, H-P. and Schumann, H., 1997, *The Global Trap: globalization and the assault on prosperity and democracy*, New York, Zed Books.

Martone, C., 1996, *The Mexican Peso Crisis: international perspectives*, in Roett, R. and Rienner, L., eds., Boulder, Colorado, Lynne Rienner Publishers.

Matthews, R. C. O., ed., 1982, *Slower Growth in the Western World*, London, Heinemann.

Maxfield, S., 1990, *Governing Capital: international finance and Mexican politics*, Ithaca, Cornell University Press.

Mayer, M., 1997, *The Bankers: the next generation*, New York, Trauma Talley Books.

McCahery, J., 1997, 'Market regulation and particularistic interest: the dynamics of insider trading in the US and Europe', in Underhill, G., ed., *The New World Order in International Finance*, New York, St. Martin's Press.

Milesi-Ferretti, G. and Razin, A., 1997, *Current Account Sustainability: selected East Asian and Latin American experiences*, IMF Working Paper 96/110, Washington, DC, IMF.

Miller, M. and Zhang, X., 1997, *A Bankruptcy Procedure for Sovereign States*, paper presented in London, based on earlier papers at IIE and the IMF.

Milward, A. S., 1984, *The Reconstruction of Western Europe 1945–5*, London, Methuen.

Minc, A., 1993, *Le Nouveau Moyen Age*, Paris, Gallimard.

Mistry, P., 1994, *Multilateral Dept: an emerging crisis*, The Hague, Fondad.

Mistry, P., 1995, *Multilateral Development Banks: an assessment of their financial structures, policies and practices*, The Hague, Fondad.

Mistry, P., 1996, *Resolving Africa's Multilateral Dept Problem: a response to the IMF*, The Hague, Fondad.

Moran, M., 1984, *The Politics of Banking*, London, Macmillan.

Mueller, J. E., 1989, *Retreat from Doomsday: the obsolescence of major war*, New York, Basic Books.

Murphy, R. T., 1996, *The Real Price of Japanese Money*, London, Weidenfeld and Nicolson.

Oxfam, 1996, *Multilateral Debt: the human costs*, Oxford, Oxfam.

Oxford Illustrated Old Testament, 1968, 1, Oxford, Oxford University Press, pp. 90–7.

Padoa-Schioppa, T., ed., *et al.*, 1991, *Europe After 1992: three essays*, No. 183.

Padoa-Schioppa, T., 1992, *Agenda for Stage Two: preparing the monetary platform*, CEPR Occasional Paper 7, London, Centre for Economic Policy Research.

Padoa-Schioppa, T., 1994, *The Road to Monetary Union in Europe: the emperor, the kings, and the genies*, Oxford, Oxford University Press.

Paoli, L., 1997, *The Pledge of Secrecy: culture, structure, and action of Mafia associations*, unpublished PhD thesis, European University Institute, Florence.

Pauly, L., 1997, *Who Elected the Bankers? Surveillance and control in the world economy*, Ithaca, Cornell University Press.

Payer, C., 1974, *The Debt Trap: the IMF and the Third World*, New York, Monthly Review Press.

Porter, M., 1990, *The Competitive Advantage of Nations*, New York, Free Press.

Prestowitz, C., 1988, *Trading Places: how we allowed Japan to take the lead*, New York, Basic Books.

Prout, C., 1976, 'Finance for developing countries: an essay', in Strange, S., ed., *International Economic Relations of the Western World 1959–1971. Volume 2: international monetary relations*, London, Oxford University Press.

Putnam, R., 1988, 'Diplomacy and domestic politics: the logic of 2-level games', *International Organization*, 42 (3), pp. 427–60.

Raw, C., Hodson, G. and Page, B.,1971, *Do You Sincerely Want to be Rich? Bernard Cornfeld and IOS: an international swindle*, London, Deutsch.

Reading, B., 1992, *Japan: the coming collapse*, London, Weidenfeld and Nicolson.

Reich, R., 1990, 'Who is US?', *Harvard Business Review*, 68,(1), pp. 53–64.

Reinicke, W. H., 1998, *Global Public Policy: governing without government?*, Washington, DC, Brookings Institution Press.

Rifkin, J., 1996, *The End of Work: the decline of the global labor force and the dawn of the post-market era*, New York, Columbia University Press.

Robbins, L. C., 1971, *Autobiography of an Economist*, London, Macmillan.

Rosenberg, N., 1994, *Exploring the Black Box: technology, economics and history*, Cambridge, Cambridge University Press.

Rostow, W. W., 1978, *World Economy: history and prospects*, London, Macmillan.

Rueff, J., 1971, *Le péché monétaire de l'occident*, Paris, Plon.

Ruggiew, V. and South, N., 1995, *Euro-Drugs: use, markets and trafficking in Europe*, London, UCL Press.

Sachs, J., 1996, *Financial Crises in Emerging Markets: the lessons of 1995*, Washington, DC, Brookings Institution.

Santiso, J., 1997, *Wall Street Face à la Crise Mexicaine*, CEPII Working Paper, Paris, Centre d'Etudes Prospectives et d'Information Internationales.

Sassen, S., 1991, *The Global City: New York, London, Tokyo*, Princeton, Princeton University Press.

Sassen, S., 1996, *Losing Control? Sovereignty in an age of globalization*, New York, Columbia University Press.

Schacht, H., 1950, *Gold for Europe*, London, Duckworth.

Schumpeter, J. A., 1939, *Business Cycles: a theoretical, historical and statistical analysis of the capitalist process*, New York, McGraw-Hill.

Schumpeter, J. A., 1961, *The Theory of Economic Development*, New York, Oxford University Press.

Shinkai, Y., 1988, 'The internationalization of finance in Japan', in Inoguchi, T. and Okimoto, D., eds, *The Political Economy of Japan: the changing international context*, vol. 2, Stanford, Stanford University Press, pp. 249–71.

Shonfield, A., 1965, *Modern Capitalism: the changing balance of public and private power*, Oxford, Oxford University Press.

Simon, H., 1948, *Economic Policy for a Free Society*, Chicago, Chicago University Press.

Sinclair, M., 1995, *The New Politics of Survival: grassroots movements in Central America*, New York, Monthly Review Press.

Skidelsky, R., ed., 1977, *The End of the Keynesian Era: essays on the disintegration of the Keynesian political economy*, London, Macmillan.

Solomon, R., 1977, *The International Monetary System, 1945–1976*, London, Harper and Row.

Soros, G., 1987, *The Alchemy of Finance: reading the mind of the market*, New York, John Wiley.

Spero, J., 1979, *The Failure of the Franklin National Bank*, New York, Columbia University Press.

Steil, B., 1994, 'International securities market regulation', in Steil, B., ed., *International Financial Market Regulation*, New York, John Wiley, pp. 1–14.

Steil, B., *et al.*, 1996, *The European Equity Markets: the state of the union and an agenda for the millennium*, London, Royal Institute of International Affairs.

Stopford, J. and Strange, S., 1991, *Rival States, Rival Firms*, Cambridge, Cambridge University Press.

Story, J. and Walter, I., 1997, *Political Economy of Financial Integration in Europe: the battle of the systems*, Manchester, Manchester University Press.

Strange, S., 1951, 'The Schuman Plan', *Journal of World Affairs*.

Strange, S., 1971, *Sterling and British Policy: a political study of an international currency in decline*, London, Oxford University Press.

Strange, S., 1976, 'International monetary relations', in Shonfield, A., ed., *International Economic Relations in the Western World 1959–1971*, vol. 2, London, Oxford University Press.

Strange, S., 1986, *Casino Capitalism*, Oxford, Blackwell. (Reprinted 1997, Manchester, Manchester University Press.)

Strange, S., 1996, *The Retreat of the State: the diffusion of power in the world economy*, Cambridge, Cambridge University Press.

Temin, P., 1976, *Did Monetary Forces Cause the Great Depression?*, New York, Norton.

Thomas, B., 1954, *Migration and Economic Growth: a study of Great Britain and the Atlantic economy*, Cambridge, Cambridge University Press.

Thompson, P. G. R., 1991, 'Donors, development and dependence, some lessons from Bangladesh, 1971–1986', unpublished PhD thesis, University of London.

Thurow, L., 1996, *The Future of Capitalism: how today's economic forces shape tomorrow's world*, London, Nicholas Brealey.

Tobin, J., 1990, 'International monetary system: pluralism and interdependence', in Steinherr, A. and Weiserbs, P., eds, *Evolution of International and Regional Monetary Systems: essays in honour of Robert Triffin*, Basingstoke, Macmillan, pp. 3–9.

Triffin, R., 1961, *Gold and the Dollar Crisis: the future of convertibility*, Yale, Yale University Press.

Tsoukalis, L., 1985, *The Political Economy of International Money: in search of a new order*, London, Sage.

Tsoukalis, L., 1997, *The New European Economy Revisited*, Oxford, Oxford University Press.

Tyson, L., 1992, *Who's Bashing Whom? Trade conflict in high-technology industries*, Washington, DC, Institute for International Economics.

Tyson, L. and Zysman, J., 1988, 'Development strategy and production innovation in Japan', in Tyson, L. and Zysman, J., eds, *Politics and*

Productivity: the real story of how Japan works, New York, Harper, pp. 59–140.

Underhill, G. R. D., 1997, 'Private markets and public responsibility in the global system: conflict and cooperation in transnational banking and securities regulations', in Underhill, G. R. D., ed., *The New World Order in International Finance*, Basingstoke, Macmillan, pp. 17–49.

United Nations, 1997, *World Drug Report*, Oxford, Oxford University Press for the UN.

van Duijn, J. J., 1983, *The Long Wave in Economic Life*, London, Allen and Unwin.

van Wolferen, K., 1989, *The Enigma of Japanese Power: people and politics in a stateless nation*, New York, Alfred A. Knopf.

Vatter, H., 1985, *The US Economy in the Second World War*, New York, Columbia University Press.

Vernon, R., 1971, *Sovereignty at Bay*, New York, Basic Books.

Vernon, R., 1977, *Storm Over the Multinationals*, London, Macmillan.

Volcker, P. and Gyohten, T., 1992, *Changing Fortunes: the world's money and the threat to American leadership*, New York, Times Books.

Wachtel, H., 1987, *The Politics of International Money*, Amsterdam, Transnational Institute.

Walter, A., 1991, *World Power and World Money: the role of hegemony and international monetary order*, London, Harvester, Wheatsheaf.

Waltz, K. N., 1979, *Theory of International Politics*, Reading, Addison-Wesley.

Walzenbach, G., 1998, *Co-ordination in Context: institutional choices to promote exports*, Aldershot, Ashgate.

Williamson, J., 1977, *The Failure of World Monetary Reform, 1971–74*, Sunbury-on-Thames, Nelson.

World Bank, 1990, *World Development Report, 1990*, New York, Oxford University Press.

World Bank, 1996, *Global Development Finance*, Washington, DC, World Bank.

Index

Note: 'n' after a page reference indicates a note on that page.